D1423426

SPIRITUAL UNION
AND COMMUNION

SPIRITUAL UNION AND COMMUNION

by
Arthur W. Pink

BAKER BOOK HOUSE
Grand Rapids, Michigan

Standard Book Number: 8010-6893-2

Library of Congress Catalog Card Number: 72-160817

Copyright, 1971, by I. C. Herendeen

PHOTOLITHOPRINTED BY CUSHING - MALLOY, INC.
ANN ARBOR, MICHIGAN, UNITED STATES OF AMERICA
1971

CONTENTS

1. Introduction 7

2. Divine Union 18

3. Mediatorial Union 31

4. Mystical Union 49

5. Federal Union 67

6. Vital Union 74

7. Saving Union 80

8. Practical Union 86

9. Experimental Union 98

10. Glory Union 135

11. Conclusion 154

1

Introduction

THE present writer has not the least doubt in his mind that the subject of *spiritual union* is the most important, the most profound, and yet the most blessed of any that is set forth in the sacred Scriptures; and yet, sad to say, there is hardly any which is now more generally neglected. The very expression "spiritual union" is unknown in most professing Christian circles, and even where it is employed it is given such a protracted meaning as to take in only a fragment of this precious truth. Probably its very profundity is the reason why it is so largely ignored in this superficial age. Yet there are still a few left who are anxious to enter into God's best and long for a fuller understanding of the deep things of the Spirit; and it is, principally, with these in mind that we take up this subject.

There are three principal unions revealed in the Scriptures which are the chief mysteries and form the foundation of our most holy faith. First, the union of three Divine persons in one Godhead: having distinct personalities, being co-eternal and co-glorious, yet constituting one Jehovah. Second, the union of the Divine and human natures in one person, Jesus Christ, Immanuel, being God and man. Third, the union of the Church to Christ, He being the Head, they the members, constituting one mystical body. Though we cannot form an exact idea of any of these unions in our imaginations, because the depth of such mysteries is beyond our comprehension, yet it is our bounden duty to believe them all, because they are clearly revealed in Scripture, and are the necessary foundation for other points of Christian doctrine. Hence it is our holy privilege to prayerfully study the same, looking unto the Holy Spirit to graciously enlighten us thereon.

The most wonderful thing of all, and yet the greatest mystery, in the natural world, is a *union*, namely, that conjunction which God has made between mind and matter, the soul and the body. What finite intelligence would or could have conceived of the joining together of an immaterial spirit and a clod of clay! What so little alike as the soul and an organized piece of earth! Who had ever imagined such a thing as animate and thinking dust! or that a spirit should be so linked with and tied to a carnal body that while *that* is preserved in health, *it* cannot free itself! And yet there *is* a union, a real union, a personal union, between the soul and the body. But that is only a *natural* mystery, and falls immeasurably below the *sacred* mystery of the union between human beings and the Lord of glory.

The Scriptures have much to say upon the union which exists between Christ and His people. "At that day ye shall know that I am in my Father, and ye in me, and I in you" (John 14:20). "He that is joined unto the Lord is one spirit" (I Cor. 6:17). "For we are members of his body, of his flesh, and of his bones. This is a great mystery: but I speak concerning Christ and the church" (Eph. 5:30, 32). What an astonishing thing it is that there should be a union between the Son of God and worms of the earth! — infinitely more so than if the king of Great Britain had married the poorest and ugliest women in all his realm. How immeasurable is the distance between the Creator and the creature, between Deity and mortal man! How wonderful beyond words that sinful wretches should be made one with Him before whom the seraphim veil their faces and cry "holy, holy, holy!"

"The union of Christ to His people is an amazing subject. It is an eternal union; it is an union made known and enjoyed in time; it is an union which will be openly and manifestatively declared, in all its glory and perfection in the latter day; it is a grace union; it is also a glory union. As it is the foundation of all the gracious actings of Christ towards His Church in a time state, so it is of all the glory He will put on His church and communicate unto His people at the last day. I cannot but lament we are most of us so great strangers to these important and heavenly truths. Depend on it, *we are great losers hereby*. The people of God lose much because they neglect truths of the greatest importance. In the present day they are too neglectful of important truths. They are willingly ignorant of them.

"We treat the Scriptures in the present day as though the less we knew of the deep things of God, so much the better. Alas! alas! this, let us think of it as we may, is to cast contempt on God himself. Nor will it serve to say, we do not so mean or intend. It is a matter of fact, we are too neglectful of those Divine truths and doctrines which concern the glory of Christ. The ancient and glorious settlements of grace are too little in our thoughts. It is sensibly felt, and by some very expressively confessed and acknowledged, that the influences of the Holy Spirit are very greatly suspended. Yet *the cause* is overlooked. Most assuredly one grand reason why we have so little of His sacred presence with us, and His power and influence manifested amongst us, may be laid to the account of neglecting to preach supernatural, spiritual truth, and the mysteries of the everlasting Gospel" (S. E. Pierce, 1812).

The vital importance of this subject of the union of the Church to Christ may be clearly seen from the place which it occupies in the High Priestly prayer of Christ. "Neither pray I for these alone, but for them also which shall believe on me through their word: that they all may *be one*, as thou, Father, art in me, and I in thee" (John 17:20, 21). Our Lord here began His prayer for the whole body of His people by speaking of the union which they had with Him and His Father in Him, and He spends the verses which follow in expressing the blessings which follow as the fruits thereof. We are *not* to conceive that Christ here prayed for an union *to be* brought about or obtained; no, for it *was* established from all eternity: rather was He praying that His beloved might be blest with the clear knowledge of it, so that they might enjoy all the benefits of the same in their own souls.

"And the glory which thou gavest me I have given them; that they may *be one* even as we are one" (John 17:22). This subject of the union between Himself and the elect was truly sweet and blessed to the heart of Christ. He knew that the knowledge and use of it is of great value and service to His people, therefore did He speak of it again and again that His saints in all ages might receive the knowledge of it into their minds and enjoy in their hearts the blessings contained in it. And, by readers, if Christ Himself esteemed this truth of union with Himself as a foundation truth, *we* should learn to think of it so also. We should bring ourselves unto the closest and prayerful study of the same, for by it our faith and hope are sustained and kept in exercise on God our Saviour.

"And the glory which thou gavest me I have given them; that they may *be one* even as we are one." This petition is the very center of Christ's prayer, expressing the supreme desire of the Saviour's mind toward His redeemed: it summed up the uttermost longing of His heart toward them. The union about which He prayed is such that thereby the Father and the Son dwell in us and we in them. It is such that the elect are so joined unto God and His Christ that it is the very highest union of which the elect are capable. It is the chiefest and greatest of all blessings, being the foundation from which all others proceed.

"I in them and thou in me, that they may be made perfect *in one*" (v. 23). A great variety of blessings are set before us in the gospel. Salvation is an unspeakable one, yet not so great as our union to the person of Christ. If we had not been united to Christ, He had not been our Saviour: it was because we stood eternally related to Him that He was most graciously pleased to undertake for us. The grace of justification is an unspeakable blessing, yet not so great as that of union, because the effect can never be equal to the cause which produces it. To be *in Christ* must exceed all the blessings which flow *from* Him which we have or ever shall partake of, either on earth or in Heaven. Communion with Christ is unspeakably blessed, yet not so great as *union*, for our union is the foundation of all communion. It is the greatest of all those super-creation "spiritual blessings" (Eph. 1:3) which the Father bestowed on the Church before sin entered the universe. It is the fruit of God's eternal love to His people.

Union with Christ is the foundation of all spiritual blessings, so that if there had been no *connection with* Him, there could be no regeneration, no justification, no sanctification, no glorification. It is so in the natural world — adumbrating the spiritual: sever one of the members from my physical body, and it is dead; only by its union with my person does it partake of life. "God is faithful, by whom ye were called unto the fellowship of his Son, Jesus Christ our Lord" (I Cor. 1:9): the word "fellowship" signifies such a co-partnership between persons that they have a joint-interest in one and the same enjoyment which is common between them. Now this fellowship or communion with Christ is entirely dependent upon our *union with* Him, even as much as the branch's participation of the sap and juice is dependent upon its union and coalition with the stock of the tree. Take away union, and there can be neither communion nor communication.

As it is for Christ's sake that God bestows upon His people all the blessings of salvation, so according to His eternal constitution those blessings could only be enjoyed in a state of communion with Him. The varied character of that communion it will be our joy to unfold, as the blessed Spirit is pleased to enable us, in the chapters which follow. But the foundation of that vital, spiritual, and experimental union which the saints have with their Beloved in a time state and which they will enjoy forever in Heaven, was laid by God in that mystical union which He established between the Mediator and His elect before the foundation of the world, when He appointed Him to be the Head and they the members of His body: when God gave Christ to them and gave them to Christ in everlasting marriage.

In consequence of God's having given the Church to Christ in marriage before the foundation of the world, He says to His people, "I will betroth thee unto me forever: yea, I will betroth thee unto me in righteousness, and in judgment, and in lovingkindness, and in mercies" (Hos. 2:19); "thy Maker is thy husband" (Isa. 54:5). And therefore does the Church exclaim, "My Beloved is mine, and I am his" (Song of Sol. 2:16). "Consider the closeness and intimacy of the union between Him and them, and let this encourage thee to lean and live on Him by faith. It is far more intimate and dear than the union between husband, and wife among men, for they are indeed 'one flesh,' but He is 'one body' and 'one spirit' (I Cor. 6:19) with His spouse; He is *in them,* and they are *in Him.* And by virtue of this intimate union, thou hast a title to Him and to His whole purchase" (Eben. Erskine, 1775).

In consequence of this eternal marriage-union between Christ and His Church there is a communion of names. In Jeremiah 23:6 we read, "And this is his name whereby *he* shall be called, The Lord our righteousness," and in Jeremiah 33:16 we are told, "and this is the name whereby *she* shall be called, The Lord our righteousness" — this by virtue of her oneness with Him. So again in I Corinthians 12:12 the Church is actually designated "the Christ," while in Galatians 3:16 and Colossians 1:24 the Head and His Church forming one body are conjointly referred to as "Christ"; hence when Saul of Tarsus was assaulting the Church, its Head protested, "Why persecutest thou *me*" (Acts 9:4). But what is yet more remarkable, we find the Lord Jesus given the name of His people: in Galatians 6:16 the Church is denominated, "the *Israel of God,*" while in Isaiah 49:3 we hear God saying *to the Mediator* "Thou art my Servant, O *Israel,* in whom I will be glorified!"

Unspeakably precious is this aspect of our wonderful subject. In Colossians 3:12 Christians are exhorted to "Put on therefore, as the elect of God, holy and beloved, bowels of mercies." Each of those titles are given to the saints because of their *union with Christ.* They are "the elect of God" because *He* is God's "Elect" (Isa. 42:1); they are "holy" because conjoined to God's "Holy One" (Ps. 16:10); they are "beloved" because married to Him of whom the Father says, "This is my Beloved Son" (Matt. 3:17). Again, we are told that God "hath made us *kings and priests*" (Rev. 1:5), which is only because we are *united to* Him who is "the Kings of kings" and the "great High Priest." Is Christ called "the Sun of righteousness" (Mal. 4:2)? So we are told, "Then shall the righteous shine forth *as the sun* in the kingdom of their Father" (Matt. 13: 42)! Does the Redeemer declare "I am the Rose of Sharon" (Song of Sol. 2:1)? Then He promises of the redeemed "The desert [their fruitless state by nature] shall rejoice and blossom *as the rose*" (Isa. 35:1) — the only two occasions the "rose" is mentioned in Holy Writ!

The union between Christ and His Church is so real, so vital, so intimate that God has never viewed the one apart from the other. There is such an indissoluble oneness between the Redeemer and the redeemed, such an absolute identification of interest between them, that the Father of mercies never saw them apart: He never saw Christ *as* "Christ" without seeing His mystical body; He never saw the Church apart from its Head. Therefore the Holy Spirit has delighted to emphasize this wondrous and glorious fact in many scriptures. In connection with Christ's birth we read, "Forasmuch then as the children are partakers of flesh and blood, He also Himself likewise took part of the same" (Heb. 2:14). Further, we are told, "In whom also *ye* are circumcised with the circumcision made without hands, in putting off the body of the sins of the flesh by the circumcision *of Christ*" (Col. 2:11) — His actual circumcision was our mystical circumcision. At His baptism Christ was "numbered *with* the transgressors," and hence, speaking as the Representative of the entire election of grace, He said, "Thus it becometh *us* [not simply "me"] to fulfil all righteousness" (Matt. 3:15).

We are told that when the Saviour was nailed to the tree "our old man was crucified *with* him" (Rom. 6:6). We are told that when He expired at Calvary "if One died for all, then all died" (II Cor. 5:14). We are told that when He was revived, we were "quickened *together with* Christ" (Eph. 2:5). He did not rise again as a single and private person, but as the Head of His Church: "since then ye be risen *with* Christ" (Col. 3:1). Nor is that all: in Ephesians 2:6 we are told, "And hath raised us up together, and made us *sit together* in heavenly places in Christ Jesus." O how surpassingly wonderful is the Christian's oneness with Christ: "Because *as* he is, *so* are we in this world" (I John 4:17). When Christ appears in glory it will not be alone: "Then shall ye also appear *with him* in glory" (Col. 3:4).

> "One in the tomb; one when He rose;
> One when He triumph'd o'er His foes;
> One when in Heaven He took His seat,
> While seraphs sang all Hell's defeat.
> With Him, their Head, they stand or fall,
> Their Life, their Surety, and their All."

II

Union and communion with the Father and His Son Jesus Christ, by the Holy Spirit who dwells personally in the saints, is a most glorious and transcendent wonder of Divine grace. Nature cannot comprehend it; carnal reason cannot grasp it; none can have the least real perception of its nature, importance, or excellency, but such as are born from above; nor can the regenerate either, except as they are Divinely enlightened and supernaturally lifted up into the true knowledge and enjoyment of the same. Spiritual life, and all its activities, is beyond the ken of mere intellect, consisting as it does in communion with God Himself. The oneness of the Church with Christ is a blessed reality, which none but the Spirit of God can open to the renewed mind and give right views of it. It is His royal prerogative so to do: it is part of His official work according to the eternal settlements of grace: His work is to glorify Christ, to enthrone Him in the hearts of His blood-bought people.

Were it not that the Holy Spirit "searcheth all things, yea, the deep things of God" (I Cor. 2:10), and that we had the unfailing promise of Christ (which needs to be laid hold of by faith and pleaded before God) that this infallible Teacher "will guide you into all truth" (John 16:13), it would be the very height of presumption for us to attempt to write upon such a subject. The very profundity of our present theme has been clearly intimated by God's designating it a "mystery." It is remarkable that twice only in the sacred Scriptures do we read of a "*great* mystery": once when the reference is to that ineffable union of the human nature with the Godhead in the person of Immanuel — "great is the mystery of godliness" (I Tim. 3:16); and once when mention is made of the mystical union subsisting between Christ and His Church — "this is a great mystery, but I speak concerning Christ and the church" (Eph. 5:32).

To aid our finite understandings, a variety of figures and natural analogies are used to express the oneness of Christ and His people. The marriage of Adam and Eve in their unfallen state, by which they became "one flesh" (Eph. 5:31) is a striking resemblance of the union between Christ and His Church, for He is the Husband (Isa. 54:5), she is the Spouse (Song of Sol. 2:1): as Adam said of Eve "this is now bone of my bone and flesh of my flesh" (Gen. 2:23), so the saints are assured "we are members of his body, of his flesh, and of his bones" (Eph. 5:30). Another resemblance or type is that of the head and members of our physical organism. In the human body there is such an intimate relation and vital connection between the head and its members that if severed the one could have no living existence apart from the other. Thus it is in the Body mystical: Christ is the Head, believers are the members (see I Cor. 12:12, 27; Eph. 4:15, 16).

A third resemblance is that of the root and the branches: there is a union between them, otherwise how should the one convey juice and nourishment to the others. So it is with Christ and believers: "I am the Vine, ye are the branches" (John 15:1). The same figure is found again in a number of passages in the Epistles: there we read of being "*graffed in* among them, and with them partakest of the root and fatness of the olive tree" (Rom. 11:17); of being *"rooted* and built up in Him" (Col. 2:7). This is a blessed analogy between Christ and believers and the root and the branches, in point of union and in point of influence: the root conveys life and nourishment to the branches; so does Christ to those who are one with Him. With this resemblance we may link the simile used by our Lord: "the corn of wheat" (John 12:24) falling into the ground, with its embryo increase of "much fruit" wrapped up within itself.

Still another resemblance is the foundation and the building which is found again and again in Scripture. Here too there is a *union,* for in a building all the stones and timbers being joined and fastened together upon the foundation, make but one entire structure. So it is here. The saints are "God's building" (I Cor. 3:9), Christ Himself being the Foundation" of that building (v. 9). And again, we are said to be "built upon the foundation of the apostles and prophets, Jesus Christ Himself being the chief corner-stone" (Eph. 2:20). The building itself is the complement of the foundation, but remove it, and the whole superstructure topples to the ground. How blessed to be assured by God, "Behold, I lay in Zion a *sure* foundation" (Isa. 28:16). Finally, Christians are referred to as "living stones, to be built up a spiritual house" (I Peter 2:5), which tells us that our union with Christ is both a mystical and a vital one.

In addition to the various figures and resemblances which God has graciously designed to employ so as to aid our feeble minds in grasping something of the mysterious and glorious union which exists between His Son and His people, there are types in the Old Testament which throw light thereon. A notable one is found in Exodus: "And thou shalt make holy garments for Aaron thy brother, for glory and for beauty. . . . And thou shalt take two onyx stones, and grave on them the names of the children of Israel . . . and thou shalt put the two stones upon the shoulders of the ephod, for stones of memorial unto the children of Israel: and *Aaron* shall bear *their* names before the Lord upon his two shoulders for a memorial. . . . And thou shalt make a plate of gold, and grave upon it, like the engravings of a signet, holiness to the Lord. And thou shalt put it on a blue lace that it may be upon the mitre; upon the forefront of the mitre it shall be. And it shall be upon Aaron's forehead, that Aaron may bear the iniquity of the holy things, which the children of Israel shall hallow in all their holy gifts; and it shall be always upon *his* forehead, that *they* may be accepted before the Lord" (28:2, 9, 12, 36-38). Thus was the whole Israel of God represented before Jehovah *in* the person of Aaron — blessed adumbration of the identification with our great High Priest. "It is like the precious ointment upon the head, that ran down upon the beard, even Aaron's beard; that went down to the skirts of his garments" (Ps. 133:2) — figure of the Holy Spirit communicated to Christ *and* His people.

Communion with Christ is our participation with Him in the *benefits* flowing from His several offices. As in marriage there must be a union before there can be any communion (sharing together) of estates and conditions, so before we can obtain anything *from* Christ we must first be one *with* Him: all is *in* Christ for us. "He that hath the Son hath life" (I John 5:12), and the term "life" sums up all spiritual blessings, just as physical "death" cuts off from all temporal mercies. We "have" the Son by God's eternal gift to us, as He possesses us by the Father's eternal gift of us to Him. Therefore it is written, "For unto us a Child is born, unto us a Son *is given*" (Isa. 9:6) — as in marriage: God made a grant of His Son to us, and *that* included all: "He that spared not his own Son, but delivered him up for us all, how shall he not with him *also* freely give us all things!" (Rom. 8:32).

"For we are *partakers* of Christ" (Heb. 3:14): He and we are made one, "*joint* heirs" (Rom. 8:17). "Being united *to* Christ we are possessed of all *in* Christ, so far as is consistent with our capacities of receiving and God's ordination and appointment in giving. Union gives us interest in the personal merits and righteousness of Christ and the benefits of His mediatory actions; they are ours to all effects and purposes, as if we ourselves had satisfied and obeyed the law. Why? because it is not in a person sundered from us; it is in our Head, in One to whom we are united by a strait bond of union (better "by a legal and vital bond of union"), therefore are they reputed as one" (T. Manton, 1670).

"But of him are ye in Christ Jesus, who of God is made unto us wisdom, and righteousness, and sanctification, and redemption" (I Cor. 1:30). To be "in Christ" is to be *united* to Him: first electively (Eph. 1:4), when God chose us in Him before the foundation of the world. Second, representatively (I Cor. 15:22), as we were in Adam. Third, vitally (II Cor. 5:17), as a branch in the vine. Fourth, voluntarily (Rom. 8:1), by faith cleaving unto Him. Of this compound union we are taught two things here in I Corinthians 1:30: its origin and its effects. As to its origin, it is "of God," He alone being the efficient cause. As to its effects, because the saints are one with Christ, they *participate* in His benefits, and so He is "made unto them wisdom. . . ."

Because of our union with Christ we are "accepted in the Beloved" (Eph. 1:6). We have the same title to enter God's presence that Christ has: "*by his own blood* he entered in once into the holy place, having obtained eternal redemption for us" (Heb. 9:12), "having, therefore, brethren, boldness to enter into the holiest *by the blood of Jesus*" (Heb. 10:19)! Because of our union with Christ we have not only a valid title or right to draw nigh unto God, but a personal *fitness*: "Giving thanks unto the Father, which hath *made us meet* to be partakers of the inheritance of the saints in light" (Col. 1:12). Our very life is "hid *with Christ* in God" (Col. 3:3), so that before we can perish, He must perish. What is yet more blessed, the Father loves us as He loves Christ: "That the world may know that thou hast sent me, and hast loved them, as thou hast loved me" (John 17:23).

"Christ is His Father's Son, and believers are Christ's sons (Isa. 8:18): He is the Father's delight (Isa. 42:1), they are Christ's: Ps. 16:3. He is the Father's glory (Heb. 1:3), and they are Christ's: II Cor. 8:23. God is Christ's Head (I Cor. 11:3), Christ is their Head: I Cor. 11:3. God always hears Christ (John 11:42), and Christ them: John 15. All power is given to Christ (Matt. 28:18), and by Christ to them: Phil. 4:13. God has committed all judgment to Christ (John 5:22), Christ makes them His assessors: I Cor. 6:2, 3." (D. Clarkson, 1685).

The oneness of Christ and His people is manifested in intimate and precious fellowship together. The whole of Solomon's "Song" sets forth this union and communion in a most wonderful and blessed way. Observe by what endearing terms the Saviour calls His Church: "thou hast ravished my heart, my sister, my spouse" (4:9) — she is His "sister" as well as His "spouse," for by taking her into union with Himself, this brings the Church into *every* relation: the saints are His "sons" (Heb. 2:10), His "brethren" (Heb. 2:12), and compare Matthew 12:48. The Divine Bridegroom says to His wife, "*eat,* O friends; drink, yea, drink abundantly, O beloved" (5:13); and she says, "Let my Beloved come into his garden and *eat* his pleasant fruits" (4:16): there is sweet entertainment on both sides. They are mutually charmed with each other's beauty: He says, "Behold, thou art fair, my love" (4:1); she exclaims, "my Beloved is white and ruddy, the chiefest among ten thousand" (5: 10).

The precious intimacy of that union which exists between Christ and His people is manifested in many Scriptures. "If any man hear my voice, and open the door, I will come in to him, and will sup with him, *and he with me*" (Rev. 3:20): there is *mutual* communion, reciprocal affections. Christ and His saints are fond of hearing each other's voices: "let me see thy countenance, let me hear thy voice; for sweet is thy voice, and thy countenance is comely" (Song of Sol. 2:14). That is Christ speaking to His spouse; her response is, "the companions hearken to thy voice: cause me to hear it" (8:13). There are also mutual complaints between them: "I have somewhat against thee, because thou hast left thy first love" (Rev. 2:4); "Lord, why castest thou off my soul? why hidest thou thy face from me?" (Ps. 88:14). O that both writer and reader may be favored with more intimate and constant communion with the eternal Lover of our souls: "Casting all your care upon him; for he careth for you" (I Peter 5:7).

Let us now seek to define and describe a little more closely the *nature* of that union which exists between Christ and His Church.

1. It is *supernatural,* being altogether beyond the powers of the creature to effectuate. It is wholly of the wisdom, grace, and power of God. All the unions we have in the natural world come infinitely short of this. The union of the body and soul in man puzzles and baffles the greatest philosophers, but the union of Christ and His Church is a far greater mystery: that persons so distant, so divided, should be made one, is a profundity which no finite intelligence can fully comprehend. We had known nothing whatever about it if God had not revealed it to us in His Word, and even now we discern it "through a glass darkly."

2. It is a *real* union, not a mere theoretical or fantastic thing, a creature of the imagination. Though it cannot be perceived by our senses,

nor visualized by the mind, it is not a mere theological fiction. It is plainly and expressly affirmed in many Scriptures, under a great variety of expressions, all of which are too clear to be misunderstood. As actually as the limbs of the body are united to their head, the wife to the husband, the branches to the root, so truly are the saints united to Christ and Christ to them. Take this away and the whole of Christianity collapses. Is not the union between God the Father and God the Son a *real* one? then so is this: John 17:22: the one is as much a verity as the other.

3. It is *spiritual.* The great design and the grand aim of God in His purpose and dealings with the elect is the communication to them of the benefits of Christ; but all communication of benefits implies communion, and all communion necessarily presupposes *union* with His person. Not that there is any confusion or transfusing of the Christian's person with Christ's person, but a real and personal conjunction between them. That conjunction is not a gross, fleshly, corporeal union, but a mystical spiritual, and inward one. The nature of this union is seen in the *bond* of it: it is entirely spiritual — the Spirit in Christ, faith in us. The husband and the wife are "one flesh" (Eph. 5:31), but "he that is joined to the Lord is one spirit" (I Cor. 6:19).

4. It is *intimate,* far closer than that existing between the branches and root of a tree, or that between husband and wife. The union between Christ and His people is so near that we know not how to conceive it, still less express it. We may borrow some light here and there from the different unions in nature, but they all, in point of nearness, fall far short of it. Believers are so united to the Lord as to be "one spirit" — What an expression is that! What could be spoken higher! So intimate is this oneness that in a coming day Christ will say, "Inasmuch as ye have done it unto one of the least of these my brethren, ye have done it unto *me*" (Matt. 25:40). So near are the saints to Christ, they are a part of Him, so that He would be *incomplete* without them — they are His "fulness" (Eph. 1:23).

5. It is *indissoluble.* The oneness between Christ and His Church is such that it cannot be broken. All the powers of Satan cannot destroy that union. "Who shall separate us from the love of Christ!" (Rom. 8: 35). "Ye *shall* abide in him" (I John 2:27). It is an inseparable, insuperable union. Death itself, though it break all other unions, does not and cannot put an end to or reach this. "Blessed are the dead which die *in* the Lord" (Rev. 14:13); "absent from the body, and to be present *with* the Lord" (II Cor. 5:8)! And this union pertains to *all* the redeemed: the least as well as the greatest Christian, the humblest as well as the highest, is *equally* united to Christ and participates in what belongs to Him.

Union with Christ *in glory* is the goal toward which we are now moving, but at present we enjoy *experimental* union with Him in grace. But experimental union with Christ is only possible as there is a *practical* union with Him, for "can two walk together except they be agreed?" Practical union with Christ presupposes a *saving* one, whereby the heart is wedded to Christ in faith and love. That, in turn, necessitates a *vital* union, for only as quickened by the Spirit and made one with Christ can any sinner savingly believe into Him. And that again denotes a *mystical* and eternal union, for the Spirit quickens none save those who had a covenant-oneness with Christ before the foundation of the world. Nor could there ever have been *any* union between the Creator and the creature but for the *mediatorial* union, whereby the Son united our nature to His own ineffable person. And the foundation of *that* was the *Divine* union, the three Persons in one God. The Lord willing, by His enabling, we shall seek to contemplate separately each of these unions in the chapters which follow, taking them up in their inverse order.

2

Divine Union

I

THAT which we shall seek to contemplate in this chapter is the revelation which God has made of Himself in His inspired Word. This ineffable subject is one which we must ever approach with bowed heads and reverent hearts, for the ground which we are to tread is indeed holy. The subject is transcendently sacred, for it is concerned with the infinite and majestic Jehovah. It is one of surpassing importance, for it is the foundation of all spiritual knowledge and faith. For any real light thereon, we are entirely shut up to what God has made known of Himself in His Word. Neither observation, science or philosophy can, in this exalted sphere, advance our knowledge one iota. We can know no more thereon except what is set forth in Holy Writ, and that must be approached with the deepest humility and reverence, with the earnest prayer, "that which I see not teach thou me."

It is not sufficient to think of God as He may be conceived of in our imagination, instead, our thoughts of Him must be formed by what He has revealed of Himself in His word. Man, unaided, cannot rightly conceive of God: all speculation concerning Him is utterly vain, yea, profane. The finite cannot comprehend the Infinite. If the "judgments" of God are "unsearchable" and if His "ways" are "past finding out," how much more so must God Himself be! Even creation cannot fully teach us what God is, because no work is able to perfectly express the worker thereof. The heathen have creation spread before them, but what do they know of *God!* The ancient Egyptians, Babylonians, Greeks, sought to delve deeply into the marvels and mysteries of "Nature," but with all their boasted wisdom the Deity was to them "the unknown God!"

It is of vast importance to the souls of God's believing people that they should have clear, spiritual, and Divine knowledge of the true and living God: without a scriptural acquaintance of the same, we are left without the very supports which are indispensable to found our faith upon. It is impossible to over-emphasize the momentousness of our present theme, for the truth thereon will alone direct us in worshipping God aright. If a person has erroneous thoughts of Deity, then he worships a false god and renders homage to a fictitious being, the figment of his own imagination. "This is life eternal: that they might know thee the only true God, and Jesus Christ, whom thou hast sent" (John 17:3): that is unspeakably blessed; it is likewise unspeakably solemn — the man who knows not the "only true God" is destitute of eternal life!

Now as we turn to and examine the Holy Scriptures we are at once impressed with their repeated and uniform emphasis upon the *unity* of God. In contrast from the polytheism (many gods) of the heathen, we read, "Hear, O Israel, the Lord thy God is *one* Lord" (Deut. 6:4), and, as we have seen above, "this is life eternal, that they might know thee the *only* true God." There can be but one infinite, self-existent Spirit, who reveals Himself as the great "I am," from whom, and through whom, and to whom, are all things, to whom be glory for ever. To think of two, or more independent and supreme Beings, would be to suppose a contradiction in terms, an utter impossibility. There can be but one *God*, with sovereign authority over all the works and creatures of His hands, having but one plan and a single administration. Such is indeed the teaching of Scripture from Genesis to Revelation.

But as we continue our examination of what God has revealed of Himself in His Holy Word, it is not long before we reach that which is profoundly mysterious, for side by side with its continuous emphasis on the *unity* of God it also reveals *three* distinct Divine persons, namely, God the Father, God the Son, and God the Holy Spirit. Here we come to an infinite depth which we have no means of sounding, for while the Scriptures are unmistakably clear in their presentation of three Divine persons, nevertheless they are equally express in denying that there are three Gods. Though no attempt whatever is made in Scripture to explain this mystery, it is unmistakable in affirming it: in affirming that God is an absolute Unity in Trinity, and Trinity in Unity; and all who refuse to bow to and acknowledge this ineffable truth must be eternally damned.

The incomprehensible nature of the truth which is now before us, so far from providing a valid motive for its rejection, supplies a most powerful argument for its being formally received. For if this truth be so sublime and mysterious, that even when revealed, it infinitely surpasses the feeble grasp of our finite powers, then it is very evident that it could never have been invented by men! What human wisdom cannot comprehend, human policy could never have proposed. It *must* have had some higher projector, and therefore the conclusion is unavoidable: in God alone we behold an adequate cause. "This also cometh forth from the Lord of hosts, which is wonderful in counsel, and excellent in working" (Isa. 28:29).

The first great truth, then, which is presented to faith — the foundation of everything — is the fact of the one living, eternal, and true God; and this we know not by any discovery of reason, but because He has Himself revealed it to our hearts through His Word. The next great truth is that, the one living and true God has revealed Himself to us under the threefold relation of Father, Son, and Holy Spirit; and this we know upon the same authority as the first. Both of these sublime truths are above reason yet their very transcendency so far from stumbling us, is a necessary condition of our confidence in the Scriptures and our faith in Him who is there revealed. Had the Scriptures professed to present a revelation of God which had no heights beyond our powers to scale, and no depth too deep for mental acumen to fathom, the writer for one would promptly spurn them as the invention of man. Personally, I would no more worship a God that my intellect could measure, than I would an idol which my hands had manufactured.

"Jesus called a little child unto Him, and set him in the midst of them, and said, Verily I say unto you, Except ye be converted and *become as little children,* ye shall not enter into the kingdom of heaven" (Matt. 18: 2, 3). A hard lesson for proud man to learn is that, yet is *must be* learned (by grace) if any entrance is to be had into the things of God. It is at *this* point we may perceive one of the radical differences between the regenerate and unregenerate: *faith receives* what reason is unable to grasp. "Great God, I desire to fall down under the deepest self-abasement, in the consciousness of my own nothingness and ignorance before Thee! I bless the Lord for that degree of information He hath been pleased to give of Himself, while here below. It is enough! O for grace, to the acknowledgement of the mystery of God, and of the Father, and of Christ, in whom dwelleth all the treasures of wisdom and knowledge, Col. 2:2, 3" (Rob. Hawker, 1810) — such is the language of every renewed heart.

Though the doctrine or truth of the Divine Trinity is properly speaking a "mystery," that affords no ground whatever for it to be disparaged by us. Some people seem to suppose that by the term "mystery," reference is made to something of which they can at best form only a vague notion, that it pertains to the sphere of half-perceived shadows, in relation to which certainty is impossible, and that it has no *practical* connection with the solid elements of knowledge and real life. This is a great mistake. The word "mystery" in Scripture is applied to that which cannot be discovered by human reason, or arrived at by any speculation, but which can only be made known by *Divine revelation,* and which can only be perceived so far as God has been pleased to unveil it. Just so far as Spiritual "mysteries" *have been* disclosed by God, they become part of the real and solid knowledge of those by whom that revelation is humbly received.

It is in the Gospel that the three Persons in the Godhead are most clearly revealed, and their respective activities in the saving of the elect are most fully made known. "The Gospel represents *God the Father* as sovereign Lord of heaven and earth: as righteous Governor of the world: as giving laws to His creatures; as revealing His wrath against all transgressions. He is represented at being injured and offended by our sins, and concerned to maintain the honor of his majesty, of His law and government, and sacred authority. He is represented as having designs of mercy towards a sinful, guilty, ruined world; and as contriving and proposing a method of recovery. He is represented as one seated on a throne of grace, reconciling the world unto Himself by Christ, ordering pardon and peace to be proclaimed to any and all who will return to Him in the way prescribed.

"The Gospel represents *God the Son* as being constituted Mediator by His Father, that in and by Him He might open a way to accomplish His designs of mercy towards a guilty world, consistent with the honor of His majesty, of His holiness and justice, of His law and government.

His Father appointed Him to the office, and He freely undertook it. His Father sent Him into this world to enter upon the difficult work, and He willingly came: 'He was made flesh, and dwelt among us.' Here He lived, and here He died, in the capacity of a Mediator. He arose, He ascended into Heaven, and sits now at His Father's right hand, God-man Mediator, exalted to the highest honor; made Lord of all things, and Judge of the world. And now we are to have access to God by Him, as our Mediator, High Priest, Intercessor, and Advocate, who has made complete atonement for sins in the days of His abasement, and has now suffiicient interest in the court of Heaven.

"The Gospel represents *God the Holy Spirit* as being sent of the Father as prime Agent, and by the Son as Mediator, in the character of an enlightener and sanctifier, in order to bring sinners effectually to see and be made sensible of their sin, guilt, and ruin; to believe the Gospel, to trust in Christ, and to return home to God through Him. It is His office to dwell in believers; to teach and lead them; to sanctify, strengthen, comfort, and keep them through faith unto salvation.

"The Father is God by nature, and God by office. The Son is God by nature, and Mediator by office. The Spirit is God by nature, and Sanctifier by office. The Father as Governor, Law-Giver, and Avenger, has all power in heaven and in earth, in and of Himself: Matt 11:25. The Son as Mediator derives all His authority from the Father: Matt. 11:27. The Holy Spirit acts as being sent by them Both: John 14:16. The Father maintains the honor of the Godhead and of His government, displaying His grace while ordaining that sin should be punished, the sinner humbled, and brought back to God and into a subjection into His will. Sin is punished in the Son as Mediator, standing in the room of the guilty. The sinner is humbled and brought into subjection to God's will by the Holy Spirit. Thus the Son and the Spirit honor the Father as supreme Governor, and all join in the same design to discountenance sin, humble the sinner, and glorify grace" (Jos. Bellamy, 1780).

By affirming that the three Divine persons are more clearly revealed in the gospel than elsewhere, it is *not* to be understood that the Old Testament saints were left in ignorance of this blessed and foundation truth. That could not be, or otherwise it had been impossible for them to know God, or to worship Him intelligently and acceptably. God must be *revealed* before He can (in any measure) be known, and He must be *known* in the distinctions of His persons, before He can be loved and adored. Those who find it hard to conceive of the Old Testament saints possessing a clear evangelical knowledge of the mystery of the Trinity, create their own difficulty by supposing the gospel is peculiar to the New Testament dispensation. This is a serious mistake. Hebrews 4:2 declares, "For unto us was the gospel preached, as well as unto *them*" — that is, unto Israel in the wilderness: see the closing verses of Hebrews 3. To go back further still, Galatians 3:8 tells us, that God "preached before *the gospel* unto Abraham."

The glorious truth of the three Persons in the Godhead is to be found as definitely and as frequently in the Old Testament as it is in the New.

On the very first page of Holy Writ it is recorded, "And God said, Let US make man in OUR image, after OUR likeness" (Gen. 1:26): how clearly do the plural pronouns there reveal the fact that there is *more* than one person in the Godhead! Nor is Genesis 1:26 by any means the only passage in the Old Testament where the plural pronoun is used of God. After Adam had fallen, we find Him saying, "Behold, the man is become as one of *Us*, to know good and evil" (Gen. 3:22) — probably that was the language of irony: God's answer to the Serpent's lie in 3:5. Again; in response to the impiety of those who had said, "Go to, let us build us a city and a tower whose top may reach unto heaven," the Lord said, Go to, let *Us* go down and there confound their language" (Gen. 11:7).

Once more; in that marvellous vision granted unto Isaiah, wherein he saw the Lord "seated upon a throne, high and lifted up, and His train filled the temple," before whom the seraphim veiled their faces, the prophet "heard the voice of the Lord saying, Whom shall *I* send, and who will go for *US?*" (Isa. 6:8). Very wonderful is that "I" and "US," intimating the Divine unity in Trinity, and the trinity in Unity. It is striking to note that the employment of this plural pronoun in connection with the Godhead, as it is consecrated by the Spirit of truth in use with the Persons in the Divine Essence, is employed by *Each* of Them to each other. By the Father in Genesis 1:26 (cf. Eph. 3:9), the Father being the *Creator*, "by Jesus Christ," by the Son of Genesis 11:7, for to Him all *judgment* is committed (John 5:22); by the Spirit of Isaiah 6:8 (see Acts 28:26 and cf. 13:2)!

The Hebrew noun is in the plural number in each of these verses: "Remember now thy Creators in the days of thy youth" (Eccles. 12:1); "For thy makers are thine husband" (Isa. 54:5); "Let the children of Zion be joyful in their kings" (Ps. 149:2); "The fear of the Lord is the beginning of wisdom: and the knowledge of the Holy Ones is understanding" (Prov. 9:10) — according to the rule of Hebrew parallelism, it is obvious that "Holy Ones" is exegetical of "Jehovah." Surely there is more that a hint of the Divine Trinity in the benediction of Numbers 6:24-26, "*The Lord* bless thee and keep thee; *the Lord* make his face shine upon thee and be gracious unto thee; *the Lord* lift up His countenance upon thee and give thee peace"; also in the "Holy, holy, holy" of the seraphim in Isaiah 6:3. In Isaiah 48:16 we hear the Messiah saying, "Come ye near unto me, hear ye this; I have not spoken in secret from the beginning; from the time that it was, there was I; and now the [1] Lord God, and [2] His Spirit, hath sent [3] me." "So *the Spirit* took me up and brought me into the inner court; and, behold, the glory of *the Lord* filled the house. And I heard *him* speaking unto me out of the house; and *the man* stood by me" (Ezek. 43:5, 6). While the prophet was adoring the manifest glory of God, the Spirit conducted him into the inner chamber, while beside him stood the One who had been instructing him — "the man": see 40:3. Thus the prophet had a vision of the three Persons in the Godhead, manifesting in different ways Their presence with him.

A plurality of persons in the Godhead was also indicated in such passages as, "Then *the Lord* rained upon Sodom and upon Gomorrah brimstone and fire *from the Lord* out of heaven" (Gen. 19:24); "the Lord said unto my Lord Sit thou at my right hand (Ps. 110:1); "And *the Lord* said unto Satan, *The Lord* rebuke thee" (Zech. 3:2). "Be strong, all ye people of the land, saith the Lord, and work: for I am with you, saith *the Lord* of hosts: *The Word* that I covenanted with you when ye came out of Egypt, so *my Spirit* remaineth among you" (Hag. 2:4, 5). The first person in the sacred Trinity was known to the Old Testament saints as *the Father*: from a number of passages we select the following, "But now, O Lord, thou art our Father" (Isa. 64:8). The second person in the Trinity was revealed as *the Son*: "The Lord hath said unto me, thou art my Son" (Ps. 2:7), and also as *the Word*: "By *the Word of the Lord* were the heavens made" (Ps. 33:6) and see Genesis 15:1 and I Kings 19:9 where the essential and personal "Word" is in view. The third person in the Trinity was revealed as *The Holy Spirit*: "The Spirit of the Lord" (I Sam. 16:13).

"Produce your cause, saith the Lord; bring forth your strong reasons, saith the King of Jacob. Let them bring them forth, and show *Us* what shall happen: let them show the former things, what they be, that *We* may consider them, and know the latter end of them; or declare *Us* things for to come" (Isa. 41:21, 22). A truly remarkable passage is that; with it may be compared, "If a man love me, he will keep my words: and my Father will love him, and *We* will come unto him, and make *Our* abode with him" (John 14:23). "For thus saith the high and lofty One that inhabiteth eternity, whose name is Holy; I dwell in the high and holy place, with him also that is of a contrite and humble spirit" (Isa. 57:15): the "high and lofty *One*" — one in the inseparable unity of the Divine Essence; "that inhabiteth eternity" — thus distinguished from all creatures; "dwelling in the high and lofty place" — true of the Father (I Kings 8:27), of the Son (Jer. 23:24 — see v. 6), of the Spirit (Ps. 139:7, 8); *indwelling His people* — true of the Father (II Cor. 6: 16, 18), of the Son (Col. 1:27), of the Spirit (I Cor. 6:19).

The title "Jehovah" — applied to the Father (Ps. 110:1), the Son (Jer. 23:6), and the Holy Spirit (II Sam. 23:2) — is *always* in the *singular* number, having no plural form, being expressive of the Unity of the Divine nature. Yet we frequently find it employed with the plural "Elohim" (God), and with plural pronouns and verbs — a thing which could never have been done consistent with the laws of grammar, except for the purpose of proving thereby, what all the parts of Scripture concur in, that Jehovah though but One in the essence of the Godhead, is nevertheless existing at the same time in a plurality or trinity of Persons. That the great God should subsist in a way *entirely different* and perfectly distinguished from all His creatures in a trinity of Persons in the unity of His essence should not stagger us, but should bow our hearts before Him in adoring wonder and worship.

"Hear, O Israel: The Lord our God is our Lord" (Deut. 6:4). This very verse which is quoted so much by "Unitarians," in their hatred of the blessed truth which we are here endeavoring to set forth, would be quite meaningless were there no Trinity of Persons in the Godhead. It is self-evident that there is no need whatever for any *Divine revelation* to teach us that *one is one*: had this text meant nothing more than that, it had been superfluous information. But inasmuch as "Elohim" (God) is in the plural number, it *was* necessary for the Deity to make known unto His people that the three Divine Persons are but *one* "Lord" or Jehovah. That Israel apprehended (in some measure, at any rate) this mystery of the great One in Three, is strikingly manifested by the fact that when Aaron made the single golden calf, the people addressed it in the *plural* number: "These be thy *gods* O Israel, which brought thee up out of the land of Egypt" (Exod. 32:4)!!

II

Right views of the Divine Being and Character lie at the foundation of all genuine and vital godliness. It should, then, be our supreme quest to seek after the knowledge of God. Without the true knowledge of Him, in His nature, persons, and attributes, we can neither worship Him acceptably nor serve Him aright. The *unity* of the Godhead is an essential part of His character. The God whom the Scriptures command us to adore and serve, love and obey, is the one only living and true God. There cannot be but *one* First Cause of all things, absolutely independent, necessarily existent, and infinite in all perfections. But this one God subsists in a *threefold*, though to us incomprehensible, manner. Though He is one simple, undivided essence, yet in the mode of His existence He subsists in three Persons. Incomprehensible as this is, yet it is no more so than as *uncaused* and eternal existence: God is infinitely above all creatures, and exists in a manner peculiar to Himself.

This truth of three Persons in the Godhead is basic, being essential to the very scheme of salvation itself, and it has been accounted the catholic doctrine of the whole Christian Church in all ages. In Scripture, the work of our salvation is represented as engaging the *joint-agency* of the Father, the Son, and the Holy Spirit. God *the Father* it was who, in infinite wisdom planned the amazing scheme, providing Himself a Lamb to purge away sin. God *the Son*, in His own person, executed the plan, by submitting to be "delivered for our offences and raised again for our justification." God *the Spirit* secures an effectual reception of this scheme of salvation, sanctifying the souls of the elect unto eternal happiness, in which it finally issues.

Each of these sacred Persons, who thus co-operate in our salvation, must of necessity be really and truly *God*, for none less could possibly execute any part of that grand scheme. Who, but the supreme Lord Himself, could admit an innocent Substitute to become Surety for criminals and bear their faction of infinite sufficiency to the Divine government, possessing such merits that, by obeying and suffering the penalty of the law, full atonement should be made for all innumerable offenses committed against the Majesty of Heaven by the entire election of grace!

And unto whom beside God Himself, the eternal and blessed Holy Spirit, doth such power belong as to change the darkness of human depravity into ineffable light, subdue rebellious wills, and bring them into loving obedience unto the Lord!

All that pertains to salvation is the gift of the Father, through the incarnate Son, by the Holy Spirit; and it is inexpressibly blessed to find in so many Scriptures how *all* the Persons in the Godhead are individually as well as unitedly concerned in the grand matter of the Church's redemption. This ought ever to be viewed as the standard of orthodoxy. Whatever is presented from pulpit or press which does not give *equal* place and ascribe equal honor to *each* of the Eternal Three is the doctrine of demons. There is not a vestige of real "Christianity" where this foundation truth of the Trinity is not known, acknowledged, and magnified. Nor is there a vestige of true piety in any heart where the Father, Son, and Holy Spirit do not dwell. Furthermore, it is not possible to obtain a clear and full view of any doctrine of the Word, unless the telescope of this transcendent truth be applied to the eye of faith and be viewed through it.

Now if the Holy Scriptures be so plain and full in declaring the interposition and operations of each Person in the blessed Trinity in the work of our salvation, it must of necessity be the bounden duty as well as the precious privilege of each Christian to pay a becoming attention to and endeavor by devout meditation and prayerful searching of the Word, to get impressed on his mind and heart what God has revealed on the subject. It most certainly behoves each one of us to spare no pains in endeavoring to attain unto a full spiritual knowledge of how the Divine Three stand related to us, how they are severally interested in us, and what we are to expect from them. This will lead us to render unto Each Divine Person that honor and praise, that loving obedience, which is His distinctive due. For "this is life eternal: that they might *know thee* the only true God" (John 17:3).

"The knowledge of God here spoken of, must include in it such a knowledge of the Holy Trinity as is revealed in the blessed gospel. The divine persons in their essential and distinctive relation to each other, and to us, must be so far known as to be believed, and acknowledged by us. The truth of their existence (not the knowledge of their subsisting in the infinite essence), is most essential to the being and to the well-being of our faith. As also how they are related unto us, and have acted for us in the everlasting covenant, in and by which they are and have revealed themselves to be the Lord our God. To know the Father, to be our Father in Christ Jesus, that He hath loved with an everlasting love, is life eternal. To know the Son, as one with the Father, of the same essence with the Father, and that He was set up to be God-man, from everlasting, this is life eternal. To know the Holy Spirit, to be personally distinct from the Father and the Son, yet of the same essence, glory, perfections and blessedness with the Father and the Son, is life eternal" (S. E. Pierce).

A distinction in the Divine nature inconceivable by us, but plainly revealed in Holy Writ, must be acknowledged by us on the all-sufficient testimony of Him who alone can instruct us in what we are concerned to know of His ineffable essence and being. "For there are three that bear record in heaven, the Father, the Word, and the Holy Spirit: and these three *are one*" (I John 5:7). To each of these three Persons the perfections of Deity are attributed and ascribed in hundreds of passages of Scripture. Each of Them, therefore, is *God*, and yet it is equally clear that there is but *one* Jehovah. Nor is there the slightest ground for us to demur in the face of this insuperable and insoluble mystery. "Let us first if we can, account for the nature, essence, and properties of the things with which, as to their effects, we are familiarly acquainted. Let us *explain* the growth of a blade of grass, or the virtues of the loadstone. Till we are able to do *this*, it becomes us to lay our hand upon our mouths, and our mouths in the dust" (John Newton).

A plurality of persons does *not* mean that the Godhead is divided, so that the Father is *one part of* Deity, the Son another part, and the Spirit still a third part. "The Divine *nature* IS the Godhead, simply and absolutely considered; a *person* is that which subsisteth IN the Godhead, as the Father, the Son, and the Holy Spirit" (W. Perkins, 1595). It is the Divine persons in the union of the Divine essence which are to be distinguished, and not the Essence itself. Jehovah is to be worshipped as a Unity in Trinity, and a Trinity in Unity: one God is to be acknowledged in the Father, the Son, and the Holy Spirit. When Scripture is compared with Scripture it is plain to be seen that the Divine Unity is *not* a unity of Persons, but of nature and essence. Though there are three in the Godhead, who are dignified with the incommunicable name of Jehovah, possessing *the same* attributes and perfections and entitled to the same adoration, yet Holy Writ does not exhibit a plurality of Deities.

That each of the Eternal Three partakes of the one Divine essence, is proved by their names. Each is called "God": the Father in Hebrews 1:1, the Son in Hebrews 1:8, the Spirit in Acts 5:4 — see v. 3. Each of them is designated "Jehovah"; the Father in Psalm 110:1, the Son in Psalm 23:1, the Spirit in Isaiah 11:2. Each of them is denominated "The Living God: the Father in Matthew 16:16, the Son in Hebrews 3:12 and I Timothy 4:10, the Spirit in II Corinthians 6:16 — cf. I Corinthians 3: 16. Each of them is addressed as "The Almighty": the Father in II Corinthians 6:18, the Son in Revelation 16:7, the Spirit in Job 32:8. Each of them is set forth as a "Fountain": the Father in Jeremiah 2:13, the Son in Zechariah 13:1, the Spirit in John 7:38. In Ephesians 1:17 the first Person is termed "the Father of glory"; in James 2:1 the second Person is termed "the Lord of Glory," while in I Peter 4:14 the third Person is termed "the Spirit of glory."

That these three names — Father, Son and Holy Spirit — are *not* so many diverse titles for one and the same august Person, but instead, belong to three distinct but equally Divine persons, is clear from the fact that in Scripture they are frequently represented as *speaking to one another*. Thus, in Psalm 2 the Messiah declares, "The Lord hath said *unto* [not "of"] me, thou art, my Son. . . . *Ask of me*, and I shall give thee the

heathen for thine inheritance" (vv. 7, 8). In Psalm 40 the Son is heard
speaking *to* the Father, saying "Lo, I come: in the volume of the book
it is written of me. I delight to do thy will, O my God; yea, thy law is
within my heart" (vv. 7, 8). In Psalm 45, the Father says to His Son,
"thy throne, O God, is forever and ever, the sceptre of thy kingdom is a
right sceptre" (v. 6). And again in Psalm 110, "The Lord *said unto* my
Lord, sit thou at my right hand, until I make thine enemies thy footstool"
(v. 1). What could possibly set forth more clearly the distinction of
Persons in the Godhead!

In the previous section of this article we called attention to a number
of passages in the Old Testament where the Eternal Three are all mentioned together: the same blessed phenomenon is presented again and
again in the New Testament. "When the [1] Comforter is come, whom
[2] I will send unto you from [3] the Father, even the Spirit of truth
which proceedeth from the Father, he shall testify of me" (John 15:26).
"I beseech you, brethren, for [1] the Lord Jesus Christ's sake, and for
[2] the love of the Spirit, that ye strive together with me in your prayers
[3] to God" (Rom. 15:30). "For through him [Christ] we both have
access by one Spirit unto the Father" (Eph. 2:18). "To the acknowledging of the mystery of God [the Spirit], and of the Father, and of Christ"
(Col. 2:2). "The Lord [the Spirit] direct your hearts into the love of
God [the Father] and into the patient waiting for Christ" (II Thess.
3:5). "Christ, who through the eternal Spirit, offered himself without spot
to God" (Heb. 9:14). "Elect according to the foreknowledge of God the
Father, through sanctification of the Spirit, unto obedience and sprinkling
of the blood of Jesus Christ" (I Peter 1:2).

"Go ye therefore, and teach all nations, baptizing them in the name of
the Father, and of the Son, and of the Holy Spirit" (Matt. 28:19). In
the name of the Triune God believers are to be baptized. What a con-
clusive confirmation of the blessed doctrine of the Holy Trinity is this!
Here are three Divine persons, but with *one* "Name" — note carefully it is
not "names!" The absolute Deity of the Son and of the Spirit are here
unmistakably intimated by their conjunction with the Father, since baptism is administered *equally* in the name of all Three as a religious or-
dinance, yea, as a part of Divine worship, which could never be were
either of the Three merely a creature. Not only is there a profession of
faith in the three Divine persons made by those who are scripturally baptized, but there is a solemn dedication unto their service and worship,
being laid under obligation of obedience unto each.

"The grace of the Lord Jesus Christ, and the love of God [the Father],
and the communion of the Holy Spirit, be with you all" (II Cor. 13:14).
This passage contains another clear proof of a trinity of Persons in the
Godhead, for here distinct things are ascribed and of them asked, as
equal Objects of prayer and worship. That comprehensive benediction
includes all the prime blessings and benefits of redemption: the "grace"
of our adorable Saviour, the "love" of our heavenly Father, and the
"communion" of our Divine Comforter. Unto what wretched shifts are
the enemies of the truth put, who would reduce the meaning of this

verse unto "the grace of a *creature* and the love of the *Creator* be joined with the communion of *an energy* of Deity, be with you all!" Unspeakably solemn is I John 2:23, "Whosoever denieth the Son, the same hath not the Father": a denial of the Trinity is a repudiation of the Deity of the Son and the Spirit, and he who is guilty of that most awful sin knows not, hath not "the Father"! In denying *one* they equally deny *all*.

"And Jesus, when he was baptized, went up straightway out of the water: and, lo, the heavens were opened unto him, and he saw the Spirit of God descending like a dove, and lighting upon him: and, lo, a voice from heaven, saying, This is my beloved Son in whom I am well pleased" (Matt. 3:16, 17). Let it be carefully observed here were presented all three persons of the Godhead, clearly distinguished from each other and manifested severally, and that, in such a way and manner as is needed to define the persons of each. Here was the person of the Father, manifested by a voice from heaven. Here was the person of the Son, manifested in our nature, coming up from the water. Here was the person of the Holy Spirit manifested in the form of a dove, lighting upon the Son. What could more clearly distinguish the Eternal Three — the Father speaking, the Son spoken of, and the Spirit manifested apart from both! Forever be His name praised that the Triune God there so gloriously revealed Himself.

Not only are the Eternal Three in one God plainly revealed in Scripture, in their distinctive personalities, but their *absolute equality* one with the other is also clearly made known. It would extend this unto too great a length were we to present a small part of the proof that each One is possessed of the same Divine perfections, and quote some of the texts which affirm that Father, Son and Spirit are alike eternal, omnipotent, omniscient, and omnipresent. Instead, we will here simply point out how their equality is evidenced by the *order* in which they are mentioned in various Scriptures. In Matthew 28:19 it is God the Father, God the Son, and God the Holy Spirit. In II Corinthians 13:14 it is the Son, the Father, and the Spirit. In Ephesians 4:4 it is the Spirit, the Son, and the Father. In Colossians 2:2 it is the Spirit, the Father, and the Son. In Revelation 1:4, 5 it is the Father, the Spirit, and the Son. What could more definitely intimate their equality than this *variation* of order!

Infidels have sought to turn into ridicule the fact of Christ praying to the Father, arguing that if both were Divine and there be only one God, then God was praying to Himself. In this they betray their ignorance, failing to discern the distinctions in the Godhead: though the Divine essence be one, there is a distinction of Persons in the undivided nature. "The language of *I* and *Thou*, and *Me* and *Thee*, so often used by Christ in John 17, are so many proofs of the Divine personalities of Himself and of the Father. The word personalities is expressive of the mode of existing in the Divine nature. The word person, besides that, implies the nature and substance in whom He subsists. A person is an individual that subsists and lives of itself, endowed with will and understanding, who is neither sustained by, nor is part of another. Such is the Father, therefore a Person; such is the Son, therefore a Person; such is the Holy Spirit, therefore a Person. The great and incommunicable name of Jehovah is always in the singular number, because it is expressive of His essence, which is but one; but the first name we meet with in the first verse of Scripture is plural" (S. E. Pierce.)

Scripture does not present the doctrine of the sacred Trinity in any way of contradiction, and affirm that God is one and three, three and one; in the *same* manner: instead, it reveals that God is one in *nature*, but three in His *Persons*. When Christ said "I and [my] Father are one" (John 10:30), He signified one in nature, not one in Person. The word "God" is sometimes expressive of the Divine Essence, and sometimes of one of the Persons in that Essence. The three Persons are one in substance, one in the depths of a common consciousness, one in purpose, and with absolute equality in power and glory. "They agree with one another in nature, being, life, time, dignity, glory, or anything else pertaining to the Divine Essence: for in all these They are one and the same, and consequently co-essential, co-equal, co-eternal" (J. Usher, 1640).

The Divine Persons are not only one, but they are *in* one another: "As thou Father art in me, and I in thee" (John 17:21) — there is an intimate inhabitation without any confusion of the three subsistences. They enjoy perfect, absolute, and Divine union and communion with each other. In the Scriptures we hear them speaking *to* each other, and *of* each other in such a way as to clearly show a distinction of Persons, while constituting one Jehovah in the indivisible Essence of the Godhead. The ineffable union between the Eternal Three is such that each one is *in* and *with* the others; each one loves, possesses, glories, in the other, and works the same thing. "The Father loveth the Son" (John 3:35); "the Son can do nothing of himself, but what he seeth the Father do; for what things soever he doeth, these also doeth the Son likewise" (John 5:19); "Believest thou not that I am in the Father, and the Father in me?" (John 14:10).

"The union of the Trinity in Godhead is an essential one. There can be no greater unity. Nothing can be more one than the Father, Son, and Holy Spirit are one. Yet it is a unity which consists with order and distinction: the Unity of the Trinity does not take away the distinction of the Persons, nor confuse their order. They are one, yet three. They keep their distinct Personalities, and their distinct Personal operations, and their different manner and order of acting. It is an eternal and inseparable union, for in the Divine nature or essence there can be no change. It is from the unity of the Persons in the same Essence ariseth their essential Inbeing in each other. All the Persons having the same Essence and being in the one Essence, it follows that in respect of the Essence, one Person is as another.

"The great and incomprehensible God is essentially and infinitely holy, happy, blessed, and glorious. His nature is a fountain of infinite perfection. He is life itself, eternity itself, love itself, and blessedness itself. His happiness arises from the knowledge which He hath of His own essential nature, persons and perfections. Nothing can be added unto Him, for 'of Him, and through Him, and to Him are all things' (Rom. 11:

36). From the in-being, society, and mutual intercourse held between the Eternal Three in the one Jehovah, flows that life of joy and bliss, which belongs to God alone. The essential union between the Persons in the Eternal Godhead is incommunicable, and the communion which they had from everlasting with each other is incomprehensible. Yet we may venture to say, their communion consisteth in the eternal life of the three Persons among themselves, in the common interests and propriety which they have in each other, in reciprocal affections, communion and enjoyment; in an equal knowledge of each other; in an alternate communication of each other's mind in mutual love and delight, and in their possession of one common glory and blessedness.

"There is an incomprehensible love borne by the Three in Jehovah to each other: it is a part of their essential perfection and blessedness. Whilst the Scripture is not altogether silent on this most sublime truth, yet it speaks but sparingly of it, because it exceeds all created conceptions; it can no more be comprehended than the life and self-sufficiency of Jehovah can. Yet, as in the order in which the Essential Three exist and co-exist in the incomprehensible Jehovah, they have been pleased to make known and manifest their Personalities in all their eternal, internal and external acts of grace in election, regeneration, sanctification, preservation and eternal glorification. So their love to each other is intimated in those distinct displays of grace which are attributed to each of them in the sacred Word. It is expressly said, 'The Father loveth the Son' (John 3:55), 'I love the Father' (John 14:31). And from the co-equality of the Father, Son and Spirit, in the Essence of Godhead, and from the unity of the Holy Ones in the whole revelation of grace, it is evident that the Spirit loves the Father and the Son" (S. E. Pierce, 1810).

We have written of the union of the Eternal Three. It is the union of distinct Persons in the unity of a single nature. It is an union which is absolute, essential, eternal, incomprehensible, ineffable. It is not only futile, but grossly impious, to attempt any *illustration* of it, for there exists *no* analogy in all the universe. GOD is unique! But though profoundly mysterious, every truly regenerated soul has *proof of this truth* in his own inward experience. He knows that he has access through Christ, by the Spirit unto the Father. He knows that the Man who has saved him from Hell, is indwelt by "all the fulness of the Godhead bodily." He knows that the invincible power which subdued his enmity and caused him to throw down the weapons of his rebellion, was exercised by God the Spirit. And he knows that he has received the spirit of adoption whereby he cries "Abba, Father."

3

Mediatorial Union

I

THAT which is now to engage our attention is the constitution of the Person of Christ, not as He existed from all eternity with the Father and the Holy Spirit, but as He was upon earth working out the salvation of His Church, and as He now is in heaven at God's right hand. It was an essential part of His covenant-engagement that the beloved Son should become the Surety of His people, and in order thereto, assume their nature into union with His Divine Person, and thus become God and man in the Person of one Christ. In consequence of that union, all the fulness of the Godhead dwells in Him bodily or personally, in a manner and to an extent it does not, will not, and cannot, in any other. This is the next greatest mystery which is revealed in Holy Writ, being the foundation upon which the Church is built (Matt. 16:18), and concerning which a belief thereof is absolutely essential unto salvation. It is therefore impossible to overestimate the importance, blessedness, and value of this truth.

This Mediatorial union — denominated the "Hypostatic (personal) union" by theologians — or the conjunction of the Divine and human natures in the God-man Mediator, is based upon that infinitely higher union which we sought to contemplate in the last chapter. Divine union — between the Eternal Three — was the foundation of the Mediatorial union. Had there been only one person in the Divine Essence or Godhead, our salvation had been utterly impossible: we could not be joined to the very nature or essence of God, without either ungodding Him or deifying us. For the elect to have been taken into *immediate* union with God would produce a change in the Divine nature — an addition to it — something which can never be. Even the Man Christ Jesus could not be taken into immediate union with the Divine Essence absolutely considered, though He could and was with One in that Essence.

We are conscious of the fact that we have just stepped into deep water, and perhaps those who are accustomed to paddle in the shallows will be unwilling to follow; but for the sake of the few who desire, by grace, to believe, and as far as God now permits, to understand the *mysteries* of our faith, we deemed it expedient to touch briefly upon this profound depth — not in a spirit of unholy boldness, but in fear and trembling. As it was impossible that the Divine nature should suffer and die, so it was for us to be joined thereto. But we could become one with a Divine *Person* who Himself subsisted *in* the Divine Essence, and Omniscience found a way whereby that should be effected. By virtue of the Son's assuming our humanity the elect have been taken into union with a

31

Divine Person, yet not into union with the Divine nature or Essence itself. Thus we have sought to point out an error against which we need to carefully guard, lest we entertain thoughts grossly dishonoring to the Godhead.

The highest union of all is that incomprehensible and yet ineffable union which exists between the three Divine Persons in the one Divine Essence. The next great union — founded, as we have briefly intimated above, upon that essential one — is the union of our nature to the second Person in Jehovah, so that the Word made flesh is both God and man in the person of Jesus Christ. This, too, is a profound and unfathomable mystery, yet is it revealed as a cardinal article of our faith. It is a subject of pure revelation, and only from the sacred Scriptures can we obtain any light thereon. It falls not within our province to *explain* this mystery, yet it is our privilege and duty to spare no pains in prayerfully seeking sound and clear views of the same, for there can be no true growing in grace except as we grow in the scriptural and Spirit-imparted knowledge of our Lord and Saviour Jesus Christ. Right thoughts of Him are to be esteemed far above all silver and gold.

Rightly did the Puritan John Flavell say of this subject, "We walk upon the brink of danger; the least tread awry may engulf us in the bogs of error." There are certain vital postulates which are necessary to the scriptural setting forth of "the doctrine of Christ" (II John 9), if the truth about His wondrous and glorious person is to be maintained; such as the following. First, that the Lord Jesus is truly God, possessing the Divine nature and all its essential attributes. Second, that He is also true Man, possessing human nature in all its essential properties and sinless infirmities. Third, that those two diverse natures are united in His unique Person, yet ever remain distinct and unmixed, so that the Divine is not humanized, nor the human deified. Fourth, that both of those natures were and are operative in all of His mediatorial acts, so that while they may be distinguished, they cannot be separated. These great verities must be held firmly by us if we are to believe in and worship *the Christ of God.*

"The Son of God, the second person in the Trinity, being very and eternal God, of one substance and equal with the Father, did, when the fulness of time was come, take upon Him man's nature, with all the essential properties and common infirmities thereof, yet without sin; being conceived by the power of the Holy Ghost, in the womb of the Virgin Mary, of her substance. So that two whole, perfect, and distinct natures — the Godhead and the manhood — were inseparably joined together in one person, without conversion, composition, or confusion. Which person is very God and very man, yet one Christ, the only Mediator between God and man" (Westminster Catechism). This is a clear and helpful setting forth of the constitution of Christ's theanthropic person, i.e., His Person as the God-man.

Let it not be supposed that because this is one of the deep mysteries of Christianity, it is a subject in which only theologians are interested, or that it is a matter upon which Christians may lawfully differ. Not so:

it is a vital truth which is to be held fast at all costs, a precious truth revealed for the nourishing of faith. Only as the Holy Spirit enables us to
receive into our minds and hearts the revelation which the Father has so
graciously made of His Son, shall we be effectually preserved from the
subtle errors of Satan. The value of *what* Christ did depended entirely
upon *who* He was, and therefore it is of the very first importance we
should attain unto right views of the constitution of His wondrous Person. If the angels "desire to look into" these things (I Peter 1:12) —
figured by the cherubim with their faces turned toward the mercy-seat
on the ark (Exod. 25) — how much more should we who are chiefly
concerned therein.

The "doctrine of Christ" or the truth concerning the constitution of
His person, is of such fundamental and vital concern that without the
belief of it no man can be a Christian: "Every spirit that confesseth that
Jesus Christ is come in the flesh is of God" (I John 4:2), that is, born of
God, one of His people, and on the side of His truth. On the other hand,
"every spirit that confesseth not that Jesus Christ is come in the flesh is
not of God" (I John 4:3). As John Newton well put it,

> What think ye of Christ? is the test
> To try both your state and your scheme,
> You cannot be right in the rest,
> Unless you think rightly of Him.

But the great majority of people have no desire to meditate upon *Him,*
wishing rather to banish all thoughts of Him from their minds, and even
among those who sing "How sweet the name of Jesus sounds," few are
willing to read *and re-read* the deeper things about His person.

That which determines our *interest* in a person is our *love* for him. I
am not much concerned about the ancestry and history of one who is a
stranger to me, but when it comes to a person who is an object of my affections, then the smallest details about him are welcomed by me. A
letter filled with little items about the person and doings of her absent
son would be dearly treasured by his fond mother, but would be point-
less and wearisome to one not acquainted with him. Does not this same
principle hold good regarding the blessed person of our Lord and Saviour.
One who is, experimentally, a stranger to Him cannot be expected to
relish a setting forth of the mysterious constitution of His person, but
those who, by grace, esteem Him as the Fairest among ten thousand to
their souls, are ready to read, meditate upon, and study, if thereby they
may be favored with clearer and fuller views *of Him.*

Surely this is a subject of thrilling interest, for it is one in which the
infinite wisdom of God is most gloriously exhibited. "To unite finite and
infinite, almightiness and weakness, immortality and mortality, immutability with a thing subject to change; to have a nature from eternity and
yet a nature subject to the revolutions of time; a nature to make a law,
and a nature to be subjected to the law; to be God blessed forever in the
bosom of His Father, and an infant exposed to calamities from the
womb of His mother: terms seeming most distant from union, most in-

capable of conjunction, to shake hands together, to be most intimately conjoined; glory and vileness, fulness and emptiness, heaven and earth; He that made all things, in one person with a nature that is made; Immanuel, God and man in one; that which is most spiritual to partake of that which is carnal flesh and blood; one with the Father in His Godhead, one with us in His manhood; the Godhead to be in Him in the fullest perfection, and the manhood in the greatest purity; the creature one with the Creator, and the Creator one with the creature. Thus is the incomprehensible wisdom of God declared in the Word being made flesh.

"The terms of this union were infinitely distant. What greater distance can there be than between the Deity and humanity, between the Creator and the creature? Can you imagine the distance between eternity and time, infinite power and miserable infirmity, an immortal Spirit and dying flesh, the highest being and nothing? Yet these are espoused. A God of unmixed blessedness is linked personally with a man of perpetual sorrows; life incapable to die joined to a body in that economy incapable to live without dying first; infinite purity and a reputed sinner, eternal blessedness with a cursed nature, omniscience and ignorance; that which is entirely independent and that which is totally dependent, met together in a personal union, the eternal Son, the seed of Abraham (Heb. 2:16). What more miraculous than for God to become man, and man to become God! That a person possessed of all the perfections of the Godhead should inherit all the imperfections of the manhood in one person, sin only excepted; a holiness incapable of sinning to be made sin. Was there not need of an infinite power to bring together terms so far asunder, to elevate the humanity to be capable of, and disposed for, a conjunction with the Deity?" (S. Charnock).

The regulation of our thoughts about Him who is Divinely denominated "Wonderful," is what every believer should pray and earnestly aim at. It is of deepest importance that we should have scriptural views concerning Him, not only in general, but in detail; not only that we may be fortified against pernicious errors touching His person, which are now so rife, but also that we may be enabled to appreciate those particular instances in which the Divine wisdom shines forth with greatest splendor. This it is which will give Christ the "pre-eminence" in our minds, revealing how high above the relation and union which exists between Christians and God, is the relation and union between Christ Himself and God. Yes, nothing short of this should be our aim and quest "till we all come in the unity of the faith, and of the knowledge of the Son of God, unto a perfect man, unto the measure of the stature of the fulness of Christ" (Eph. 4:13).

Before seeking to contemplate, separately, the various aspects of and elements in the great mystery of "God manifest in flesh," we will devote the remainder of this chapter to a consideration of some of the reasons *why* it was needful for the Son of God to become the Son of man. The union of two distinct natures in the person of the Lord Jesus was a fundamental requisite for the union of sinners to God in Christ. We were once with God in Adam, but when he fell, a breach was made: as it is written, "They are all *gone out of* the way" (Rom. 3:12), which clearly implies that they were once found in "the way." That breach being made, we cannot be restored unto God, unless and until He came to us. A Divine person must take our nature in order to reconcile our persons to God, and therefore do we read of Christ that He "once suffered for sins, the Just for the unjust, that he might *bring us to God*" (I Peter 3: 18). But let us enter a little into detail, even though the ground here be familiar to most of our readers.

First, it was requisite that one of the Divine persons should be made under that very law which was originally given to man, and which man transgressed. "When the fulness of the time was come, God sent forth his Son, made of a woman, made under the law" (Gal. 4:4). Observe the order: He was "made of a woman" in order to be "made under the law." He who was "in the form of God" took upon Him "the form of a servant," that is, entered the place of subjection. He came to repair our lost condition, and in order thereto it was needful that He submit Himself unto the Divine precepts, that by His obedience He might recover what by their disobedience His people had lost. And by the perfect obedience of this august Person, the law was more "magnified" than it had been insulted by our rebellion.

Second, it was requisite that He who would save His people from their sins should suffer the penalty of that law which they had broken. There was an awful curse pronounced upon those who broke the law, and the Saviour must take His people's place and undergo it: "Christ hath redeemed us from the curse of the law, *being made a curse for us*" (Gal. 3:13). That curse was death, but how could God the Son die? Only by assuming a mortal nature. Third, it was requisite that in delivering Satan's captives the great Enemy should be conquered by One in the same nature as had been defeated by him. Accordingly it is written, "Forasmuch then as the children are partakers of flesh and blood, He also Himself likewise took part of the same; that through death He might destroy him that had the power of death, that is, the devil" (Heb. 2:14).

Fourth, it was requisite that the Redeemer should take possession of Heaven for us in our nature, and therefore did He say, "I go to prepare a place for you" (John 14:2). Blessed indeed is that word in Heb. 6, "That by two immutable things, in which it was impossible for God to lie, we might have a strong consolation, who have fled for refuge to lay hold upon the hope set before us; which hope we have as an anchor of the soul, both sure and steadfast, and which entereth into that *within the veil*. Whither the Forerunner is *for us entered*, even Jesus" (vv. 18-20). Fifth, it was requisite that the mighty Redeemer should also be capable, and how could this be had He never encountered them in His own person? "For we have not an high priest which cannot be touched with the feeling of our infirmities; but was in all points tempted like as we are, sin excepted" (Heb. 4:15).

Not only was it necessary for God the Son to assume a *human* nature, but also that His humanity should be derived from *the common root* of our first parents. It would not suitably have answered the Divine purpose that Christ's humanity should be created immediately out of nothing, because there had then been no such alliance between Him and us as to lay a foundation of hope of salvation by His undertaking. No, it was essential that He should sustain the character and perform the work of a *redeemer*, that He should be our Goal or *near Kinsman*, for to him alone belonged the *right* of redemption: see Leviticus 25:48, 49; Ruth 2:20 and 3:9, margin. So it was declared at the beginning: He was to be *the woman's* "Seed" (Gen. 3:15), and thus become our Kinsman. "For both he that sanctifieth, and they who are sanctified, are *all of one* (i.e., one stock): for which cause He is not ashamed to call them brethren" (Heb. 2:11).

Yet, it was also absolutely necessary, notwithstanding, that the nature in which redemption was to be performed should not only be derived from its original root, but also by *such* derivation that it should not be tainted by sin or partake in any degree of that moral defilement in which every child of Adam is conceived and born. It was requisite that our High Priest should be "holy harmless, undefiled, and separate from sinners." "If the human nature of Christ had partook, in any measure, of that pollution which, since the fall, is hereditary to us, it would have been destitute of the holy image of God, as we are prior to regeneration: and, consequently, He would have been rendered incapable of making the least atonement for us. He who is himself sinful, cannot satisfy Divine justice on the behalf of another; because, by one offense, He forfeits his own soul. Here, then, the adorable wisdom of God appears in its richest glory. For though it was necessary our Surety should be man, and the seed of the woman, yet He was conceived in such a manner as to be entirely without sin" (A. Booth).

God brought a clean thing out of an unclean. The manhood of Christ was derived from the common stock of our humanity, yet was it neither begotten nor conceived by carnal concupiscence. Original sin is propagated by ordinary generation, but the Son of man was produced by extraordinary generation. It is by the father's act that a child is begotten in the image and likeness of our first fallen and corrupted father. But though real Man, Christ was not begotten by a man. His humanity was produced from the substance of Mary by an extraordinary operation of the Holy Spirit above nature, and hence His miraculous and immaculate conception is far above the compass of human reason to either understand or express. Through the supernatural agency of the Holy Spirit, the humanity of Christ was conceived by a virgin who had never known a man. It was an act of Omnipotence to produce it; it was an act of Divine holiness to sanctify it; it was an act of Omniscience to unite it unto the person of the eternal Son of God.

II

We shall now endeavor to consider *the nature of* the Divine incarnation itself — exactly what took place when the Word became flesh. Here it behoves us to tread with the utmost reverence and caution, for the ground is truly holy. Only by adhering closely to the Scriptures themselves can we hope to be preserved from error; only as the Holy Spirit Himself is pleased to be our Guide may we expect to be led into the truth thereof; and only as we attend diligently to every jot and tittle in the revelation which God has graciously vouchsafed, will it be possible to obtain anything approaching a complete view of the same. May the Lord enable us to gird up the loins of our mind, and grant that in His light we may see light, as we approach our happy but difficult task.

In Old Testament times God granted various intimations that the coming Deliverer should be both Divine and human. At the beginning God announced to the Serpent (not "promised" unto Adam, be it noted), "I will put enmity between thee and the woman, and between thy seed and her seed; it shall bruise thy head, and thou shalt bruise his heel" (Gen. 3:15). This was a clear indication that the Saviour should be human, for He would be the woman's seed"; yet it as definitely intimated that the Saviour would be more than a man, for it is the work of Omnipotence to destroy Satan's power, hence we read, "The *God* of peace shall bruise Satan under your feet shortly" (Rom. 16:20). Expressly was it revealed that "a virgin shall conceive, and bear a son, and shall call His name Immanuel" (Isa. 7:14), "For unto us a child is born, unto us a Son is given; and the government shall be upon His shoulder: and His name shall be called Wonderful, Counseller, The mighty God . . ." (Isa. 9:6). In the ancient "Theophanies" such as in Genesis 18:1, 2; 32:24; Joshua 5:13, 14, etc., the Divine incarnation was anticipated and adumbrated, for in each case the "man" was obviously the Lord Himself in temporary human form.

Now there were three distinct things which belonged to the Word's becoming flesh: the actual production of His humanity, the sanctifying thereof, and His personal assumption of it. The production of it was by miraculous conception, whereby His human nature, was under the supernatural operation of God the Spirit framed of the substance of Mary, without man's help: "The Holy Spirit shall come upon thee, and the power of the Highest shall overshadow thee: therefore also that holy thing which shall be born of thee shall be called the Son of God" (Luke 1:35). But let it here be pointed out that in no sense was the Spirit the "father" of Jesus, for He contributed no matter to the making of His manhood, but only miraculously fashioned it out of the seed of His virgin mother. "Although the human nature of Christ was individualized and personalized by a miraculous conception, and not by ordinary generation, yet there was as really and truly a conception and birth as if it had been by ordinary generation. Jesus Christ was really and truly the Son of Mary. He was bone of her bone, and flesh of her flesh. He was of her substance and blood. He was consubstantial with her, in as full a sense as an ordinary child is consubstantial with an ordinary mother" (W. Shedd, 1889).

That which was conceived by Mary, under the mighty power of the Holy Spirit was *not* a human *person*, but a human *nature*; hence was it said "that holy *thing* which shall be born" (Luke 1:35). It is most important to clearly grasp this fact if we are to be preserved from error. When contemplating the ineffable mystery of the Holy Trinity, we saw how necessary it was to distinguish sharply between *nature* and *person*, for while there are three persons in the Godhead, their essence or nature is but one. In like manner, it is equally essential that we observe this same distinction when viewing the Person of the Mediator, for though He assumed human nature, He did not take a human person into union with Himself. Thus, we may correctly refer to the *complex person* of Christ, but we must not speak of His *dual personality*.

At the first moment of our Lord's assumption of human nature, that human nature existed only as the "seed" or *un*-individualized substance of the Virgin. But it was not for that reason an *incomplete* humanity, for all the essential *properties* of humanity are in the human nature itself. Christ assumed the human nature *before* it had become a particular person by conception in the womb: He "took on Him the *seed* of Abraham" (Heb. 2:16). The personalizing of His humanity was by its miraculous union with His Deity, though that added no new properties to human nature, but gave it a new and unique *form*. Nor was it simply a material body He assumed, but a human spirit and soul and body; for He was made "in all things like unto His brethren, sin excepted."

That it was an *impersonal* human nature which the Son of God assumed is clear from His own words in Hebrews 10:5: "A body hast thou prepared *me*." The "body," put metonymically for the entire human nature was *not* the "me" or "Person," but something which He took unto Himself. "For the love of Christ constraineth us: because we thus judge, that if One died for all, then the all died" (II Cor. 5:14): note carefully it is *one* who died: though possessing two natures, there was but a single Person. The humanity of Christ — consisting of spirit, and soul and body — had no subsistence in itself or by itself, but only as it was taken into union with a Divine Person. In answering the question, "What was the cause that the Person of the Son of God *did not* join Himself to a perfect *person* of man," the renowned James Usher (1654) replied, "1. Because then there could not be a personal union of both to make *one* perfect Mediator. 2. Then there should be four Persons in the Trinity. 3. The works of each of the natures, could not be counted the works of a whole Person."

"The *personality* of Jesus Christ is in His Divine nature, and not in His human. Jesus Christ existed a distinct, Divine person from eternity, the second person in the adorable Trinity. The human nature which this Divine person, the Word, assumed into a personal union with Himself, is not and never was a distinct person by itself, and personality cannot be ascribed to it, and does not belong to it any otherwise than as united to the Logos" (S. Hopkins, 1795). As a woman has no *wifely* personality until she is married, so the humanity of Christ had no personality till it was united to Himself: "that holy thing which shall be born of thee (Mary) shall be called *the Son of God*" (Luke 1:35) — receiving its name from the Divine Person with which it was made one. Just as my personality and your personality, from first to last, centers in our *highest* part — the soul — and is only shared in by the body, so the personality of the Mediator centers in His highest part — His Deity — His humanity only sharing in it.

The second thing pertaining to the Mediatorial union was the *sanctifying* of that "seed" which was miraculously conceived in the womb of the Virgin. To sanctify signifies to set apart unto God. For that two things are required: the cleansing of the object or person from pollution, and the enduing it with excellency to fit for the Divine service — typified under the ceremonial economy by the washing and then the anointing of the priests, and the sacred vessels. In connection with the humanity of our Lord, the first, was secured by God's miraculously preserving it from the slightest taint of defilement, so that the Lamb was "without blemish and without spot" (I Peter 1:19). Nothing with the least trace of corruption in it could be joined to the immaculate Son of God. Original sin could not be transmitted to Him, because He was never in Adam nor begotten by a man. The immediate interposition of the Holy Spirit (Luke 1:35) prevented all possiblity of any corruption being transmitted through Mary.

The enduing of Christ's humanity was also by the gracious operation of the Spirit (see Isa. 11:1, 2). "God, in the human nature of Christ, did perfectly renew that blessed image of His on our nature, which we lost in Adam; with an addition of many glorious endowments which Adam was not made partaker of. God did not renew it in His nature, as though that portion of it whereof He was partaker, had ever been destitute or deprived of it, as it is with the same nature in all other persons. For He derived not His nature from Adam in the same way that we do; nor was He ever in Adam as the public representative of our nature as we were. But our nature in Him had the image of God implanted in it, which was lost and separated from the same nature, in all other instances of its subsistence. It pleased the Father that in Him *all fulness* should dwell, that He should be full of grace and truth,' and in all thngs have the pre-eminence.

"The great design of God in His grace is, that as we have borne the 'image of the first Adam' in the depravation of our natures, so we should bear the 'image of the second' in their renovation. As we have borne 'the image of the earthy,' so we shall bear 'the image of the heavenly' (I Cor. 15:49). And as He is the pattern of all our graces, so He is of glory also. All our glory will consist in our being 'made like unto Him,' which what it is doth not yet appear (I John 3:2). For 'He shall change our vile body, that it may be fashioned like unto His glorious body' (Phil. 3:21). Wherefore the fulness of grace was bestowed upon the human nature of Christ, and the image of God gloriously implanted thereon, that it might be the prototype and example of what the church was through Him to be made partaker of" (John Owen).

The Holy Spirit infused into our Saviour's humanity *every* spiritual grace in its fulness and perfection. Each child of God is lovely in His sight because of some spiritual excellence which has been imparted to him — in one it is faith, in another courage, in another meekness; but the humanity of Christ was *"altogether* lovely." This was foreshadowed of old in the meal offering (Lev. 2): not only was the fine flour "un-leavened" (v. 5), but the fragrant "frankincense" was put thereon as a "sweet savor to the Lord" (v. 2). Christ was more holy in His human nature than was Adam when he was first created, and than are the unfallen and pure angels in Heaven, for it received the Spirit "without measure" (John 3:34), and because it was taken into personal union with the Son of the Living God. "His body and mind were the essence of purity. His heart was filled with the love of God, His thoughts were all regularly acted on what was before Him, His will was perfectly sanctified to perform the whole will of God, His affections were most correctly poised and properly fixed on God" (S. E. Pierce).

The third thing pertaining to the Mediatorial union was *the actual assumption* of that human nature which the Holy Spirit framed in the womb of the Virgin, and which He endowed with a fulness of grace and truth, whereby the eternal Son took the same upon Him, that it might have a proper and personal subsistence. A remarkable adumbration of this mystery seems to have been made in the natural world for the pur-pose of aiding our feeble understandings. This was set forth by one of the earlier Puritans thus: "As the plant called mistletoe *has no root of its own*, but grows and lives in the stock or body of the oak, or some other tree, so the human nature having no personal subsistence, is, as it were, ingrafted into the person of the Son, and is wholly supported and sus-tained by it, so as it should not be at all, if it were not sustained in that manner" (W. Perkins, 1595).

We believe this act of assumption took place at the very first moment of conception in the Virgin's womb: certainly it was months before the birth, as is clear from Luke 1:43, where Elizabeth, "filled with the Holy Spirit" (v. 41), exclaimed "And whence is this to me, that the mother of my *Lord* should come to me?" This assumption was purely a *voluntary* act on the part of the Son of God: He did not assume human nature from any necessity, but freely; not out of indigence, but bounty; not that *He* might be perfected thereby, but to perfect *it*. It was also a *permanent* act, so that from the first moment of His assumption of our humanity, there never was, nor to all eternity shall there be, any separation be-tween His two natures. Therein the hypostatic union differs from the conjunction between the soul and body in us: at death this conjunction is severed in us; but when Christ died, His body and soul were still united to His Divine person as much as ever.

As to *how* this act of assumption took place, we cannot say, The Scriptures themselves draw a veil over this mystery: "the power of the Highest shall *overshadow* thee" (Luke 1:35), so that from Mary and from us was hidden that ineffable work of the Most High, forbidding us to make any curious and unholy attempts to pry into it. The Divine transaction occurred, the amazing work was performed, and we are called upon to believe and adore. That unique act whereby the Maker of all things "took on Him the seed of Abraham (Heb. 2:16), when the

Sovereign over angels "took on Him the form of a servant" (Phil. 2:7), was the foundation of the Divine relation between the Son of God and the man Christ Jesus. Concerning the blessedness, the marvel, the unfathomable depths, the transcendent wisdom and glory of the act of assumption, we cannot do better than quote again from that prince of theologians, John Owen:

"His conception in the womb of the Virgin, as unto the integrity of human nature, was a miraculous operation of the Divine power. But the prevention of that nature from any subsistence of its own, by its assumption into personal union with the Son of God, in the first instance of its conception, is that which is *above all miracles*, nor can be designed by that name. A *mystery* it is, so far above the order of all creating or providential operations, that it wholly transcends the sphere of them that are most miraculous. Herein did God glorify all the properties of the Divine nature, acting in a way of infinite wisdom, grace, and condescension. The depths of the mystery hereof are open only unto Him whose understanding is infinite, which no created understanding can comprehend.

"All other things were produced and effected by an outward emanation of power from God: He said, 'Let there be light, and there was light.' But this assumption of our nature into hypostatical union with the Son of God, the constitution of one and the same individual person in two natures so infinitely distinct, as those of God and man, whereby the eternal was made in time, the infinite became finite, the immortal mortal, yet continuing eternal, infinite, immortal, is that singular expression of Divine wisdom, goodness, and power, wherein God will be admired and glorified unto all eternity. Herein was that change introduced into the whole first creation, whereby the blessed angels were exalted, Satan and his works ruined, mankind recovered from a dismal apostacy, all things made new, all things in heaven and earth reconciled and gathered into one Head, and a revenue of eternal glory raised unto God, incomparably above what the first constitution of all things in the order of nature could yield unto Him."

"And the Word became flesh" (John 1:14): not by His Deity being converted into matter, nor simply by His appearing in the outward semblance of man; but by actually assuming that "holy thing" which was framed by the Spirit and conceived by the Virgin. The Word "flesh" in John 1:14 includes more than a physical body — compare Romans 3:20 and I Corinthians 1:29 for the scope of this term. The eternal Word took upon Him a complete and perfect human nature, with all the faculties and members pertaining to such. "Choosing from the womb of the Virgin a temple for His residence, He who was the Son of God became also the Son of man: not by confusion of substance, but by a unity of person. For we assert such a connection and union of the Divine with the humanity, that each nature *retains* its properties entire, and yet both together constitute one Christ. (John Calvin, *Institutes*).

This union of the Divine and human natures in the Mediator is not a *consubstantial* one such as pertains to the three Persons in the Godhead, for they are united among themselves in one Essence: They all have but one and the same nature and will; but in Christ there are two distinct natures and wills. Nor is the Mediatorial union like unto the *physical*, whereby a soul and body are united in one human being, for that constitution is dissolved by death; whereas the hypostatic union is indissoluable. Nor is the Mediatorial union analogous to the *mystical*, such as exists between Christ and His Church, for though that be indeed a most glorious union, so that we are in Christ and He in us, yet we are not *one person* with Him; and thus the mystical union falls far below that ineffable and incomprehensible oneness which exists between the Son of God and the Son of man.

Thomas Goodwin, of blessed memory among lovers of deep expository works, was wont to call this Mediatorial union "the *middle* union," coming in as it does between the union of the three Divine persons in the Godhead, and the Church's union with God in Christ. We may also perceive and admire the wisdom of the eternal Three in selecting the middle One to be the Mediator; as we may also discern and adore the propriety of choosing the *Son* to be the one who should enter the place of *obedience*. He who eternally subsisted between the Father and the Spirit, has, by virtue of His incarnation, entered the place of "Daysman" between God and men; for in consequence of His union with the Divine Essence, He is able to "take hold" of God on the one side, and in consequence of His union with our humanity, He is able to take hold of us on the other side; so that He "takes hold of both" as Job desired (9:33).

III

Christ is not now two persons combined together, but one Person having two natures. He is both God and man, as many Scriptures plainly affirm, possessing in Himself both Deity and humanity. "Unto us a child is born," there is His humanity; "Unto us a Son is given, and his name shall be called The Mighty God" (Isa. 9:6), there is His Deity. "That holy thing which shall be born of thee," there is His humanity; "shall be called the Son of God" (Luke 1:35), there is His Deity — "*called* the Son of God" means He shall be *owned* as such: "all shall so acknowledge Him: either here in gracious confession, or in glorious confusion hereafter" (Thos. Adams, 1660). "God sent forth His Son," there is His Deity; "made of a woman" (Gal. 4:4), there is His humanity. "Made of the seed of David according to the flesh," there is His humanity; "And delcared the Son of God" (Rom. 1:3, 4), there is His Deity, both making up the one Person of "Jesus Christ our Lord."

Having considered the needs-be for the Divine incarnation, having sought to contemplate the nature thereof, we now turn to some of the *effects and consequences* of the same. We shall seek to examine, first, the effects of the Mediatorial union with respect to the Divine nature of Christ; second, with respect to His human nature; and third with respect to His complex Person.

When the eternal Word became flesh, His Divine nature underwent

no change whatsoever. Such a thing could not be: God is no more subject to alteration or variation than He is to death. Being God the Son,
the Word was immutable, and must remain forever the same. To say that
His Deity was humanized, is to assert an utter impossiblity. The incarnation of the Beloved of the Father, despoiled Him of none of His
perfections. Had He lost (or "emptied" Himself of) any of those attributes proper to the Divine nature, He could not have been a sufficient
Mediator. That is properly a "change," when anything ceases to be what
it was before; but such was not the case with Immanuel. It was none
other than *God* who was "manifest in flesh" (I Tim. 3:16), so that the incarnate Son could say, "He that hath seen me, hath see the Father"
(John 14:9).

When it is affirmed "the Word was made flesh and tabernacled
among us," the Spirit was careful to move John to add at once, "and we
beheld his glory." *What* "glory?" the "glory" of His meekness, gentleness,
compassion? No, but "the glory as of the Only-begotten of the Father."
Though He now became what He was not previously — united to manhood — yet He ceased not to be in Himself all that He was before. "He
assumed our nature without laying aside His own. When the soul is
united to the body, doth it lose any of those perfections that are proper
to its nature? Is there any change either in the substance or qualities of
it? No; but it makes a change in the body; and of a dull lump it makes
it a living mass, conveys vigor to it, and by its power quickens it to sense
and motion. So did the Divine nature and human remain entire: there
was no change of the one into the other, as Christ by a miracle changed
water into wine, or men by art change sand or ashes into glass" (S.
Charnock).

During the days of His humiliation, the Divine *glory* of the Mediator
was partly veiled. There was no halo of Divine light encircling His
head, to mark Him out as Immanuel. There was no visible retinue of
angels in attendance upon Him, to signify the Lord of Heaven was tabernacling upon earth. Instead, He was born in a manger, grew up in the
home of a peasant family, and when He began His public ministry His
forerunner was clothed in a garment of camel's hair and His ambassadors
were humble fishermen. Yet even then His Divine glory was not completely eclipsed. The character He displayed was "Fairer than the children of men" (Ps. 45:2). His teaching was such that even the officers
sent to arrest Him testified, "never man spake like this Man" (John 7:
46). His miracles witnessed to His Almightiness. Even in death He
could not be hid: the centurion exclaiming, "Truly this was the Son of
God" (Matt. 27:54).

Yet the partial veiling of His Divine glory in nowise wrought any
change in, still less did it injure the Divine nature itself, any more than
the sun undergoes any change or is to the slightest degree injured when
it is hid by the interposition of a cloud. "When He prays for the glory
He had with the Father before the world was (John 17:5), He prays
that a glory He had in His Deity might shine forth in His person
as Mediator, and be evinced in that height and splendor suitable to His

dignity, which had been so lately darkened by His abasement; that as He had appeared to be the Son of man in the infirmity of the flesh, He might appear to be the Son of God in the glory of His person, that He might appear to be the Son of God and the Son of man in one person" (S. Charnock). At His ascension, nothing was added to His essential person: His Divine glory did but shine forth more distinctly when He sat down at the right hand of the Majesty on high.

We turn next to consider the consequence of His human nature being taken into union with the Son of God. And, first negatively. His humanity was not invested with Divine attributes. As the Divine nature was not humanized at the incarnation, neither was the humanity deified: there was no communication of properties from one to the other; both preserved their integrity, and remained in possession of their distinctive qualities. "I do not hereby ascribe the infusion of omniscience, of infinite understanding, wisdom, and knowledge into the human nature of Christ. It was and is a creature, finite and limited, nor is a capable subject of properties absolutely infinite and immense. Filled it was with light and wisdom to the utmost capacity of a creature. But it was so, not by being changed into a Divine nature or essence, but by the communication of the Spirit unto it without measure. The Spirit of the Lord did rest upon Him: Isa. 11:1-3" (John Owen).

There were three respects in which the humanity of Christ underwent no change by virtue of its union with His Divine person. First, with respect to its *essence*: intrinsically and integrally it was and forever remains a real and true humanity. Second, in respect to its *properties*: "And Jesus increased in wisdom and in stature, and in favor with God and man" (Luke 2:52); when He prayed "not my will, but thine be done" (Luke 22:42), it was the subjecting of the human unto the Divine. Third, with respect to its *operations*: every human faculty was normally exercised by "the man Christ Jesus." He hungered and thirsted, ate and drank; He wearied and slept; He sorrowed and wept; He suffered and died. Some things as a man He knew not (Mark 13:32), except as they were *given* Him by revelation (Rev. 1:1).

Positively, the humanity was elevated unto a state infinitely surpassing that of every other creature in earth and Heaven. Though the Godhead received nothing from the manhood, yet the manhood itself — taken into union with the second Person in the Trinity — was immeasurably enriched and exalted to unspeakable dignity, infinitely above that of the angels. He who is the Head of the Church has, in all things, "the pre-eminence." Not only was the Divine *wisdom* more illustriously displayed in the wondrous constitution of the Mediator than in any or all the other works of God, but His *grace* was also more gloriously evidenced unto the man Christ Jesus than it was in the saving of sinners. The highest act of Divine favor was exercised when the woman's "seed" was raised high above all other creatures, and made Jehovah's "fellow." Wherein could the seed of Abraham merit such an inestimable honor! It was *grace*, pure and simple, grace in its most superlative exercise, which conferred upon the humanity of Christ a dignity and glory immeasurably exceeding that possessed by the cherubim and seraphim.

The Man Christ Jesus was fore-ordained before the foundation of the world (I Peter 1:20) unto union with the second Person in the Godhead, and therefore the Divine grace shown unto Him in *His* predestination was greater far than that shown unto *us*, by how much more the privileges ordained were greater. Marvellous grace indeed is it that we should be elevated to a place in the family of God and "brought nigh" (Eph. 2: 13) unto Him; but that falls far, far short of the Man Christ Jesus being actually united to the immediate person of the Son of God; and in consequence thereof being not only "the *firstborn* [Chief] of every creature," but "the Man that is *my fellow*, saith the Lord of hosts" (Zech. 13:7) — advanced unto a fellowship in the Society of the blessed Trinity. This it was which stamped an infinite worth upon the whole work of the Mediator.

"Behold my servant, whom I uphold: *mine elect*, in whom my soul delighteth" (Isa. 42:1). God's "elect" was the Man whom He eternally chose to be taken into personal union with His co-essential and co-equal Son. This is the One in whom He eternally delighted, ever viewing Him in the glass of His decrees. This is "the man of his right hand, the son of man whom he made strong *for himself*" (Ps. 80:17). This was indeed grace worthy of God, such as can never be fully conceived by any finite intelligence, no not by the saints in Heaven through the ages of eternity. In the person of the God-man, grace, sovereign grace, was exercised in its first and greatest act, shining forth in its utmost splendour and discovered in its utmost freeness. For again we say, there could be nothing whatever in the unindividualized "seed" of the woman which could be, to the smallest degree, entitled to such supernal glory.

It was therefore meet and requisite that grace and glory should be communicated and bestowed upon the humanity of Christ, proportionably to the high dignity of its being taken into union with the Son. "1. Pre-eminence, to all other individuals of human nature: the humanity of Christ was chosen and preferred to the grace of union with the Son of God, above them all; it has a better subsistence than they had, and has obtained a more excellent name than they, and is possessed of blessings and privileges above all creatures. All which is not of any merit in it, but of the free grace of God. 2. Perfect holiness and impeccability: it is called *that holy Thing*: it is eminently and perfectly so, without original sin, or any actual transgression; it is not conscious of any sin, never committed any, nor is it possible it should. 3. A communication of habitual grace to it in the greatest degree; it is, in this respect, fairer and more beautiful than any of the sons of men: grace being poured into it in great plenty; it is anointed with the oil of gladness above its fellows; that is, with the gifts and graces of the Holy Spirit" (John Gill, 1770).

Consider, briefly, some of the super-excellent perfections of the man Christ Jesus. There is a *wisdom* in Him which is far above what all other creatures have attained or can reach unto, so that in Him "Are hid all the treasures of wisdom and knowledge" (Col. 2:3). It is true those treasures of wisdom are not of that richness and extent as the wisdom that dwells in God Himself, for the manhood of Christ is not omniscient; yet by virtue of its union with the Son of God, it has been taken into all the counsels of the Godhead, and knows all decrees concerning, the past, the present, and the future.

The same holds good of His *power*. Though the manhood of Christ has not been endowed with omnipotence, yet it approximates as closely thereto, as any creature could, for all power has been given to Him, both in Heaven and earth (Matt. 28:18), so that the rule of the universe is committed to Him, He upholding all things by the word of His power (Heb. 1:3). God "hath given authority to execute judgment also, because he is the Son of *man*" (John 5:27).

The image of God shines brightly in Christ's *independency* and *sovereignty*. This incommunicable attribute of Deity is reflected to a high degree in Him who has been made "both Lord and Christ" (Acts 2:36), being one of the brightest jewels in the crown of His glorified humanity. This personal prerogative of the Son of God is now shared in by the nature which He took into union with Himself, as the queen shares the palace of the king. A dependent "thing" has been made an independent creature — what a marvel of marvels!

So too of His *holiness*. There is that transcendency of holiness in the man Christ Jesus that is not found in all other creatures put together, and in this respect also He is "the image of the invisible God" (Col. 1:15). There is in Him a holiness over and above that grace communicated to Him "without measure" by the Spirit: it is a relative holiness of a man united to the second Person of the Godhead, which casts the shine of its superlative glory upon that which is habitual or communicated. It is *this* which gave infinite value to all He did.

Coming now to the consequences of the Divine incarnation as it respects *the complex Person* of the Mediator. First, there is a communion between the two natures in Him which is far more intimate than that enjoyed by husband and wife, or even that which obtains between Christ and His Church: it is exceeded only by that ineffable fellowship which exists among the eternal Three. While the properties of each several nature preserve their distinctness, yet they are so united as to form one Person, who may be denominated according to either nature. Sometimes the Mediator is called "man" as in Acts 17:31, etc., and at others He is designated "God," as in Romans 9:5, etc. Thus, what cannot be said of Christ in the abstract, can be predicated of Him in the concrete — His Deity could not be tempted, nor is His humanity omnipresent: yet as a *Person* He was tempted and is omnipresent.

Second, in consequence of the two natures in His Person, Christ holds the office of Mediator. "But He is not Mediator only in His human nature, and only exercises it in that; He took upon Him, and was invested with this *office* before His assumption of human nature; and could and did exercise some parts of it without it; but there were others that required His human nature; and when, and not before it was requisite, He assumed it; and in it, as united to His Divine person, He is God-man, is Prophet, Priest, and King, Judge, Lawgiver, and Saviour; and has power over all flesh, to give eternal life to as many as the Father has given Him" (John Gill). This it is which stamped infinite worth, dignity and glory on what He did. He being both God and man in one Person, His life was the life of God (I John 3:16), His righteousness was the righteousness of God (Phil. 3:9), His blood was the blood of God (Acts 20:28).

Thirdly, there is a communion *of operations* in both natures of the discharge of His Mediatorial office. The work performed by Christ was the work of the God-man: there was a concurrence of both natures in the performance of it. "In the work of atonement, as well as in all the other parts of His mediatorial activity, Christ acted according to both natures. They ever acted conjointly, but in their several spheres. It is important to keep in mind that they never acted apart in anything that concerned the mediatorial function. And this it is the more necessary to mention, because the notion has obtained currency in modern times that the Divine nature was for the most part in abeyance during His humiliation" (Geo. Smeaton, 1868). "The perfect complete work of Christ in every act of His mediatory office, in all that He did as the King, Priest, and Prophet of the Church, in all that He continueth to do for us, in or by virtue of whether nature soever it be done, is not to be considered as the act of this or that nature in Him alone, but it is the act and work of *the whole person*" (John Owen).

Fourth, though the human nature of Christ, distinctively considered, is not a formal object of worship, since it is a creature, yet as taken into union with God the Son, and both natures together forming the one Person of the Mediator, Christ is to be adored and worshipped. Thus, at His birth it was said, "Let all the angels ·of God worship Him" (Heb. 1:6). So at His ascension He was given a name which is above every name, "that at the name *of Jesus* every knee should bow" (Phil. 2:9, 10), that is, in a way of religious adoration. Accordingly we read "And every creature which is in heaven, and on the earth, and under the earth, and such as are in the sea, and all that are in them, heard I saying, Blessing, and honor, and glory, and power, be unto him that sitteth upon the throne, *and unto the Lamb* for ever and ever" (Rev. 5:13).

Fifth, in consequence of the hypostatic union, all the fulness of the Godhead dwells personally in Jesus Christ, and in Him there is such an outshining of the perfections of Jehovah as contain the utmost manifestation of Deity which can be made either unto the angels or unto men. The "glory of God" shines "in the face of Jesus Christ" (II Cor. 4:6). Much may be seen of God, in creation, in providence, in grace, but in and by *Jesus Christ alone* is He fully and perfectly revealed. Therefore could He say, "He that hath seen me, hath seen the Father" (John 14:9).

The particular points which most need to be guarded in connection with this mysterious and glorious subject are: 1. The eternal Son of God united to Himself human nature. 2. Every particular man is a separate person, because he subsists of himself; but the manhood of Christ never subsisted of itself, but only in union with the second Person of the Godhead. 3. Christ, the Mediator, is but one Person; God and man being perfectly united in Him. 4. The two natures remain distinct in Him, preserving their own properties and characteristics. 5. Christ's human nature was *not* created in Heaven (as the early Plymouth Brethren taught): "The Lord from heaven" (I Cor. 15:47) refers to His *Divine Person,* and not to the descent of His humanity. If Christ's humanity had not been formed out of Mary's substance, it had belonged to another class of creatures, and Christ had not been "the Son *of man*" and so could not have been our Kinsman-Redeemer. 6. The humanity of Christ was not begotten by generation according to the ordinary course of nature, but was produced by the extraordinary operation of the Holy Spirit, and therefore it is high above the compass of human reason to understand or explain. 7. As man, Christ is neither "the Son of God" (Luke 1:35) by nature or by adoption, but only *by personal union* – as the wife receives the name of her husband. 8. The humanity of Christ had to be united to His Divine Person, in order that His work should possess infinite merits. 9. Each nature acts separately, yet in conjunction with the other: as man Christ "laid down" His life, as God He "took it again" (John 10:18). 10. A *whole* Christ, God and man, is the Object of our faith, is our Saviour and Lord, and is to be worshipped and served as such.

In conclusion, let us marvel at, admire and adore this transcendent wonder and mystery. First, that a *human* nature was produced without the instrumentality of any man. Second, that that human nature was produced out of a woman without contracting the slighest taint of sin. Third, that it had no separate personality subsisting by itself. Fourth, that it should be, nevertheless, "the Son of man." Fifth, that a Divine Person should unite unto Himself such a frail and lowly nature. Sixth, that that Divine Person was in no wise injured by such an union. Seventh, that each nature should continue to preserve its own separate properties and functions.

4

Mystical Union

I

In the introduction we pointed out that "There are three principal unions revealed in the Scriptures which are the chief mysteries and form the foundation of our most holy faith. First, the union of three Divine persons in one Godhead: having distinct personalities, being co-eternal and co-glorious, yet constituting one Jehovah. Second, the union of the Divine and human natures in one person, Jesus Christ, Immanuel, being God and man. Third, the union of the Church to Christ: He being the Head, they the members, constituting one mystical body. Though we cannot form any exact idea of any of these unions in our imaginations, because the depth of such mysteries is beyond our comprehension, yet it is our bounden duty to believe them all because they are clearly revealed in Scripture, and are the necessary foundation for other parts of Christian doctrine. Hence it is our holy privilege to prayerfully study the same, looking unto the Holy Spirit to graciously enlighten us thereon."

Having shown in the previous chapters — very stumblingly and inadequately — how that a plurality of persons in the Godhead made possible the Mediatorial union, we are now ready to consider how the Son of God taking upon Himself our nature made possible the union of the Church to Him. While orthodox theologians have written clearly on the Divine union which exists between the three persons in the Godhead, and while they have treated helpfully the nature of the Mediatorial union, the same can hardly be said of their discussion of the union which exists between God's elect and their glorious Head. Though not a little has been written thereon, most men have generalized far too much, failing to distinguish between the various aspects of that oneness which exists between Christ and His people. Not a few have jumbled together what needs to be considered apart, if a clear view is to be obtained thereof.

It is not to be expected that Arminians should have any clear grasp of the exceedingly precious subject which is now to engage our attention. Making man, rather than God, the center of their system, they necessarily begin at the wrong place. They make the union of the believer with Christ to commence at his conversion, when faith lays hold of and makes Him ours. But this is to start at the middle, instead of at the beginning. They fail to recognize that there must be a *vital* union before there can be a fiducial one, that the soul must first be made alive spiritually before it is capacitated to trust savingly in Christ. One who is dead in trespasses and sins has no more ability to perform spiritual acts — and appropriating the Lord Jesus as his own *is* a spiritual act — than a corpse in the grave is qualified to perform physical acts. Life itself must be present before there can be any evidences and exercises of it.

Calvinists do not fall into the error just pointed out above. They perceive that the sinner must first be quickened before he can savingly believe the gospel. They insist that the Holy Spirit must unite the soul vitally to Christ ere there can be any drawing from the fulness which is in Christ. We must be livingly united to Him before any of His benefits become ours. I must be a son before I can be an heir. So far so good. But at this point not a few modern Calvinists fail to trace the effect back to its proper source. It is not sufficient to point out that faith necessarily presupposes spiritual life, for that spiritual life itself presupposes something else prior to the communication of it. The Holy Spirit does not regenerate all. *Who* are the ones He brings from death unto life? Galatians 4:6 tells us, "Because ye are *sons*, God hath sent forth the Spirit of His Son into your hearts." There is, then, a relation to God *prior to* regeneration.

Now a relation to God previous to regeneration necessarily presupposes *a relation to Christ* previous to regeneration, for we have no spiritual relation to God Himself apart from the Mediator. The elect are God's "sons" because united to His Son: "Behold I and the children which God hath given me" (Heb. 2:13) is His own language. Before He came into this world it was said, "Thou shalt call his name Jesus, for he shall save his people from their sins" (Matt. 1:21) — those who were to be saved by Him were "his people" *before* He became incarnate. They were one with Him by an indissoluable bond long ere the Lord of glory took upon Himself human nature. There was a mystical and eternal union subsisting between Christ and the Church, which formed the basis of that vital union which is effected by the Holy Spirit during a time state, the latter *making manifest* the former, the former being the ground upon which the latter is effected.

Not a few of the older Calvinists firmly adhered to this foundation truth of the mystical union subsisting between Christ and His Church, but it is to be regretted that they did not define more definitely the *real nature* of that mystical union, and distinguish between the different elements which composed it, or rather, the various aspects which it comprises. Some have narrowed it down to a mere legal or federal union, failing to see that this also presupposed a prior relationship. Some have confined the oneness between Christ and His people to that of the Surety and those whom He represented. Others have spoken of the *covenant-union* between Christ and His Church, without stating in detail *of what* that covenant-union consists. Still others employed the expression "election-union," which though coming nearer to the mark, still leaves the subject clouded in a certain vagueness.

The one writer who appears to have been blest with a clearer insight into this great mystery than most of his fellows was John Gill — to whom we are indebted for some of the leading thoughts in what follows — though he, in turn, received help, no doubt, from the writings of James

Hussey, the high Calvinist of the seventeenth century. Those men rightly traced back the covenant and federal union which the Church has with its Head to the eternal *love* of the Triune God, which, operating by His everlasting decree, gave them an *election union* with Christ. It needs to be pointed out that the eternal decree of Jehovah gave Christ — as the God-man Mediator — a real subsistence before Him before the foundation of the world, and a real subsistence unto the elect in Him, so that "*before* the mountains were settled. . . . while as yet He had not made the earth," He could say "My delights were with the sons of men" (Prov. 8:24, 26, 32).

The technical name by which the oneness between Christ and His people is designated by theologians is "mystical union." This term has been employed — for want of a better — not because the union is vague or unreal, but because it far transcends all earthly analogies in its intimacy of fellowship and reciprocal partnership, both in the very nature of it, the power of its influence, and the excellency of its consequence. "On the one hand, this union does not involve any mysterious *confusion* of the person of Christ with the persons of His people, and, on the other hand, it is not such *a mere association* of separate persons as exists in human societies" (A. A. Hodge). It is a relation far more intimate than any which may be formed by any external bonds. This union is presented to us in Scripture as a matter of fact, without any explanation, to be credited on the ground of Divine testimony.

But though the union between Christ and His Church far transcends all natural analogies, the Scriptures set forth its variety and fulness, element by element, by means of several partial analogies. Because this union is so high and mysterious, it has pleased God to make use of various resemblances for the describing of it, that He might thereby make it more credible and intelligible to us. It is observable that the Holy Spirit has referred to various unions, natural, relative, and artificial, that He might by all of them more clearly and distinctly shadow out the grand union betwixt Christ and His saints. Yet let it be pointed out that useful as are these particular analogies as to the end designed, yet they all come short of the mystical union to which they refer. They may indeed illustrate it — so far as temporal and natural things can — but they cannot reach or equal it.

The first of these typical resemblances which may be mentioned is that of husband and wife. Upon the conjugal relation there is a very close and intimate conjunction. Now Christ and His people stand in this conjugal relation each to the other. He is their "husband" (Isa. 54:5), they are His "wife" (Rev. 19:7). They are "espoused" to Christ (II Cor. 11:2), "married" to Christ (Rom. 7:4), "betrothed" to Him "forever" (Hos. 2:19); their name is "Hephzibah" ("my delight is in her") and "Beulah" — "married" (Isa. 62:4). This marriage-union Paul applies to Christ and believers: "So ought men to love their wives as their own body. He that loveth his wife loveth himself. For no man ever yet hated his own flesh; but nourisheth and cherisheth it, even as the Lord the church: for we are members of his body, of his flesh, and of his bones" (Eph. 5:28-30), to which the apostle adds, "This is a great mystery: but I speak concerning Christ and the church" — I am using this union between husband and wife to point to that higher and spiritual union which exists between Christ and His people: the husband and the wife are "one;" and Christ and the Church are so much more.

The second of these natural analogies is found in the physical head and members. In the human body there is a close conjunction between these two, for they are joined the one to the other, and together form one and the same organism. Thus it is with Christ and believers in the body mystical, to which the Holy Spirit has repeatedly applied the terms pertaining to this physical adumbration: Christ is the Head, they are the several members belonging to that Head. Of Christ it is said, God "gave him to be the head over all things to the church, which is his body" (Eph. 1:22, 23), "and he is the head of the body, the church" (Col. 1:18). Of the members it is said, "Now ye are the body of Christ and members in particular" (I Cor. 12:27), and "So we, being many, are one body in Christ, and every one members one of another" (Rom. 12:5). As truly and as intimately as the head and members of the physical body are united, so truly and intimately are Christ and believers united also.

The third of these earthly adumbrations is found in that of the root and the branches growing out of the same. There is not only a connection between them, but a vital oneness, otherwise how should the one convey life, sap, growth to the other? So it is with Christ and His people: He is the Root, they are the tendrils issuing therefrom. "I am the vine, ye are the branches" (John 15:5). To this analogy the Holy Spirit frequently makes reference: "We have been *planted together* in the likeness of his death" (Rom. 6:5); "If the root be holy, so are the branches; and if some of the branches be broken off, and thou, being a wild olive tree, wert graffed in among them, and with them partakest of the root and fatness of the olive tree" (Rom. 11:16, 17); "rooted and built up in him" (Col. 2:7). Thus there is a blessed resemblance between Christ and His Church and the root and its branches, both in point of union and of influence: the root is united to the branches and they to it; the root conveys life, nourishment and fruitfulness to the branches; so does Christ to believers.

Another resemblance is found in the foundation and the building. Here again is union, for in a building all the stones and timbers are joined and fastened together upon the foundation, making but one entire structure. So it is with believers and Christ. This figure is also used in Scripture again and again. The Lord Himself likened the one who heard and obeyed His sayings to "a wise man who built his house upon a rock" (Matt. 7:24). The apostle Paul reminded the saints, "Ye are God's building" and added, "other foundation can no man lay than that is laid, which is Jesus Christ" (I Cor. 3:9, 11); and again they are said to be "built upon the foundation of the apostles and prophets, Jesus Christ himself being the chief cornerstone" (Eph. 2:20). As a man builds upon the foundation, laying the weight of the whole building upon it, so the faith and confidence of the Christian is built upon that "sure foundation which

God has laid in Zion" (Isa. 28:16).

Now as there is nothing in this natural world which more sweetly and securely knots souls together than *love*, so the cementing bond which unites Christ and the Church must be traced back to the love of God. If love can be so effectual among men in binding one heart to another, how infinitely more powerful must love in the heart of God attract and unite the objects of it to Himself, giving them a nearness to Him such as finite minds are quite incapable of fully comprehending. *This* is the bond of union of saints one to another, for their hearts are "knit together in love" (Col. 2:2), and therefore is love called "the bond of perfectness" (Col. 3:14). *Love*, then, the everlasting love of the Father, Son, and Spirit, is the *origin* of the Church's union with Christ. "This is that cement which will never loosen, that union-knot which can never be untied, that bond which can never be dissolved, from whence there can be no separation" (John Gill).

Now *election* was the first and fundamental act of God's love toward His people, giving them a subsistence in Christ from everlasting, "according as he hath chosen us in him before the foundation of the world" (Eph. 1:4). God does not love His people because He elected them, rather did He elect them because He had set His heart upon them. The Divine order is plainly intimated in II Thessalonians 2:13, "Brethren, *beloved* of the Lord, because God hath from the beginning *chosen* you unto salvation." The same precious truth is brought out again in Ephesians 1. "*In love* having predestinated us unto the adoption of children by Jesus Christ to himself, according to the good pleasure of his will" (vv. 4, 5). This was the supreme act and instance of everlasting love, by which the elect were considered in Christ and one with Him, He being chosen as the Head, they as His members — obviously we could not be *in* Christ without being one *with* Him.

"He is the head of the body, the church, who is the beginning, the firstborn from the dead; that in all things he might have the pre-eminence" (Col. 1:18). Yes, *Christ* was "the beginning" even in connection with election: there too He had "the pre-eminence."

> Be Thou My first elect He said,
> Then chose the Church in Christ its Head.

Christ was not chosen for the Church, but the Church for Him. There was an *order* in God's counsels, as there is in all His works; and *Christ* occupies the first place therein. The ever-blessed and all-sufficient God was pleased to desire *creature* fellowship and society, instead of dwelling alone for ever in His own infinite immensity. The eternal Father therefore ordained that His co-essential Son should take unto Himself a created nature, uniting the man Christ Jesus into indissoluable union to His Divine person. God fixed upon the person of Christ, as God-man, as the one great and everlasting object of His love, delight and complacency. He was as God-man "set up from everlasting," being possessed by Jehovah as "the beginning of his way" (Prov. 8:22, 23).

Next, God was pleased to decree that an elect number of Adam's race should be united to Christ and be for His glory. As the man Christ Jesus was Jehovah's "Elect" in whom his soul "delighteth" (Isa. 42:1), and as He was (by infinite grace) taken to be Jehovah's "fellow" (Zech. 13:9), so those who were elected in Christ became His "delight" (Prov. 8:32) and were to be *His* "fellows" (Ps. 45:7), to be everlastingly glorified in and with Him. Though in the order of time Christ and His church were elected together, to form one complete mystical Body, yet in the order of God's counsels Christ was elected first, and then His people were chosen in Him. "Christ was *the Head* of election, and of the elect of God; and so in order of nature elected first, though in order of time we were elected with Him. In the womb of election He, the Head, came out first, and then we the members. He is therefore said *in predestination* to be the Firstborn of all His brethren — see Rom. 8:29" (Thos. Goodwin). This is a profound depth, yet a most important truth, and needing further amplification.

"God in the act of election looked not at us apart and singly as in ourselves, so as by one act to choose us, and by another act to give us to Christ. But as of the soul it is by one and the same act of God's both created and infused into the body, as so subsists not one moment apart; likewise God in the act of choosing us gave us to Christ, and in giving us to Christ He chose us. And thus, He never considering us apart, but as members of Christ and given to Him in the very act of choosing, hence our very choice itself is said to be "in him." And so, on the other side, in the first view and purpose God took up concerning Christ, and in electing Him, He looked not at Him apart as a single person in Himself, but as a Head to us His body, chosen in Him and with Him. So it is not that Jesus Christ was chosen by one act to be man, and then to be a Common Person by another; but at the very *same instant* that He was chosen the one, He was chosen the other, under that very consideration to be a Common Person.

"It was in this as in the creation of Adam, Christ's shadow; who when he was first made, was not made as a single man, he was made 'a living soul' (I Cor. 15:45). What is that? To be a *public* person, to convey life to others as well as to have life personally in himself. That is the meaning, as appears by the following words, 'The last Adam,' that is, Christ 'was made a quickening spirit,' that is, not for Himself, but to others. So that the very first view that God in election took of Christ, was not of Him only as a single person considered, but as a Common Person. In a word, as in the womb head and members are not conceived apart, *but together,* as having relation each to other, so were we in Christ, as making up one mystical body unto God, formed together in that eternal womb of election. So that God's choice did completely terminate itself on Him and us; us with Him, and yet us in Him; He having the priority to be constituted a Common Person and root to us" (Thos. Goodwin).

Now God's eternal decree gave His elect a super-creation subsistence before Him, so that they were capable of being "loved" (Jer. 31:3) and of receiving a grant of grace: "Who hath saved us, and called us with a holy calling, not according to our works, but according to his own purpose and grace, which was given us in Christ Jesus before the world began" (II Tim. 1:9) — note well, it was not simply that God purposed to give His chosen people grace, but that grace *was* given us in Christ" before the world began." If, then, grace was actually "given us in Christ" ere time commenced, then we must have had a real subsistence in Him before God from everlasting. This too, is above our powers to fully comprehend, yet is it a truth to be held fast on the ground of the Divine testimony. In God's eternal thoughts and foreviews, the elect were conceived and contemplated *in the Divine mind* as real entities, in a state of pure creaturehood, above and beyond the consideration of the fall.

II

The everlasting love of the Triune God is *the origin of* the Church's union to Christ, election being the first and fundamental act of that love toward its members, that election giving them a subsistence in their Head: "According as he hath chosen us in him before the foundation of the world" (Eph. 1:4). In election God made it manifest that He was pleased to desire *creature* fellowship and society, instead of dwelling alone forever in His own infinite self-sufficiency. First, He ordained that His beloved Son should take manhood into union with His own person, and that as God-man He should be the Head of a people given to Him for His glory. This *order* in the Divine counsel is marvellously adumbrated in the physical realm: the head and members of the human body are conceived *together* in the womb, as Christ and the members of His Church were chosen to form one Body; yet as the head comes out *first,* so Christ was given the pre-eminence from the womb of God's decrees.

However, difficult it be for us to grasp, it is important we should recognize that God's eternal decree gave the elect a super-creation subsistence before Him, so that they were capable of being loved and of receiving a grant of grace. In other words, in God's eternal thoughts and foreviews, the elect were conceived and contemplated by Him in the Divine mind as real entities in a state of pure creaturehood, above and beyond any consideration of the fall. Even then they were "Blessed with all spiritual blessings in the heavenlies in Christ" and "accepted in the beloved" (Eph. 1:3, 6). It is of great moment that the Church should thus be first considered by us, that we never lose sight of the *original* dignity and loveliness of the Church, anointed and blessed in Christ before the foundation of the world. Her state by the fall *was not her original one,* any more than her present state is the final one.

"Behold I and the children whom the Lord hath given me" (Isa. 8: 18). Such were "sons" *before* God sends forth the Holy Spirit into their hearts (Gal. 4:6); they were "children" while "scattered abroad" *before* Christ died for them (John 11:51, 52); they were "children" *before* the Redeemer became incarnate (Heb. 2:14). The elect were "children" *from* all eternity and decreed to be so *unto* all eternity. They did not lose their sonship by the fall, neither by any corruption derived from that fall in their nature. "Children" they continued, though *sinful* children, and as such, justly exposed to wrath. Nevertheless, this relationship could not be revoked by any after-acts in time: united to Christ from all eternity, they were always one with Him. It is a remarkable fact that never once has the Holy Spirit used the prepositional form "into Christ" with reference to God's *election* of the Church, although *eis* occurs in the epistles over six hundred times: it is always in "(Gk. *en*) Christ," because the Church was *never out of Christ!*

From all eternity the Church stood in Christ as His mystical Body and Bride. A union between the members and their Head was then established which neither sin, Satan, nor death could sever. We say again, it is of vast importance that we do not lose sight of the original glory and beauty of the Church. The fall of the Church in Adam did not and could not alienate the Church from Christ, but it gave occasion for redemption, thereby affording the means and opportunity for the honor of Christ, by His work, death and resurrection bringing a greater revenue of glory to the Almighty Author of salvation than had the fall of man never taken place. Wondrous indeed are all the ways of God: in the ultimate outcome, He was no loser by Adam's defection, but the gainer; as it is written, "The Lord hath made all things *for himself*: yea, even the wicked for the day of evil" (Prov. 16:4); and again, "Surely the wrath of man shall praise thee" (Ps. 76:10).

"God's love to His elect is not of yesterday; it does not begin with their love to Him, 'We love Him, because He first loved us' (I John 4:19). It does not commence in time, but dates back from eternity, and is the ground and foundation of the elect's being called in time out of darkness into marvellous light: 'I have loved thee,' says the Lord of the Church, 'with an everlasting love; therefore with loving kindness have I drawn thee' (Jer. 31:3); that is, in effectual vocation. Many are the instances which might be given in proof of the antiquity of God's love to His elect, and as it is antecedent to their being brought out of a state of nature. God's choosing them in Christ before the foundation of the world, was an act of His love towards them, the fruit and effect of it. His making an everlasting covenant with His Son, ordered in all things and sure, on account of those He chose in Him; His setting Him up as the Mediator of the covenant from everlasting; His donation of grace to them in Him before the world began; His putting their persons into His hands, and so making them His care and charge, are so many demonstrative proofs of His early love to them.

"There are also instances to be given of God's love to His elect while they are in a state of nature. 'When we were yet without strength, in due time Christ died for the ungodly. . . . God commendeth His love towards us, in that while we were yet sinners, Christ died for us' (Rom. 5: 6, 8). Now certainly these persons were in a state of nature who are said to be 'without strength' etc., and yet God commended His love towards them when and while they were such, in a matchless instance of it. John makes use of this circumstance respecting the state of God's elect, to magnify the greatness of God's love: 'Herein is love, not that we loved God, but that He loved us, and sent His Son to be the propitiation for our sins.' Again, the quickening of God's elect when dead in trespasses and sins, the drawing of them to Christ with the cords of powerful and efficacious grace in effectual vocation, are instances of His special grace and favour, and fruits and effects of His everlasting love to them.

"If God did not love His elect while in a state of nature, they must for ever remain in that state, since they are unable to help themselves out of it; and it is only the love, grace and mercy of God, which engage His almighty power to deliver them from thence. There are three gifts and instances of God's love to His people before conversion, which are not to be matched by any instance or instances of love after conversion. The one is the gift of God Himself to them in the everlasting covenant, which covenant runs thus: 'I will be their God, and they shall be My people.' The second is the gift of His Son to suffer and die in their room and stead, and so obtain eternal redemption for them. The third is the gift of His Spirit to them, to convince them of sin, of righteousness, and of judgment. And now what greater instance is there of God's love to His people after conversion? If the heavenly glory, with all the entertaining joys of that delightful state, should be fixed upon, I deny it to be a greater instance of God's love, than the gift of Himself, His Son, and Spirit; and, indeed, all that God does in time, or will do to all eternity, is only *telling* His people how much He loved them *from everlasting*" (John Gill).

Now it was this eternal love of the Triune God which gave the Church an election-union in Christ from everlasting, for that love ever considered them in Christ. As it is written, Nothing "shall be able to separate them from the love of God *which is in Christ Jesus our Lord*" (Rom. 8:39). Christ, as God-man, was loved by the Father as the supreme object of His complacency (Prov. 8:30; Isa. 42:1), which was manifested in His election of Him; and the Church was the secondary object of God's love as viewed in Christ. The Lord Jesus declared to the Father, Thou "hast loved them *as* thou hast loved me. . . . thou lovedst me before the foundation of the world" (John 17:23, 24). Therefore as eternal election is a display of God's everlasting love to His people, so it is also an instance and evidence of their eternal union to Christ. The one cannot be without the other: if loved *in* Christ the Church must have been one *with* Him.

It is not that election was a fore-appointing of persons *unto* an union with Christ, as stones are selected *to be* used in a building, or as a slip is chosen for engrafting into a tree. Ephesians 1:4 *does not* say, "According as he had chosen us to be in him" or "that we should be in him." Instead we read, "Blessed be the God and Father of our Lord Jesus Christ, who hath blessed us with all spiritual blessings in the heavenlies in Christ, according as he hath chosen us in him before the foundation of the world" — the Church was blessed with all spiritual blessings *in Christ* "according as" they were chosen in Him. Election was not the original uniting act, for *that* was the everlasting love of God; yet the two must not be separated: they went together. Nevertheless, as in election the Church is considered *in Christ*, so it is a proof of their eternal union to Him. Now there are several things which *arise from* and are *branches of* this everlasting love-union of the Church to Christ, which it will now be our joy to consider. First and chief of these is *the marriage* between Christ and the Church.

It pleased the Father to choose for His Son, as God-man, the Church, to be not only His Body, but also His Bride, who was to receive from Him and share with Him His honors, glories, and privileges. Having chosen the Church in Christ, the Father set her before Him in the glass of His decrees, according to the uttermost purpose of His love and grace toward her, causing her to shine with excelling brightness and loveliness in the view of His Son, giving Him to see how high she was in the Father's estimation, and presenting her to Christ as His choicest gift to Him. This drew out the heart of the God-man towards her, caused Him to open His arms and heart to receive her, to set His affections and delight upon her, to regard and esteem her according to the high value which the Father Himself had placed upon her.

"Thine they were," said Christ to His Father, "And thou *gavest them me*" (John 17:6), to be My heritage, My portion, My bride. Here was the grand originating cause of Christ's love for His Church; the fact that she was the Father's love-gift to Him. Viewing the Church from eternity as thus presented to Him by the Father, He could not but regard her as supremely worthy of His affection and delight. His language was "I will betroth thee unto me forever; yea, I will betroth thee unto me in righteousness, and in judgment, and in lovingkindness, and in mercies, I will even betroth thee unto me in faithfulness, and thou shalt know the Lord" (Hos. 2:19, 20) — let it be carefully borne in mind that the record of His words in Holy Scripture are but the *open* transcript of what He said in secret before the world began: many examples of this might be given, but we here only state the bare fact.

"The king's daughter is all glorious within: her clothing is of wrought gold" (Ps. 45:13). Observe well the glorious title which the Church here bears, and mark carefully what is necessarily presupposed and clearly implied in it. The "king" is God the Father, of whom we read "a certain king, which made a marriage for his son" (Matt. 22:2). That "marriage" was made from everlasting, and therefore could the Divine Bridegroom say to His celestial Bride, "thy maker is thy husband" (Isa. 54:5). Now it is by virtue of this marital union between Christ and His people that the Church is here designated "the king's *daughter:*" because the Father is *Christ's* "Father," He is the Church's "Father" (John 20:17); because Christ is the Father's *Son*, and the Church is wedded to Him, therefore the Church is the Father's "daughter!"

Most marvellously and blessedly was all of this shadowed out in connection with our first parents. Adam, in his creation and formation, was a type of Christ; Eve of the Church. Before Adam's creation we read of a council held between the Eternal Three concerning him: "And God said, Let *us* make man in our image, after our likeness" (Gen. 1:26) So it was in connection with the last Adam (Heb. 10:5, 9). Adam's body was supernaturally produced out of the virgin earth, as Christ's body was miraculously conceived by the Virgin Mary. The union between the soul and body of Adam (Gen. 2:7) adumbrated the incomprehensible union between the eternal Son of God and His assumption of our nature into oneness with His own person. Adam's lordship, or his being given dominion over all mundane creatures (Gen. 1:28), prefigured Christ's universal headship over all things to His Church (Eph. 1:22, 23). But it is the formation of Eve and her union with Adam to which we would now direct particular attention.

"And the Lord God said, It is not good that the man should be alone: I will make him a help meet for him. . . . And the Lord God caused a deep sleep to fall upon Adam, and he slept; and he took one of his ribs and closed up the flesh instead thereof. And the rib, which the Lord God had taken from man, builded he a woman, and brought her unto the man. And Adam said, This is now bone of my bones, and flesh of my flesh: she shall be called woman, because she was taken out of man" (Gen. 2:18, 21-23). First, behold here the tender solicitude of God toward Adam: "It is not good that man should be alone." In this, a deeper mystery is opened unto those who have eyes to see: it is a revelation on the earth plane of what had passed secretly in the eternal councils of Heaven. Christ, as God-man — "the Beginning" of Jehovah's way (Prov. 8:22, Col. 1:18), the Fountain-head of all His decrees (Isa. 42:1; Eph. 3:11) — was the grand Object of Jehovah's love: all His vast designs concentrated in Him, concerned Him, and were designed for His manifestative glory from all eternity — "all things were created by him *and for him*" (Col. 1:16).

Second, we discover here God's purpose to provide a suitable companion for Adam: "I will make an help meet for him." This affords us a yet fuller insight into that which had passed in the Divine mind before the foundation of the world: God thought it not meet that the God-man ("set up" in heaven before the world was: Prov. 8:23, 24) should be alone, therefore did He ordain and choose a Bride for Him. Third, God created Eve *out of Adam*, taking one of his ribs and from it and the flesh cleaving thereto made He the first woman. This also was a most striking acting out in time of what had transpired ere time began. God had chosen the Church in Christ, she was *in Him* before the foundation of the world" (I Peter 1:20) to become incarnate, and His human nature having a covenant subsistence before God, the Church, as thus considered in Him, received her human nature from Him, and hence that expression "We are members of his body, of his flesh, and of his bones" (Eph. 5:32) is language which most evidently refers us back to Genesis 2:22.

Fourth, out of Adam's rib the Lord God made, or as the margin more correctly renders it *"builded"* the woman, for she is of a more curious and delicate frame than the man. Now Christ is "the foundation" (I Cor. 3:11) and the Church is His "building:" built up for Him and upon Him, with heavenly art, by an infinitely wise Architect — "Ye also as living stones, are built up a spiritual house" (I Peter 2:5). Fifth, God then set Eve before Adam, "and brought her unto the man," and this, in order to effect *a marriage union* between them. What blessed light this casts upon the high mystery of grace, when God the Father presented the elect unto Christ. It was *to that* He referred when He said, "Thine they were, and thou *gavest them me*" (John 17:6) — as He gave Eve to Adam!

In our endeavor to view the eternal transactions of Divine love and grace, we must contemplate the Church as she was before Adam's defection. We must view her first, not as fallen, but as unfallen; not as involved in sin and ruin, but as the pure and spotless bride of Christ, given by the Father to Him as His spouse. Most blessedly was this typed out in Eve as she was brought and given to Adam in all her spotless innocency. O how surpassingly fair must Eve have appeared in the morning of her creation, as she came fresh from the hand of her Maker! What could Adam do but love her and delight in the admirable bride which the Lord God had so graciously provided for him! So Christ viewing, in the glass of God's decrees, the Bride selected for Him, loved and delighted in her, betrothed Himself unto her, took her as thus presented by God unto Himself in a deed of marriage-settlement as the gift of the Father.

Let it be fully noted that Adam was joined to Eve in marriage *before* the fall, and not after it. How this exposes the makeshift compromise of sublapsarians! Ephesians 5:31, 32 in the light of Genesis 2:23 unequivocally establishes the fact that the making of Adam and Eve *before* sin entered the world, prefigured the marriage-union of Christ and His Church, decreed of God prior to any consideration of the fall. Nor does this stand alone. In Leviticus 21:13, 14 is another precious type equally definite and plain. There we read, "And he [namely, the high priest of v. 10] shall take a wife in her virginity. A widow, or a divorced woman, or profane, or a harlot, these shall he not take: but he shall take *a virgin* of his own people to wife." Now as the high priest under the law was a figure of the great High Priest over the House of God, we must see in this Divine prohibition a typical intimation that the Church was espoused to the God-man in all her *virgin purity* as she stood before Jehovah in her native innocency.

But to return to the exquisite scene set before us in Genesis 2. We observe, sixth, that Adam *owned* the relation which now existed between himself and Eve: "This is now bone of my bones and flesh of my flesh: she shall be called woman, because she was taken out of man." In like manner Christ received the elect at the Father's hands, became their Husband, and from thence owned them as His everlasting Spouse. His love for her is blessedly told out in "As the Father hath loved me, so have I loved you" (John 15:10) — eternally, infinitely, unchangeably. He speaks of her as "in whom is all my delight" (Ps. 16:3); and "How fair and how pleasant art thou, O Love, for delights!" (Song of Sol. 7:6). Seventh, as Adam was not created for Eve, but she for him, so God did not foreordain and "set up" Christ, as God-man, for the Church, but the Church was ordained for Him: "For the man is not of the woman, but the woman of the man; neither was the man created for the woman, but the woman for the man" (I Cor. 11:8, 9).

Finally, though Adam was not taken out of the woman nor created for her, nevertheless it was not good that he should be "alone:" Eve was his necessary complement, his companion, his helpmeet; yea, as we are told, "the woman is *the glory of* the man" (I Cor. 11:7). In like manner, Christ, as God-man, would be incomplete without His Bride: considered as His mystical Body, she is called "the fulness of him that filleth all in all" (Eph. 1:23). Christ needed a vessel which He might fill, that should reflect His glory; hence we read, "the messengers of the churches, *the glory of Christ*" (II Cor. 8:23); and again, "Israel *my glory*" (Isa. 46:13) He calls her. In the last reference made to her in holy Writ we read, "Come hither, I will show thee the bride, the Lamb's wife . . . descending out of heaven from God, having the glory of God, and her light is like unto a stone most precious" (Rev. 21:9-11). In and by and through the Church Christ will be glorified to all eternity.

III

We have pointed out that the everlasting love of the Triune God is *the origin* of the Church's union to Christ, and that election was the first and fundamental act of that love toward its members; that election giving them a super-creation subsistence in their glorious Head. In God's eternal thoughts and foreviews, the elect were conceived and contemplated in the Divine mind as real entities in a state of pure creaturehood, above and beyond any consideration of the Fall. Even then they were "blessed with all spiritual blessings in the heavenlies in Christ" and "graced in the beloved" (Eph. 1:3, 6). It is much to be deplored that this *original* dignity and loveliness of the Church, as anointed, graced, and blest in Christ before the foundation of the world, has almost entirely disappeared from the theology even of the "orthodox" during the past century. A glorious relationship was established between Christ and the Church in eternity past, which neither sin, Satan, nor death could sever. This alone provides the key to all of God's dealings with her in a time state.

We also pointed out that several things arise from and are branches of the everlasting love-union between Christ and the Church. First and chief of these is the *marriage* between them, marvellously and blessedly shadowed out in connection with our first parents before the Fall. We will now endeavor to point out how that that marital union gave the Church *communion with Christ* in His honors and interests. A wide field — hinted at in the Introduction — is here set before us, which, because of our spiritual feebleness, we are not able to fully explore. Christ admits His Church into fellowship with Himself in His names, titles, relations, grace, fulness, salvation, blessings, and benefits. As God in choosing the Church in Christ gave her a relation to His person, giving her being in Him, so in accepting her in Him God gave Christ to her, so that she should live with Him, have communion with Him, and be like Him forever, the everlasting object of His unchanging love.

See how this is exemplified in the Church's sharing of Christ's names and titles. As Christ is by His co-existence in the Godhead, the essential *Son of God*, so by predestination His brethren are the adopted *sons* of

God, and by virtue of the marriage-union between Christ and them, they have His Father as their Father, and His God for their God (John 20:17). In Colossians 1:15 Christ, as God-man, is designated "*the firstborn* of every creature," while on Hebrews 12:23 His people are said to be "the church of the *firstborn* which are written in heaven." Is Christ the "heir of all things" (Heb. 1:2), so believers are "heirs of God and joint-heirs with Christ" (Rom. 8:17). Is Christ denominated "the *stone* of Israel" (Gen. 49:24), His people are also called "living *stones*" (I Peter 2:5). As Christ acquired "a name which no one knoweth but himself" (Rev. 19:7), so also has the believer: "To him that overcometh will I give to eat of the hidden manna, and will give him a white stone, and in the stone a new name written, which no man knoweth saving he that receiveth it" (Rev. 2:17). So precious is this aspect of the truth that we take leave to copy from our Introduction:

"In Jeremiah 23:6 we read, And this is his name whereby *he* shall be called, The Lord our righteousness, and in Jeremiah 33:16 we are told and this is the name whereby *she* shall be called, the Lord our righteousness — this by virtue of her oneness with Him. So again in I Corinthians 12:12 the Church is actually designated 'the Christ,' while in Galatians 3:16 and Colossians 1:24 the Head and His Church forming one body are conjointly referred to as 'Christ'; hence when Saul of Tarsus was assaulting the Church, its Head protested 'Why persecutest thou *me?*' (Acts 9:4). But what is yet more remarkable, we find the Lord Jesus given the name of His people: in Galatians 6:16 the Church is denominated 'the *Israel* of God,' while in Isaiah 49:3 we hear God saying *to the Mediator* 'Thou are my Servant, O *Israel*, in whom I will be glorified!' "

In Colossians 3:12 Christians are exhorted to "Put on therefore, as the elect of God, holy and beloved, bowels of mercies." Each of those titles is given to the saints because of *their union with Christ*. They are "the elect of God" because *He* is God's "Elect" (Isa. 42:1); they are "holy" because conjoined to God's "Holy One" (Ps. 16:10); they are "beloved" because married to Him of whom the Father says "This is my Beloved son" (Matt. 3:17). Again, we are told God "hath made us *kings and priests*" (Rev. 1:5), which is only because we are *united to Him who is* "the King of kings" and the "great High Priest." Is Christ called "the Sun of righteousness" (Mal. 4:2)? So we are told "Then shall the righteous shine forth *as the sun* in the kingdom of their Father" (Matt. 13:42)! Does the Redeemer declare "I am the Rose of Sharon" (Song of Sol. 2:1)? Then He promised of the redeemed "The desert [their fruitless state by nature] shall rejoice and blossom *as the rose*" (Isa. 35:1) — the only two occasions the "rose" is mentioned in Holy Writ!

Having sought to show that the Church had a super-creation excellency, that before the foundation of the world its members were chosen in Christ, united to Christ, and blessed with all spiritual blessings; we must now point out that *sin has drawn a veil* which makes it very difficult for us to discern the *original* purity, dignity and glory of Christ's mystical Body and Bride. It is much easier for us to apprehend our ruin and misery, and our redemption from it by the incarnation, obedience and sacrifice of the Son of God, than it is to realize what the Church was in the purpose, counsel and mind of God before sin entered the world. It is only by receiving into the mind what is revealed thereon in the Scriptures of Truth and by mixing faith therewith, that we can in any measure obtain a conception of this transcendent and glorious mystery. It is only as the Holy Spirit is pleased to shine upon our understandings that we can see the light in His light.

As Eve was united to Adam in her virgin purity and became his wife *before* she ate of the forbidden fruit, so in the will and eternal counsels of God the Church was wedded to Christ, over and above any foreviews of the Fall. As Eve disobeyed the Divine prohibition and fell from her pristine uprightness, and lost her original beauty, so the Church shared in the defection of the whole human race when its federal head (Adam) apostatized from his Maker. In God's infinite prescience He foresaw the Fall, having predetermined to permit it, and upon the foresight of that Fall, He entered into an everlasting covenant with Christ, the spiritual Head of the elect, to raise them up from the ruins of the Fall, by the incarnation and finished work of Christ. In this the illustrious wisdom of God was discovered and displayed in a way which would serve to be the marvel of time and the admiration of saints in Heaven to all eternity.

In Adam, the Church was brought into this world by creation pure, holy and righteous. From that *creature* purity, holiness and righteousness, she fell by Adam's first act of transgression, and became in her own nature and person, simply considered (that is, viewed apart from her eternal standing and state in Christ), impure, unholy and unrighteous. Therefore do we read that the elect are "by nature the children of wrath even as others" (Eph. 2:3); that is, because of sin, their *nature* is repellent unto Divine holiness, and falls under the condemning sentence of Divine justice. It was to redeem or deliver the Church from the state of sin and misery, and in order to raise her up again to the enjoyment of her original state and glory, to which she was decreed or predestinated, that her Head and Husband, her Lord and Saviour, became actually incarnate, taking upon Him humanity, tabernacling personally in the same, and having imputed to Him the transgressions of His people, with all the guilt thereof.

Herein we may behold not only the fathomless love and amazing condescension of Christ, but also the wondrous wisdom of God, who designed that there should be *an accurate conformity of* the Church *to* its Head, between the mystical Wife and her celestial Husband. By their fall in Adam, a veil was drawn over the elect, so that they cannot in their ruined state be known by themselves or by others, to be the Lord's. In their natural condition there is nothing to distinguish the elect from the non-elect: their "life is *hid* with Christ in God" (Col. 3:3). They are born into this world the same as others, with no halo of glory around their heads to mark them out as the high favorites of Heaven, with nothing to show that they are the beloved Bride of Christ. Instead, according to human observation, there is everything to the contrary: they are shapen in iniquity, conceived in sin, and live in a way of open revolt from the Lord.

In like manner, a veil was drawn over Christ when He appeared on the earth. As the God-man, He had a glory with the Father "before the world was" (John 17:5), and lived a life of blessedness inconceivable by us; yet He laid aside that glory and took upon Him the form of a servant. When He was born into this world, it was not in a palace, but a cattle-shed. Ah, my reader, what was there about the Babe of Bethlehem, hanging upon His mother's breast, to indicate that He was the Maker of Heaven and earth? Witness the vile attempt upon His life and the consequent flight into Egypt, and what was there to show that He had previously been worshipped by all the hosts of Heaven? See Him later, in the lowly peasant-home of Joseph and Mary in Nazareth, and who among the companions of His boyhood dreamed He was the incarnate Son of God? View Him in early manhood, laboring at the carpenter's bench, and wherein did it appear that He was Jehovah's "fellow?" Was not the Sun of righteousness eclipsed for a season when He was in all things "made like unto His brethren"? (Heb. 2:17).

When the Lord of glory became incarnate, He came under a cloud, if we may so express it. He suspended the shinings forth of His essential glory, due to the dignity of His person, and appeared in the likeness of sinful flesh, coming not to be ministered unto, but to minister, and give His life a ransom for many, that He might complete the work of redemption by which He was to redeem His Spouse, and wash away her deformity and stains. In this lay the depths of Christ's humiliation: that the Father's co-equal should make Himself "of no reputation," be made in the likeness of men, be made "under the law," and so humble Himself as to be "obedient unto death, even the death of the cross." In Him "dwelt all the fulness of the Godhead bodily," but for a season — except when its beams darted forth on the Mount of Transfiguration — the breakings forth thereof were withheld. Incomprehensible grace! such as will fill the saints in Heaven with astonishment through the ages of eternity. Alas, that our hearts are so feebly moved by it now.

Herein, then, we may perceive *the conformity* between Christ and the Church: each had a celestial glory before the foundation of the world: a veil was cast over that glory when each appeared on the earth. When the elect were brought forth into creature-existence and open being (having subsisted previously in the secret counsels of God), they were pure, holy, righteous, perfect in their natural head. Yet, being in Adam, not only by seminal union but by federal representation, when he broke the Covenant of Works and fell from God, the elect also fell in and with him into a state of sin, misery and alienation from the Lord. Therefore the Spouse of Christ became wholly unlike herself and unlike her Divine and Heavenly Bridegroom, so that she became in her natural head, and inherently in herself, altogether unholy and unrighteous, becoming sinful and impure, having undergone an eclipse of her glory, suffering the loss of the moral image of God, in which she was created: all of which is to be justly ascribed to the mutability of the creature's will — proving that no creature has whereof to glory before God.

Estranged as the Church became in her affections and obedience to her Lord, by reason of her sunken and degraded condition through the Fall, yet the union existing between her and her celestial Husband remained the same. The very fall of the whole human race in Adam, by virtue of the mutability of the creature, only made more evident the absolute necessity of *Christ's* Headship, to the end that *by Him* the elect were so united to God by everlasting bonds as to be beyond the possibility of hazard or miscarriage or of finally falling from Him; having been blessed with super-creation grace, and that, that Christ might be the more honored and magnified. It is His sole prerogative, as God-man, to have life *in Himself*: "For as the Father [the self-existent One] hath life in himself, so hath he *given* to the Son [as Mediator] to have life in himself" (John 5:26). No creature, either angel or man, "anointed cherub" or Adam when made "very good," is able to stand one moment of himself. Those who have an eternal standing before God owe it alone to Christ.

The fall of the elect of mankind (in the decree of Jehovah) was *subordinated to the glory of Christ*, it being thereby contrived to show forth and exalt His wondrous perfections. To mention here only one: consider Christ's *love for the Church*. Christ had a view of the Church in the glass of God's decrees before the world began. He saw her as graced in Himself, and destined to eternal glory. He saw her as presented to Himself by the Father as His love gift. This drew out His heart to her. He saw her as "the king's daughter all glorious within" (Ps. 45:13). She was given to Him: they were made one by marriage-union in the everlasting settlements of Heaven. The Father blest her in Christ with all spiritual blessings. Hear Him speak as God-man before time began: "Then I was by him, as one brought up with him: and I was daily his delight, rejoicing always before him; rejoicing in the habitable part of his earth; and *my delights were with the sons of men*" (Prov. 8:30, 31).

Certainly Christ's "delights" were *not* with "the sons of men" regarded as *fallen* creatures. No, He was there contemplating them in their supralapsarian state, in their original purity and beauty. Oh how vastly different must the Church have next appeared in His eyes, when He viewed her as fallen, depraved and filthy! Yet so knit was His heart to her, such was His affection for her, that it neither destroyed nor abated the same by the foreviews He took of her apostasy in Adam. Yea, as He viewed the members of His body in their debased and vile condition, His heart was drawn out in pity and compassion toward them. Therefore was He willing to be their Surety, assume all their liabilities, fully discharge their debts, and make a complete atonement for them. Their fall in Adam occasioned an opportunity for their eternal Lover to display the changelessness of His infinite love for and to them.

"It is among the mysteries of grace, such as belong to the deep things of God, that the elect, though they fell from God by reason of sin, through the fall of the first man, by means of their union to him and interest in him; from whence they received and partook of the same equal corruption and total ruin of their natures by the infection of sin, with the rest of mankind — having in themselves the same fountain and principle of sin which the very reprobate hath: *yet they fell not from* the grace of personal election, nor from the everlasting favor of God; nor did they lose their interest in their Heavenly Father's love thereby.

"Their union and relation to the person of Christ, their eternal Head, and interest in Him, were not dissolved nor impaired hereby; nor did they cease to be the beloved of Immanuel's soul. Though they, by the fall, lost all that was given them in Adam as their nature-head, and nature-root, yet, the grace of election still continued the same as ever; and Jesus Christ, their ever-living Head, in whom is their spiritual, everlasting life, happiness, and glory, was Alpha and Omega to them; their beginning, their eternal spring, who, as such, broke forth towards them in their fallen state, and still continues His kindness in dispensing all grace to them, to whom it will be continued with all its glorious fruits and blessings by Him to eternity" (S. E. Pierce).

Christ was first the "Head" and then the "Saviour" of the Church (Eph. 5:23). All is eternally secured in the person of the Lord Jesus. When God permitted the fall of all mankind in Adam, the elect fell in him; yet they fell not from the heart and arms of Christ. They lost in Adam the creature blessings of purity, holiness and righteousness, which as their natural head he should have conveyed to them, and received from him instead an impure and sinful nature, the fruits of which are as justly deserving of Divine wrath as are the sins of the non-elect. In that state they are, in themselves, without hope and help. This it is which made way for their need of redemption, to be delivered out of it, and which provided an occasion for their Husband to become their Redeemer, which He engaged to be before the foundation of the world. "On his head are *many* crowns" (Rev. 19:12), each representing a separate and distinctive glory, which it is the joy of saints to separately contemplate.

"The elect lost their all that was given unto them and bestowed upon them in their nature-head. But they lost not their interest in the grace of election in the person of Christ, in the supernatural spiritual blessings which had been bestowed upon them in Christ their eternal Head; and this secured them from everlasting ruin and misery. The love of God to His elect in Christ was not weakened, nor the union-knot between Christ and His Church loosed, by all which befel them and came upon them by the Fall. Christ being the Head of the Church, the life, light, grace, holiness, righteousness, glory, and blessings in Christ, could not undergo any hazard or damage by the Fall.

"The Body being defiled with sin, the glorious Head and Husband who had loved His Spouse as Himself, having viewed her as the object of His Father's complacency and delight, descended from Heaven, by His mysterious incarnation, to fulfill His covenant stipulations on her behalf, and act a part of Redeemer and Saviour" [From *Christ's Love to His Church* by S. E. Pierce, to whom we gladly own our indebtedness for much in this chapter].

5

Federal Union

ONCE more we would point out that *the origin* of that union which subsists between the Church and Christ was the everlasting love of God: this it was which cemented Head and members together. The loving purpose of God gave the Church an election-union to Christ, which (for the want of a better term) we have styled the "mystical." Inseparably connected with the election-standing of the Church before God, was its marriage to Christ, and upon that marital relationship we have dwelt at length. We are now to consider further what branched out of the mystical union in view of the Church's fall in its nature-head. Having in His high sovereignty predetermined the apostasy of Adam, upon His foreviews of the same, God engaged in an everlasting covenant with Christ, the spiritual Head of the elect, to raise them up from the ruins of their fall. What that involved and included it will now be our joy to consider.

In contemplating the Covenant of Grace which was made between God and the Mediator, it is very necessary to recognise that Christ acted therein as *the Head* of the Church. This it is which determined the title of this chapter. The elect had not only a mystical union with Christ in the womb of God's decrees, but they had an actual oneness together in the sight of the Divine law. That oneness has been variously designated by different writers: "covenant union," "legal union," "representative union," "federal union," all which signify much the same. The grand point to be apprehended here is, that Christ and His people were one in Divine election, He the Head and they the members of the mystical Body, and so likewise they are to be regarded in the everlasting covenant. The covenant was made with Christ not as a single person, but as a common Head, representing all the elect who were given to Him in a federal way; so that what He promised in the covenant, He promised for them and on their account; and what He was promised, He received on their behalf.

This federal oneness which exists between Christ and the elect from everlasting, means that they are one in a legal sense: or to state it yet more simply, Christ and His people are looked at as one by the eyes of the law, as surety and debtor are one. The bond of this union is Christ's *suretyship.* "A relation is formed between a surety and the person for whom he engages, by which they are thus far considered as one, that the surety is liable for the debt which the other has contracted, and his payment is held as the payment of the debtor, who is *ipso facto* absolved from all obligation to the creditor. A similar connection is established between our Redeemer and those who are given to Him by His Father. He became answerable for them to the justice of God; and it was stipulated that, on acount of His satisfaction to its demands, they should receive the pardon of their sins" (John Dick).

The federal union between Christ and the elect gave them a covenant-subsistence in Him, for it was as their Head and Representative that He contracted to serve. The everlasting covenant flowed from and was the fruit of the love and grace of God. The ordering thereof pre-supposed *sin*, for its provisions had respect to the fall, and its effects upon the Church. It was made with Christ not as a private or single person, but as a public and common Person. As the Covenant of Works was made with the first Adam as the federal head of his posterity — so that he was "a figure of him that was to come" (Rom. 5:14) — so the Covenant of Grace was made with Christ as the last Adam as the federal Head of His spiritual offspring. The elect, then, had a representative union to Christ in the Covenant, for all that He engaged to do, He engaged in their name and on their account; and when *He* performed its stipulations it was the same with God as if it had been done by *them*.

The bond, then, of the federal, legal and representative union between Christ and His people, is suretyship for them. Christ's entering upon that office on their behalf gave full proof of His deep and unchangeable affection to them. He loved them "with an everlasting love" (Jer. 31:3), and as Song of Solomon 8:7 declares, "Many waters cannot quench love, neither can the floods drown it." So it was here: not even His foreviews of the Church's apostasy in Adam, its fall into a state of degradation and defilement could change the heart of Christ toward His Bride. Her defection in Adam and her alienation from God, only provided opportunity to her eternal Lover to manifest the infinite affection He bore to her. Christ drew nigh unto God on behalf of His Church, gave His bond, and placed Himself under obligation to pay all the debts of His people and satisfy for their sins.

Though the Church fell in Adam from her state of native innocency, she did not fall from the heart or arms of her heavenly Bridegroom. "Christ also loved the church, and gave himself for it" (Eph. 5:25): note "loved" *before* "gave himself for it." And when did He first love the Church? Hear His own answer: "I have declared unto them Thy name, and will declare it; that the love wherewith thou hast loved me may be in them, and I in them" (John 17:26). That declaration establishes two points: the eternality and the nature of Christ's love for His Church. Christ has been loved by the Father "before the foundation of the world" (John 17:24), and He had been loved with a love which delighted in the excellency of His person. Such was Christ's love toward His Church: it was not a love of compassion in view of the wretchedness occasioned by her fall in Adam, but a love of *complacency*, when He first viewed her as "all glorious within" (Ps. 45:13). His "delights" with the sons of men (Prov. 8:31) were precisely the same as the Father's "delight" in Him (Prov. 8:30). Blessedly did He display that love when, in foreviews of the Fall, He presented Himself to the Father to serve as

"Surety" on behalf of His Church, who was immersed in debt which she could never discharge.

Then it was that the Father said, "Who is this that *engaged* [or, as the Hebrew word is rendered, "be surety for" in Ps. 119:122; Prov. 11:15] his heart to approach unto me?" (Jer. 30:21). That the reference here is to Christ Himself, and that His undertaking to serve as Surety was infinitely well-pleasing to God, is clear from the first part of the verse: "their Governor shall proceed from the midst of them: and I will cause him to draw near, and he shall approach unto me." It was then that Christ became "the Surety of a better testament" (Heb. 7:22), substituting Himself in the place and stead of His fallen people, placing Himself under obligation to fully discharge their legal responsibility, pay their debts, satisfy for their sins, and procure for them all the blessings of grace and glory. It was then that Christ offered to "finish the transgression, and to make an end of sins, and to make reconciliation for iniquity, and to bring in everlasting righteousness" (Dan. 9:24). This being accepted of by God, henceforth Christ and His elect were looked upon by the law as one person.

What was then transacted in the secret councils of eternity was, "when the fulness of time was come" (Gal. 4:4), openly manifested on earth. In order to discharge His suretyship, it was necessary for there to be a natural union (a union in human nature), between Christ and His people, for "both he that sanctifieth and they who are sanctified are all *of one*" — one nature (Heb. 2:11). Before the Son of God could take upon Him the sins of the elect, He must first assume their nature. It was meet that the Divine law should be magnified and made honorable by One in the same nature as those by whom it had been disobeyed and dishonored. Moreover, it was only by becoming incarnate that the second Person in the Trinity could be "made under the law." Therefore do we read, "Forasmuch then as the children are partakers of flesh and blood, he also himself likewise took part of the same; that through death He might destroy him that had the power of death, that is, the devil" (Heb. 2:14).

The incarnation of Christ may therefore be called "manifestative union," for at His birth there was *openly displayed* the oneness which existed between Him and His Church. "Wherefore in all things it behoved him to be made like unto his brethren, that he might be a merciful and faithful High Priest in things pertaining to God, to make propitiation for the sins of *the people*" (Heb. 2:17). The elect, who had fallen in Adam, could not be conformed unto the image of Christ until He had — by amazing grace — been conformed to their image. The nature which Christ assumed was the same as that which we have, for it was the "seed" of the woman — save that it was entirely free of sin's taint. Though this union was supernaturally affected in time, yet it was the fruit of Christ's love for the Church and the fulfillment of His covenant-engagements on her behalf before time began. Though the nature Christ assumed is one that is common to all mankind, yet as Hebrews 2 so plainly intimates, it was taken by Him with a peculiar regard to the elect — His "brethren," — the "children," the seed "of Abraham."

Before proceeding further, let it be pointed out that the election union, the marital union, the federal union which the Church had with Christ, and the manifest union which the incarnation gave Him to the Church, are only so many branches of and all take their rise from the everlasting *love union*. Everything is founded upon and grows out of the eternal love of the Triune God unto the elect: *this* is the grand original, the strong and firm bond of union between the Head and His members, and is the spring of all that communion and fellowship which the Church has with Christ (and God in Him) in time, and shall have to all eternity. All is antecedent to our faith union with Christ. It is from hence that the Holy Spirit is sent down into their hearts to renew them and work faith in their souls. Faith does not give them a being in Christ, but is only one of the fruits, effects, and evidences of their being in Christ and of their union to Him.

It is true that the elect do not, and cannot, *know of* their being eternally in Christ, nor of their union to Him before the foundation of the world, until they are given to savingly believe in Him; and that, by Christ's sending the quickening Spirit into their hearts. Only then is that which before was concealed from them, revealed to them. "Therefore if any man be in Christ, he is a new creature" (II Cor. 5:17): but being made a "new creature," does not put a man into Christ, rather is it *the evidence of* his being there, and without which he cannot know it. "Now if any man have not the Spirit of Christ, he is none of his" (Rom. 8:9): nevertheless, I may be one of Christ's chosen and redeemed ones, though I have not yet the Spirit indwelling me. The *full* manifestation of our union to Christ will only appear in Heaven itself, when His prayer in John 17:20-24 is fulfilled. But to return unto the present aspect of our subject.

Christ is the Friend who "*sticketh closer* than a brother" (Prov. 18: 14) to His people. Nothing could dissolve the tie which had been established between them ere the world began. Nothing could quench His love to them, for "having loved his own which were in the world he loved them unto the end" (John 13:1). Therefore, when He viewed the Church in its fallen estate, He willingly became incarnate, entered the office of Surety on their behalf, and engaged to put away all their sins and bring in a perfect righteousness for them. Christ undertook to conquer Satan, death, and Hell for His Church, and to present her before the high throne of God holy and without spot, as though she had never been defiled. This is a greater work than His making all things out of nothing, or the upholding of all things by the Word of His power. This work is the admiration and marvel of angels, and the theme of Heaven's new song.

Jehovah Jesus, the God-man, with all the love of Godhead in His heart, in His incarnate state, stood in the law-place, room and stead of, His sinful people as their Sponsor, lived and obeyed the law for them. He was here as their Representative, and His perfect fulfillment of the law in thought and word and deed, constitutes their everlasting righteousness. When Christ had magnified the law and made it honorable, the Lord caused to meet on Him the iniquities of all His people, so that He was, imputatively, "made sin" (II Cor. 5:21) for them. Jehovah the Father alone could dispose of iniquity, and gather all the sins of all the elect and place them on Christ: He "the Judge of all" (Heb. 12:23) was the One immediately sinned against, and therefore the only One who could provide and accept an atoning sacrifice. "*God was in Christ* reconciling the world unto himself, not imputing their trespasses unto them" (II Cor. 5:19).

As "the Lamb of God" Christ was appointed and prepared from eternity, as is clear from Revelation 13:8 and I Peter 1:19, 20. The atoning death of Christ, then, was a grand article of the everlasting covenant between the Father and the Son. This was decreed by God, agreed upon by the Mediator, and published by the Spirit in the Scriptures. The transferring of sin from the persons of the elect to the person of Christ was shadowed forth under the Old Testament sacrifices, they being substituted in the room of sinners and offered for sin — the sins of the offenders being laid upon them in a typical way (see Lev. 4:4 and 16:21). The curse and vengeance of God's wrath which was to fall upon Christ when He should have the sins of His people laid upon Him, and be borne by Him in His own body to and on the Tree, was set forth by the fire which lighted upon and consumed the sacrifices under the law.

The covenant oneness of Christ and His Church was adumbrated by the relation which obtained between Adam and the human race, for though Christ's actual discharge of His suretyship was historically afterwards, yet in the order of God's decrees it was before it. This is clear from Romans 5:18, 19, "Therefore *as* by the offense of one judgment came upon all men unto condemnation; *even so* by the righteousness of One the free gift came upon all men unto justification of life. For *as* by one man's disobedience many were made sinners, *so* by the obedience of One shall many be made righteous." Believers are made righteous through the obedience of Christ on precisely the same principles as all of Adam's posterity were made sinners by the disobedience of their natural head: there was an identity of legal relations and reciprocal obligations and rights. In each case it was the one that was acting on the behalf of many, and doing so because of his federal union with the many.

When God accepted Christ as the federal Head of His people, they were henceforth considered as legally one: this, and this alone, being the foundation for the imputation of their sins to Him and of His righteousness to them. *This* was the foundation of all which Christ did and suffered for them, and for them alone; and for all the blessings of grace which are or shall be bestowed on them; which blessings are denied all others. To discharge their legal liabilities, Christ entered upon the office of Surety, in consequence of which He became responsible to the law for His people: so truly so, that the benefit of His transactions redounds to them. As Adam's transgression was imputed to us because we were legally one with him, so our iniquities were imputed to Christ because He stood before the law as our Sponsor; and in like manner, His obedience and its reward is reckoned to our account: "For he [God] hath made him [Christ] to be sin for us, who knew no sin; that we might be made the righteousness of God in him" (II Cor. 5:21).

It is of vast importance to perceive that the saving-work of Christ was performed not only *for* His people, but that He did it as *in union with* them, so that the Church has such an interest in all her Head did and suffered for her sake, that she was one with Him, yea, *in Him*, in all His actions and sufferings. He loved *them*, was born for them, lived for them, died for them, rose from the grave for them, and ascended into heaven for them. But more: they were one with Him at every point. They were crucified *"with Christ"* (Gal. 2:20), "buried with him" (Col. 2:12), "and hath raised us up *together*, and made us sit together in the heavenlies in Christ Jesus" (Eph. 2:6). These expressions indicate not only the *intimacy* of the federal union, but the *efficacy* of the same, for the validity and virtue of His actions are reckoned to her. In Christ the Church is holy and righteous, pure and spotless: "ye are complete *in him*" (Col. 2:10).

In the grand fact of federal union, and nowhere else, do we obtain an adequate answer to the age-long question of infidels, "How could Christ, a perfectly innocent person, *justly* suffer the curse of the law? If He were guiltless in Himself, then how could the Judge of all the earth *righteously* cause His sword to smite Him?" This objection loses its air of plausibility once the clear light of Christ's Covenant Headship is thrown upon it. Christ *voluntarily* suffered in the room and stead of others. If it be asked, What righteous principle justified His dying as a *Substitute?* "the Just for the unjust?" the answer is, that gracious substituting of Himself as a victim for His people was the discharge of His *Suretyship*. If the inquiry be pressed further back still, And what justified Christ's entering upon His office of Surety? the answer is, *His Covenant-oneness* with His people. And what moved Him to enter into His covenant engagement? LOVE, love to His Bride as He foresaw her fallen into sin.

In view of what has just been pointed out, must we not join the apostle in exclaiming "O *the depth* of the riches both of the wisdom and knowledge of God!" (Rom. 11:33). Contrariwise, are we not also obliged to lament "O the dreadful *superficiality* of present-day preaching [?] of the Cross!" It was by a voluntary act on Christ's part, out of love to God and His people, that He offered to serve as the Surety of His elect, substitute Himself in their fallen stead, and bear the full punishment due their sins. Because their guilt was imputed to Him, the Father, without the slightest impeachment of His holiness and justice, exacted satisfaction from the Sponsor. In like manner, in perfect righteousness, God imputes Christ's merits to them. Therefore, no one considered as innocent, suffered; and none, considered guilty, escaped. The blood shed by Christ was "the blood of the everlasting covenant" (Heb. 13:20), and therefore has God promised Christ "By the blood of

Thy covenant I have sent forth *Thy* prisoners out of the pit wherein is no water" (Zech. 9:11).

The *effect* of this federal union is the Church's *communion* with Christ in all the benefits which His infinitely-meritorious work as Surety procured. "There is therefore now no condemnation to them which are in Christ Jesus" (Rom. 8:1); "In the Lord have I righteousness and strength" (Isa. 45:24); "And of his fulness have all we received, and grace for grace" (John 1:16). The elect have a community with their Head in His covenant standing and rights: *His* God and Father is *their* God and Father (John 20:17). The one Spirit who sanctified, anointed, sealed, and graced Him, does the same (according to their measure) for them. They have fellowship with Him now in His sufferings, and shall have fellowship with Him in His glory throughout eternity. May writer and reader be enabled to "mix faith" with this blessed truth to the praise and glory of Him "who loved us and gave himself for us."

6

Vital Union

I

GOD established a legal or federal union between the Redeemer and those who were to be redeemed by Him, so that He became answerable for them to the Divine justice. But something more was neccessary in order to *their actual enjoyment* of the benefits of Christ's representation. God not only determined that His Son should sustain the character of their Surety, but also that a vital and spiritual relation should take place between them, through which there should be *conveyed to them* the benefits of His purchase. God ordained that as Christ and the Church were one in law, so also they should be one experimentally: that not only should His righteousness be imputed to His members, but that His very life should also be imparted to them.

Though the elect were federally united to Christ in the everlasting covenant, yet until they are regenerated they are personally and experimentally *far from* God and Christ, so far as their actual state is concerned. This is abundantly clear from, "Wherefore remember, that ye being in time past Gentiles in the flesh. . . . that at that time ye were *without Christ,* being aliens from the commonwealth of Israel, and strangers from the covenants of promise, having no hope, and without God in the world" (Eph. 2:11, 12). But at the new birth, Christ unites them to Himself in a vital way: this He does by sending His Spirit to take possession of them and communicate to them a principle of spiritual life, namely, His *own* life, whereby they are made *living* members of His body, the Church. Previously we were "in Christ" mystically (Eph. 1:4) and representatively (I Cor. 15:22), now we are "in Christ" vitally (II Cor. 5:17; 12:2; Rom. 16:7).

As we were not the actual possessors of Adam's guilt until we were conceived by our mothers and thereby united to him by carnal generation, neither are we the actual possessors of Christ's merits until we are quickened by His Spirit and thereby united to Him by regeneration. While there was a legal union between Adam and us in Eden, yet not until we are born into this world do we enter into personal communion with what his conduct entailed. In like manner, though there was a federal union between Christ and us when He served as our Sponsor, yet not until we are born again do we begin to enjoy that which the discharge of His Surety-engagement obtained for us. Though there was a mystical and federal union between Christ and His people, not until their regeneration can they have any *communion* with Him.

The human race was inseparably linked to Adam in a *double* way —

federally and naturally, as he was both the legal representative and father of his posterity. So too the elect are related to Christ in a double way — federally and vitally, as He is both their legal Representative and their spiritual Quickener: "For as by one man's disobedience many were made sinners, so by the obedience of one shall many be made righteous." (Rom. 5:19). Those whom Adam represented (the first "many") were "made sinners" judicially the moment he fell, but they were only "made sinners" experimentally when they were "shapen in iniquity" (Ps. 51:5). Those whom Christ represented (the second "many," which is *not* co-extensive with the first) were "made righteous" judicially when He rose again from the dead, but they are only "made righteous" experimentally when they are born again and believe.

This is only another way of saying that Christ's *Headship* is of a two-fold character: He is unto His mystical body both a Head of government and a Head of influence. The term "head" has a twofold extension in our common speech: it is that by which we name the highest part of our physical organism, and it is also that by which we describe the chief ruler, be he over a family, a corporation, or a nation. Such is its significance as applied to Christ: He is both the Life and the Lord of His people. Remarkably has God caused this to be adumbrated in the natural realm: sever the head from the physical organism, and all its members are at once reduced to a state of lifelessness. Likewise, if the brain were removed, the members become incapable of action — they are regulated and dominated by the mind.

In the natural body the head is the seat of sensation, and from it feelings and motions are communicated to all of its members by means of the nerves, which have their origin in the brain. Here again the natural supplies an object-lesson of the spiritual. It is from Christ, the Head, there flows that life and grace by which the members of His mystical body are enabled to perform the various functions of the Christian life. "May grow up into him in all things, which is the head, Christ: *from whom* the whole body fitly joined together and compacted by that which every joint supplieth, according to the effectual working in the measure of every part, maketh increase of the body unto the edifying of itself in love" (Eph. 4:15, 16). It is from the Head there proceeds that which causes "the effectual working in the measure of every part" of His body.

The same blessed truth is set before us again in, "And not holding the Head, *from which* all the body by joints and bands having nourishment ministered, and knit together, increaseth with the increase of God" (Col. 2:19). Here the apostle was setting forth the evil tendency of one of the errors of Gnosticism, which now occupies a prominent place in the vile system of Romanism. Under the pretense of honoring Christ and abasing man, the Gnostics taught that He was so far above us in the scale of being that access could only be obtained to Him via the angels (v. 18). In like maner, Romanism introduces various mediators between Christ and the sinner. But this is failing to hold fast the doctrine of the Head. It is only by *immediate* union and communion with Christ Himself that His members are nourished and strengthened.

Christ, then, is not only the Head of authority, the Lord and Ruler of His Church, but He is also the Head of influence — its Quickener and Nourisher. In God's appointed time, the Lord Jesus sends down the Holy Spirit into the hearts of His people when they are dead in trespasses and sins, imparting spiritual life to their souls, and thus making them one with Himself in a *vital* way; and this He does by virtue of the prior mystical and federal union existing between them. It is our *eternal* union with, interest in, and relation to the person of Christ in the ever-lasting covenant, which is the foundation of the Spirit's work in our souls during the time-state. It is by communicating His own life into the members of His body, the Church, that their mystical and legal union with Him is then made real and actual to them in their own experience.

As Adam is the root of generation, so Christ is the root of regeneration: note "his seed" and "the travail of his soul" in Isaiah 53:10, 11. If we had not been in Adam by Divine creation, we would not have been produced from him by generation; and had we not been given a super-creation being in Christ by Divine election, we had never been manifested in Him by regeneration. Had there been no *oneness with* Christ, there could be no *life from* Him; and if no life, then no justification, salvation, or glorification. And in order to our having life from Christ, we must receive His Spirit; for as our physical bodies are lifeless without the natural spirit (James 2:26), so the soul is spiritually dead without the Spirit of God. At regeneration the Holy Spirit becomes to the soul — though in a far more excellent manner — what the soul is to the body with respect to its animal and rational life.

The vital union which is effected between Christ and His people is a work of God by which His elect are made spiritually one with their Head, for the same Spirit which indwells Him now takes up His abode within them. Herein we may perceive how each person in the Holy Trinity is distinctively honoured, and endeared unto us. God the Father gave us a mystical union to Christ when He chose us in Him before the foundation of the world. God the Son gave us a legal union to Himself when He took upon Him the office of Surety. And God the Spirit gives us a vital union to Christ by imparting to us His life and making us living members of His Church. It is only by means of this third union that the first and second are made manifest to us: "*Hereby know we that we dwell in Him, and He in us, because* He has given of His Spirit" (I John 4:23).

This union has also been variously designated by different writers. It has been called the "new-creation" union, because it is effected by our being born again. It has been called the "influential" union, because only through it do we receive the virtues of the mystical and federal unions. It has been called the "manifestative" union, because by it is revealed to us our eternal oneness with Christ. We have called it the "vital" union because it is that which gives us a living relation with Christ. This it is which capacitates the Christian to know Christ, to receive Him, to have communion with Him, to live upon and enjoy Him. The Spirit unites us to Christ at the very first moment the "good work" of God is "begun"

(Phil. 1:6) in the heart. Then it is that we are "delivered from the power of darkness, and translated into the kingdom of God's dear Son" (Col. 1:13), so that we are brought into open and actual fellowship with Him.

Then also it is that we are "made meet" for the inheritance of the saints in light" (Col. 1:12). It was Christ's work *for* us which secured our *title* to the heavenly inheritance, but it is the Spirit's work *in* us which supplies the *fitness* or capacity to enjoy the same. This is confirmed by what we read in II Corinthians 5:5: "Now he that hath wrought us for the selfsame thing is God, who also hath given unto us the earnest of the Spirit." The context here is also speaking of the heavenly inheritance of the saints, when "mortality shall be swallowed up of life." And "for" that inheritance (the "selfsame thing") God hath "wrought us" or fashioned and fitted us, for we are "His workmanship created in Christ Jesus" (Eph. 2:10). In addition to the *evidence* which His work in our souls gives us, that we are vessels of mercy "prepared unto glory," the Spirit Himself indwells us as an *earnest* or guaranty of our future bliss.

Christ has a threefold union with the Church, and the Church has a threefold union with Him. First, He had a mystical union, when God elected Him to be the Head of His Church. Second, He had a legal union, when He agreed to serve as our Representative and Sponsor. Third, this began to be *openly effected* when He became incarnate, entering into a natural union with us by being made flesh. In like manner, our mystical and federal union with Christ becomes manifest and efficacious when we are vitally joined to Him by the person and work of the Holy Spirit. The entrance of Christ into our nature capacitated Him to discharge His office-work of Surety, and fitted Him to be a merciful High Priest who could be touched with the feeling of our infirmities. The communication of Christ's nature unto us qualifies us for communion with Him and fits unto the discharge of our Christian duties: "he that is joined unto the Lord is one spirit" (I Cor. 6:17).

As in our natural bodies, the members receive life (the animal spirits) from their head, so in the mystical body of Christ the members receive the life-giving Spirit from their Head. This, we believe, is the meaning of John 1:16, "And of His fulness have all we received, and grace for grace." What is signified *here* by Christ's "fulness?" Let it be noted that in John 1:16 Christ is not presented absolutely as the second person in the Godhead, but as incarnate (v. 14), as the God-man, Mediator, as the next verse shows. What, then, was His "fulness" as Mediator, *furnishing Him* for the discharge of that office? Was it not His being "anointed with the Holy Spirit" (Acts 10:38)? Is not the key to this word "fulness" in John 1:16 found in John 3:34, "For God giveth not the Spirit by measure unto him"? — Christ, as God-man, was capacitated to receive the Spirit *without* "measure," to receive Him in all His fulness.

Therefore, it is that Christ is represented as "He that *hath* the seven Spirits of God" (Rev. 3:1), that is, the Spirit in His plenitude or fulness — see the sevenfold reference to the Spirit as given to Christ in Isaiah

11:1, 2! Thus, Christ's *Mediatorial* "fulness" is the Holy Spirit indwelling Him *without* "measure." But let it be observed that, Christ received the Spirit not for Himself alone, but also for and in order to communicate Him to His people. This is clear from Acts 2:33, "having received of the Father the promise of the Holy Spirit, he hath shed forth this [at Pentecost], which ye now see and hear." Thus "out of [Greek] his fulness have all we received" signifies that, Christ has communicated to us the same Spirit He received — called "the Spirit of Christ" (Rom. 8:9) and "the Spirit of his Son" (Gal. 4:6). A beautiful illustration of this is found in John 20:22, "He breathed on them, and saith unto them, *Receive ye* the Holy Spirit."

Perhaps a word should be given upon the last clause of John 1:16, for we have never seen any interpretation of it which quite satisfied us: "and grace for grace." Just as the same life which is in the vine is in each of its branches producing "after its *own* kind," so the same "grace" (the same in nature, though not in degree) which the Spirit produced in Christ (*see* Luke 2:40 and 52!) He reproduces in His people. Was the lovely "fruit" of Galatians 5:22, 23 found in its *fulness* in Christ? — then the Spirit works the same in us *in measure*. "Grace for grace," then, means grace *answerable* to grace: the same spiritual excellency which abides in the Head, is communicated to the members of His Body; and thus are they being "conformed" unto His "image."

"The first man Adam was made a living soul: the last Adam, a quickening spirit" (I Cor. 15:45). It is as such that He sends forth the Holy Spirit into the hearts of His own. "He saved us by the washing of regeneration and renewing of the Holy Spirit, which He shed on us abundantly *through Jesus Christ* our Saviour" (Titus 2:5, 6). "But ye have received an Unction from the Holy One" (I John 2:20): the "Unction" (the Greek word for which is rendered "anointing" in II Cor. 1:21 and I John 2:27) is the Holy Spirit and He comes to us from "the Holy One," that is, Christ (Ps. 16:10, Mark 1:24). A blessed type of this is seen in Psalm 133:2, "The precious ointment upon the head, that ran down upon the beard, Aaron's beard; that went down to the skirts of his garments." Here we behold the high priest of Israel anointed unto his holy office, and the "precious ointment" — emblem of the Holy Spirit — proceeding from his head to that part of his vestments which touched the earth!

"There is one body, and one Spirit" (Eph. 4:4) which animates it: "For by one Spirit are we all baptised into one body, whether Jews or Gentiles, whether bond or free; and have been all made to drink into one Spirit" (I Cor. 12:13). As the soul and body of man are so united as to form one entire person, so God's elect and their Head are so united as to form one mystical and spiritual Body, the Church. Just as the human soul gives a living union between the most widely separated members — the head and the feet — so the Divine Spirit livingly unites together the Head in Heaven and His members on earth. "If a man were never so tall that his head should reach the stars, yet having but one soul, he would be but one man still. Though Christ in His nature be exceedingly distanced from us, yet there being but one and the selfsame Spirit in Him and in us, we are one mystical Christ" (John Owen).

The distance between Christ in Heaven and believers on earth is no obstacle to their vital union, for being God, the Spirit is *omni-present,* and therefore does He indwell both Head and members. A very striking proof of the Spirit's being the living bond of union between Christ and the Church is found in Romans 8:11: "But if the Spirit of Him that raised up Jesus from the dead dwell in you, He that raised up Christ from the dead shall *also* quicken your mortal bodies, *by His Spirit* that dwelleth in you." The saints will not be raised from the dead by the naked power of God *without* them, but by virtue of their risen Head sending forth the quickening influences of His Spirit *within* their bodies. This is wonderfully adumbrated in the natural: when awakening out of sleep, the animal spirits arouse the *head* first, and then the senses are awakened throughout the whole body!

A real living union is effected between Christ and His members, not (as it were) by soldering two souls together, but by the Spirit anointing and indwelling *both,* for He being *infinite* is able to conjoin those who, in themselves, are so far apart. The whole person of the Christian (I Cor. 6:15) is united to the whole person of Christ: "At that day ye shall know that I am in my Father, and ye in me, and I in you" (John 14:20). The same Spirit who lives in our exalted Redeemer, lives in His people on earth. By this spiritual union a far more blessed relation is established than which obtains between a king and his subjects, or even between a husband and wife: the tie connecting Him with His people is so intimate that He indwells them — *"Christ liveth in me"* (Gal. 2:20).

"The grace of the Lord Jesus Christ, and the love of God, and the communion of the Holy Spirit be with you all" (II Cor. 13:14). Let it be duly noted that as "grace" is predicated of Christ and "love" of God (the Father), so "communion" is as expressly ascribed to the Holy Spirit; and, as we said so often in the preceding chapters, there can be no "communion" unless there first be *union.* It is by the Spirit there is union and communion between Christ and the Church. "Now if any man have not the Spirit of Christ he is none of his" (Rom. 8:9), that is, he is not yet grafted as a *living* member into His mystical body. Let it be pointed here that, blessed and glorious as is this vital union, yet it falls far below the "mediatorial" union: that was two distinct natures (the Divine and the human) forming together *one Person;* this is of different persons being joined together so as to make *one Body,* the Church.

7

Saving Union

THAT which unites the believer to Christ may (for the purpose of simplification) be likened to a golden chain, a chain possessing a number of distinct links, yet inseparably welded together. The first of these links we denominated "mystical," having reference to our original uniting to Christ, when the Father chose us in Him before the foundation of the world. The second link we denominated "federal," having reference to our covenant-oneness with Christ, wherein He served as our Surety, we having a representative or legal being in Him. The third link we denominated "vital," having reference to the Spirit's quickening us, whereby we became livingly united to our Head in Heaven. Now, this wondrous chain is let down still lower, for the fourth link in it is formed by *our* personally cleaving unto Christ. This is a union *unto* Christ, as the previous ones were *in* Him.

We have pointed out that it is by means of the vital union that our mystical and federal oneness with Christ is made manifest. Not until the Holy Spirit has brought us from death unto life can we have any experimental knowledge of the Father's love and the Son's work for us. In like manner, it is not until we have a *saving* union with Christ by our believing in Him, that we have any personal evidence we have been vitally joined to Him. In other words, we are only able to apprehend the outworking of God's eternal purpose *in the inverse order* to His execution of it: He proceeds from cause to effect, but we have to work back from effect to cause. Or, to use the terms of our illustration: as we grasp the lowest link in the chain *that* brings into our view the one next above it.

Thus, the whole of this chapter will supply answer to a question which may have been raised in exercised readers by the last one, namely, *How* may I ascertain whether or not spiritual life has actually been communicated to *my* soul? O how urgently it behoves each one of us to earnestly and prayerfully examine ourselves on this all-important matter. Before developing the distinctive theme of this article, and as a suitable introduction thereto, let us offer one or two observations by way of determining the above matter. First, where there is spiritual life, there is spiritual *sensibility*: "senses exercised to discern both good and evil" (Heb. 5:14). Just as our natural senses recognize and feel the difference between cold and heat, so the spiritual senses of a quickened soul perceive and feel the difference between good and evil, sin and holiness. If there be spiritual life within, the soul cannot but be sensible of and groan under the burden of sin.

What we have just alluded to is something radically different from

His entire character, as Prophet, Priest, and King" (J. Dick). Saving faith is the heart going off all others and cleaving to Christ alone.

Now Christ's design in quickening us is that we should turn to and put our trust in Him, for we are not *saved* until we do so. "For by grace are ye saved *through faith*" (Eph. 2:8). True, we are not saved because of our faith; yet, we cannot be saved without it. Rightly did Thomas Brooks, the Puritan, affirm, "Faith in its place is as necessary as the blood of Christ is in its place." "To him give all the prophets witness, that through his name whosoever *believeth* in him shall receive remission of sins" (Acts 10:43). The righteousness of God which is by faith of Jesus Christ is "unto all and upon all them that *believe*" (Rom. 3:23), and it is not upon them until they do. Christ is "a propitiation through *faith* in his blood" (Rom. 3:25), for His blood avails none but those who *plead* it. To the Hebrew Christians Paul wrote, We are "of them that *believe to the saving of the soul*" (Heb. 10:39).

Let us not confuse things that differ. Though it be true that the elect were saved in the purpose of God before the world began (II Tim. 1:9), and that they were saved representatively when their Head rose again from the dead (Eph. 2:5), yet they are not saved personally and actually until they "come unto the knowledge of the truth" (I Tim. 2:4). Trusting in Christ obtains something more than a *knowledge* of our salvation: it brings salvation itself to us. Surely there is no salvation actually bestowed where an individual's sins have not yet been "remitted," and no one's sins are remitted until he has believed (Acts 10:43). Nor is this making a saviour of faith: Christ is the Saviour, but faith must lay hold of Him for salvation. Nothing but food will save a starving man from death, yet food untouched will serve him nothing. It is not his *eating* which saves him, yet the food *must* be eaten if he is to be saved!

While it be true, on the one hand, that faith does not give us a being in Christ, but rather is our cleaving to Him an evidence and effect *of* our being in Him; yet, on the other hand, faith does *unite* us to Christ, as is clear from His own words: "Neither pray I for these alone, but for them also which shall *believe* on me through their word; *that* they all *may be one;* as thou, Father, art in me, and I in thee, that they also may be one of us" (John 17:20, 21). Moreover, do we not read, "That Christ may dwell in your hearts *by faith*" (Eph. 3:17): it is faith which gives Him a real subsistence in the soul. Here, then, is the principal difference between what was before us in the last chapter and the present aspect of our subject: in the forming of the vital union we were *passive,* but in the making of the saving union we are *active.* Here is the order: "That I may apprehend that for which also I am apprehended of Christ Jesus" (Phil. 3:12).

Having been "apprehended" or "laid hold of" by Christ (through His quickening Spirit), we now apprehend Him. We cannot lay hold of Him, until He has first laid hold of us. But having been laid hold of by Christ, the soul now draws near to Him, joins itself to Him, appropriates Him by faith as its very own. And from *this* union there follows our justification, sanctification, preservation, and glorification. The *federal* union was necessary so that the demands of the law might be met by our Surety. The *vital* union was necessary so that a principle of life, grace, holiness, might be imparted to the soul, qualifying its recipient to perform spiritual acts and live a spiritual life. The *believing* union is necessary so that we may personally receive the salvation of God and have His receipt for it written in our own hearts.

Our believing in Christ is the sequel to His "I will betroth thee unto me forever" (Hos. 2:19), for faith is it which ties the marriage-knot between us, for there must be a personal consent on our part. In the gospel Christ offers Himself to us, and saving faith is our acceptance of Him. Saving faith, therefore, presupposes a turning from all others — from the seductions of the world and from trusting in my own righteousness — and yielding myself to Christ as my only Lord. It is a willingness to receive Christ on His own terms. It is turning our backs upon our idols, and saying with Ruth, "Entreat me not to leave thee, or to return from following after thee: for whither thou goest, I will go; and where thou lodgest, I will lodge: thy people shall be my people, and thy God my God" (Ruth 1:16). Since a mediator is not a mediator of one, but requires the mutual consent of both parties, so there must be a personal acceptance of Christ as Mediator on our part. This makes the union *reciprocal*. As a woman, by her free consent, accepts a man for her husband, so the believer accepts Christ as his only Lord and Saviour.

This union also has been variously designated by the older writers — for alas! most modern writers seem to know little or nothing of this wondrous and blessed subject. Some of them call it the "voluntary" union, in order to distinguish it from the previous ones, which are quite involuntary on our part; and because this one is consummated by an act of our own wills. Some call it the "fiducial" or "believing" union, because it is brought about by faith, defining more definitely the nature of our voluntary act. Others call it the "conjugal" union, because it signifies our acceptance of Christ as our loving Lord or Husband. We have preferred to designate it the *saving* union, because a section of our readers need to have this aspect of the Truth pressed upon their notice; and also because it seems to express more than the other terms do.

The manner in which this saving union is brought about may be illustrated from the meaning of the names borne by the first three sons of Jacob. Reuben signifies "See! the Son." It is as such the gospel sets forth Christ, and its call is, "*Behold* the Lamb of God which taketh away the sin of the world" (John 1:29), for it is only as we are favored with spiritual and believing views of Him that spiritual blessings flow into the soul. Simeon signifies "Hearing," and it is only as we hear the voice of Christ Himself speaking to us through the gospel that peace comes to our conscience and joy fills the heart. Levi signifies "Joined:" as we see the Son responsively and hear Him believingly, we become *connected with Him*. It was well put by Witsuis when he said, "Faith in its actings is the echo or repercussion of the Divine voice speaking to the soul."

It is only the quickened soul which sees, hears, and receives Christ in a spiritual way. A distressed child's cleaving to and hanging upon its beloved father with entreaties and expectations of succor, are in consequence of a relation and union between them *prior to* those actings. So it is with the elect sinner: having been joined to Him by the Spirit, he now looks to Christ, lays hold of, embraces, and cleaves unto Him; and thus his saving union is effected. As a woman accepts the marriage proposal of her wooer by yielding herself and all her future interests into his care, so the believer is able to say, "I know whom I have believed, and am persuaded that He is able to keep that which I *have committed unto him* against that day" (II Tim. 1:12). And again, "My beloved is mine, and I am his" (Song of Sol. 2:16) — His by my own consent and acceptance.

"Who shall separate us from the love of Christ?" (Rom. 8:35). Separation necessarily implies a joining together, for nothing can be "separated" but what was first united. Union with Christ is by the Spirit on His part, and by faith on our part; and both of them are made known *by love,* and this it is which makes the union indissoluble. The Spirit is given to us as the great proof and fruit of Christ's love to us, and He sheds abroad God's love in our hearts. The faith which lays hold of Christ for salvation is a "faith which worketh *by love*" (Gal. 5:6), for it is "with the *heart* that man believeth unto righteousness" (Rom. 10:10). And nothing can unclasp those mutual embraces. The believer is now united to Christ by his affections, for he loves what Christ loves and hates what He hates. "A Christian is held by his heart rather than by his head" (Thos. Manton).

Vital union takes place at regeneration: in it we were entirely passive, and at the time thereof had no knowledge at all of it. Saving union takes place when the awakened sinner receives Christ as He is offered to him in the gospel: in it he is active, and has a definite consciousness of what he is doing. As the Israelite of old gave a personal consent to God's gracious provision by laying his hand on the head of his sacrifice (Lev. 1:4), so the believer rests upon Christ as an all-sufficient Sacrifice for all his sins. Saving union takes place when the returning prodigal falls into the arms of his loving Father in Christ (Luke 15:20); when the fugitive, chased by the avenging law (Num 35:11, 12) crosses the threshold of the City of Refuge (Heb. 6:18); when the sin-sick soul is able to stretch forth the hand of faith and receive healing from Christ by personal contact with Him (Mark 5:27-29).

8

Practical Union

I

WHAT is Divine "salvation"? It is a rescuing or deliverance. From what? From the penalty, power, and presence of sin. How is it effected? By the joint-operations of the Father, the Son, and the Holy Spirit. May a real Christian regard himself as a "saved" person? In one sense, yes; in another sense, no. What do you mean? This, that God's salvation is presented to us in Scripture under three tenses, past, present, and future. There is a real sense in which every Christian has already been saved; there is a real sense in which every Christian is now being saved; and there is a real sense in which the salvation of every Christian on earth is yet future. Every Christian on earth has been saved from the penalty of sin, because Christ suffered it in his stead. But the sinful nature is left within, and though its complete dominion over us has been broken, it is still active and operative, and from its power and defiling effects we need saving.

Now the design of God in saving His people is to recover them from the fall, to deliver them from its effects, to restore them to their state of happy fellowship with Him. It is true, blessedly true, that the redeemed gain far more through the last Adam than they lost by the first Adam; yet that in nowise conflicts with what we have said in the preceding sentence — the surpassing gain through Christ will be discussed in the last chapter. Before the fall, we, in Adam, were in blissful communion with God: our nature was in tune with His, our joy lay in a ready responsiveness to His will. God and man were then of one accord, each finding delight in the other, yet the difference between the Creator and the creature being suitably sustained by the relation which was appointed — that of Sovereign and subject.

Only as Sovereign and subject could God and man maintain their relative positions: there must be the exercise of *authority* on the part of the former, and of *submission* on the part of the latter: thereby there was a mutual indwelling of the one and the other — God ruling, man obeying. Such mutual indwelling and concord would daily become more intimate and confident: man increasingly perceiving the exceeding excellency of the commandments he was keeping (and of Him whose nature and will those commandments discovered), and God having increasing delight in the growing intelligence and love by which His subject obeyed. Thus at the beginning, holiness and happiness were made inseparable in the experience of the creature: holiness in walking in complete subjection to his Maker's revealed will, happiness in the joyous fellowship which this secured. Thus, too, were the relative positions and relations of Creator and creature perfectly sustained.

But alas, sin entered: entered by Eve's entertaining the Serpent's suggestion that God's restraints were tyrannical and irksome, and freedom from them being greatly to be desired; culminating in the overt act of rebellious disobedience. In consequence thereof a breach was made: harmony no longer existed between God and man; and happy fellowship which already obtained was broken. Henceforth, God and disobedient man must dwell apart; so Adam and Eve were driven out of paradise. Outside paradise *away from God,* were all their descendants born: "afar off" (Eph. 2:23) are the awful words written over the brow of all the first Adam's offspring, *"alienated from* the life of God" (Eph. 4:18). "Behold, I was shapen in iniquity; and in sin did my mother conceive me" (Ps. 51:5) is true of all alike; and because this is so "the wicked are *estranged* from the womb" (Ps. 58:3).

How this terrible situation is counteracted by God in the saving of His people we have endeavored to show in the preceding chapters of this series. Christ was made their Head, and their redemption was entrusted to Him: a union was established between them. First, a mystical union, when they were chosen in Him before the foundation of the world. Second, a federal union, whereby Christ should act as their Representative and Surety. Third, a vital union: by the incarnation, when He assumed their nature; and by regeneration, when they became partakers of His nature. Fourth, a saving union, when the soul (previously quickened) exercises faith, lays hold of and cleaves unto Christ. Then is it that the trusting sinner enters into the legal benefits which the Saviour's atonement secured for him: "By him all that believe are justified from all things" (Acts 13:39). Saving union is the personal acceptance of Christ on His own terms: the penitent heart now rests upon Christ as an all-sufficient sacrifice for all his sins.

A new relation has been entered into by the believer which radically changes the course of his life, and which is to regulate all of his future conduct. He is no longer his own: he has given himself to the Lord (II Cor. 8:5); henceforth to please and honor Him must be his paramount concern. As the wedding, when the knot is tied, is but the beginning of married life, so the soul's surrender to and acceptance of Christ as Lord, is but the commencement of the Christian life. As the bride has turned her back upon all other lovers and solemnly vowed to be faithful to and obey her husband in all things, so the believer has disowned all other lords and promised to be in subjection to Christ alone (Isa. 26:13). As the purpose of marriage is the production of offspring, so we read, "ye also are become dead to the law by the body of Christ, that ye should be *married* to another; to him who is raised from the dead, that we should *bring forth fruit* unto God" (Rom. 7:4).

Marriage, then, is a new beginning, the entering into a new order of things, the startingpoint *of a fresh life.* Before her marriage the woman, perhaps, was alone in the world; without father or brothers to defend her. She had to look after herself and plan her own career and course.

But now she has taken upon her the marriage-yoke: she has given herself up to the one who loves her more dearly than any other creature, to the one who has won her heart, and who has now assumed the sole responsibility of being her provider and protector. It is now *for her good* to meekly submit to her husband's loving rule (I Peter 3:1-6), to seek and promote his interests, to adorn the home he has made for her. His will is supreme; her good is his concern; and it is her welfare to act in submission to his wishes. Such is the ideal of married life: on the one hand, love's authority maintained by the head of the home; on the other, love's obedience joyously rendered by the dutiful and devoted wife — a shadowing forth of the relation which exists between the Redeemer and His redeemed, and the new order of things into which the saved soul enters.

Marriage is a means to an end, the making possible of wedded union, with its responsibilities and privileges, its duties, and joys. In like manner, saving union with Christ is a means to an end, the making possible of *the Christian life,* which is to *evidence* the new relationship that has been entered into. In other words, just as the vital union between Christ and the Christian (effected by the Spirit at the new birth) capacitates the soul for a saving union with Christ (accomplished by believing in Him), so that saving union, in turn, makes way for a *practical* union with Him. Thus, at the very outset, the Lord Jesus says to the sin-weary and conscience-burdened sinner who comes to Him for relief, "Take my *yoke* upon you, and learn of me; for I am meek and lowly in heart: and ye shall find rest unto your souls!" (Matt. 11:29). Now a "yoke" is that which harnesses two oxen, that they may walk and work *together,* and the Lord employed this figure to denote the relation now obtaining between Himself and His people.

In the preceding chapter we pointed out that one of the main characteristics which distinguishes the saving from the vital union is, that in the latter the soul is *active,* whereas in the former the soul was *passive.* That is to say, in regeneration something was wrought *in* us, but in connection with salvation something is required *of* us, namely, our voluntary act of surrendering to, laying hold of, and cleaving unto Christ. So is it in connection with the *practical* union which exists between the Saviour and the saved: He does not place the yoke upon us, but says "*Take* my yoke upon you." It is a voluntary and conscious act upon *our* part. The figure is a very plain one. Previously the ox roamed at large in the fields, but now it is no longer free to please itself — it is subservient to the will of its owner and master. The "yoke," then, speaks of *subjection,* and thus it is with the believer: he has yielded himself to the claims of Christ, bowed to His Lordship, and entered into the place of submission, to be directed and used of Him.

But, alas, we now witness very little in actual realization of what we have said above, either in the natural or the spiritual sphere. The "yoke" is looked upon as something which is objectionable. Our lot is cast in a day when the spirit of lawlessness is rife on every hand, when any restraints are regarded as irksome and repellent. The equality of the sexes, the woman's rights, the repudiation of the man's headship, is being proclaimed in almost every quarter. The modern wife is "willing to be led" (providing the leading suits her whims), but refuses to be ruled; the idea of meekly *obeying* her husband is altogether foreign to her disposition and ideas. And, my readers, *that* is only an adumbration on the lower plane of what now obtains so widely in the religious sphere. Multitudes profess to be resting on the finished work of Christ, but they *refuse* His "yoke"; they want to be saved from Hell, but they do not want His commandments; and the two cannot be separated.

In days gone by preachers frequently made it plain that "No cross, no crown"; alas, the pulpit is now pandering to a self-indulging generation. But God has not changed, nor has He lowered the claims of His holiness. Christ *must be followed* if ever we are to arrive at the Place where He has gone; and to "follow" Christ is to take upon us *His* "yoke" — to enter the same position of servitude and subjection which He did. Christ "pleased not himself" (Rom. 15:3), and His imperative word is, "If any man will come after me, let him deny himself, and take up his cross, and follow me" (Matt. 16:24). Christ lived in full submission to the revealed will of God, and He left us an "example" that we should "follow his steps" (I Peter 2:21). We must "suffer *with* him" if ever we are to be "glorified *together*" (Rom. 8:17).

"Can two walk together, except they be agreed?" (Amos 3:3). Here again is brought before us the *practical* union which exists between Christ and His people. If there is to be true fellowship there must first be harmony, oneness of accord in mind and will. All real communion is based upon union, and as the "*walk* together" intimates, it is not the vital or the saving union which is there in view, but the practical — the actual living out of the Christian life. And the Christian life (alas that the life of the average Christian falls so far short) is summed up in one word: "For to me to live *is Christ*" (Phil. 1:21). But Christ is holy, and He will not walk with us in any of the by-paths of unrighteousness: "For what fellowship hath righteousness with unrighteousness? and what communion hath light with darkness? and what concord hath Christ with Belial?" (II Cor. 6:14, 15).

Just as the ideal married life can only be maintained by the exercise of love's authority on the one hand and love's obedience on the other, so it is in the Christian life. "If ye love me," says Christ, "keep my commandments" (John 14:15). *Obedience* is not only the prime condition of practical union and communion with Christ, but it is of its very essence, for only thus is restored the relation which existed between God and His creature before sin entered — love's rule and love's submission. Before the fall there was perfect complacency on both sides, Creator and creature dwelling in each other with unalloyed satisfaction, as the "very good" of Genesis 1:31 clearly denotes. Yet that mutual indwelling of God in man and man in God was *not procured* by man's keeping God's commandments, rather was that the channel of its outgoing and conscious realization; and only thus could they maintain their relative positions of Sovereign and servant.

We repeat what was said in an earlier paragraph: the grand design in salvation is to bring us back again into communion with God in Christ: not merely into a nominal communion, but into a real, intelligent, and joyous one. But "Can two walk together, except they be agreed?" — walk together in a way of holy and spiritual fellowship? No indeed, for *that* we must be of one mind and will with Christ Himself. For *that* we must receive His commandments into our hearts, be well-pleased with them, and live under their controlling influence. "God is light, and in him is no darkness at all. If we say that we have fellowship with him, and walk in darkness, we lie, and do not the truth; but if we *walk in the light,* as he is in the light, *we have fellowship* one with another" (I John 1:5-7).

"And the hand of the Lord was with them, and a great number believed, and turned unto the Lord. Then tidings of these things came unto the ears of the church which was in Jerusalem: and they sent forth Barnabas, that he should go as far as Antioch. Who, when he came, and had seen the grace of God, was glad, and exhorted them all, that with purpose of heart they would cleave unto the Lord" (Acts 11:21-23). Having *"turned unto* the Lord" these young converts were now exhorted to *"cleave unto* the Lord": that is, since a saving union with Christ had been effected, they were bidden to "with purpose of heart" maintain a practical union and communion with Him. To "cleave unto the Lord" is to live a life of dependence upon and devotedness unto Him: having "come" to Him, they are now to diligently "follow" Him, or "to walk even as he walked" (I John 2:6). Only by the continued exercise of faith, a bold profession of His name, and obedience to His commands, can we "follow on to know the Lord" (Hos. 6:3).

Practical union with Christ consists in the exercise of *obedience,* and that was impossible till there has been a saving union. The only kind of obedience which is acceptable to God is evangelical obedience, that is the obedience *of faith"* (Rom. 16:26) — an obedience which springs from faith, which is animated by faith. There can be no true obedience before faith, for "without faith it is impossible to please God" (Heb. 11:6), and therefore without faith it is impossible to obey Him. Faith is (from our side) the bond of union which unites with Christ, and obedience is the fruit of that believing union: see Romans 7:4 again — all "fruit" before marriage is bastard. Our persons must first be accepted in Christ before our services can be pleasing to God. All the good works recorded in Hebrews 11 were the fruits or obedience of faith.

Though inseparably connected, faith and obedience are quite distinct. Faith is the principle, obedience is the product; faith is the cause, obedience is the effect; faith is the root, obedience is the fruit. By faith we receive and own Christ as our rightful Lord; by obedience we regulate our conduct according to His commands. By faith a saving union with Christ is effected, by obedience a practical union with Him is maintained. "He that hath my commandments and *keepeth* them, he it is that loveth me: and he that loveth me shall be loved of my Father, and I will love him, and will manifest myself to him" (John 14:21): Christ only *manifests* Himself in the intimacies of His love to those who are treading the path of obedience. A striking illustration of this is seen by a comparison of Genesis 18 and 19: "*the Lord* appeared unto" Abraham (Gen. 18:1) accompanied by two angels, manifesting Himself in human form. But only the "two angels" came to Lot (Gen. 19:1), who was not walking in practical union with the Lord. O how much we miss by allowing self-will to dominate and regulate us.

There is another spiritual grace which is inseparably connected with faith: "Faith which *worketh by love*" (Gal. 5:6). The reality and sincerity of faith is only evidenced by the presence and operations of love. Faith is the hand which works, but love is the power that moves it. Faith is the feet walking, but love is the energy that stirs them into action; hence we find the Psalmist declaring, "I will run the way of thy commandments, when thou shalt *enlarge my heart*" (119:32). Now as there can be no saving union with Christ without faith, so there can be no practical union with Him without love. Love must be answered by love: "My son, give me thine heart" (Prov. 23:26) is our loving Lord's call. Love is the mainspring in the soul which moves every faculty and grace, and therefore is love denominated "the *fulfilling of* the law" (Rom. 13:10).

True repentance also flows from love. The warmer our love to God, the stronger will be our hatred of sin, as contrary to Him. The sweeter the fellowship of Christ to our hearts, the more bitter the realization of our offenses against Him. This is that "*godly* sorrow" which worketh repentance to salvation "not to be repented of" (II Cor. 7:10): it is a sorrow issuing from a heart that truly loves the Lord, and which is grieved for having displeased and dishonoured Him. Love mourns the breaking of fellowship and the hiding of the Lord's countenance. Then it is that the agonized soul cries, "The Enemy hath persecuted my soul; he hath smitten my life down to the ground; he hath made me to dwell in darkness, as those that have been long dead. Therefore is my spirit overwhelmed within me; my heart within me is desolate. I remember the days of old . . . I stretch forth my hands unto thee: my soul thirsteth after thee, as a thirsty land. Selah. Hear me speedily, O Lord; my spirit faileth; hide not thy face from me, lest I be like unto them that go down into the pit" (Ps. 143:3-7).

In what has been said above we have sought to indicate the relation between the saving and the practical union between the believer and Christ; what practical union actually consists of, and how it is to be restored when broken — by true repentance and humble confession. As this branch of our subject is so much neglected to-day, as it so intimately concerns the glory of Christ, and the wellbeing of our souls, a further chapter thereon seems called for.

II

Our practical union and communion with Christ grows out of our having cleaved to Him for salvation. A union to Christ by faith is designed by God to issue in a practical conformity to the image of His Son. We are "delivered out of the hand of our enemies" (sin, Satan, the world, the curse of the law, the wrath of God) in order that we "might *serve* [be in subjection to and obey] him without fear, in holiness and righteousness before him all the days of our life" (Luke 1:74, 75). God does not save us in order that we may henceforth indulge in the lusts of the flesh without fear of fatal consequences; but He brings us to Christ in order that we should take His "yoke" upon us, and live for His pleasure and glory. Our initial salvation is but a means to an end: to melt our hard hearts, that out of gratitude we may gladly render Him love's obedience, and be the monuments and witnesses of His transforming power.

The union which exists between the Redeemer and the redeemed is not a simple, but a compound one: that which binds us to Him is not a single strand, but made up of several combined together. In a previous chapter we likened the bond of union between the believer and Christ to a golden chain, possessing a number of distinct links, yet inseparably welded together. That chain is led down all the way from God Himself, through Christ, to each of His people on earth. As the hand of faith lays hold of each separate link, the one immediately above it is revealed in turn. We have followed that chain, link by link, as it descended from above; but in our actual experience, *we*, of necessity, apprehend them in their inverse order — grasping first the lowest link and then ascending higher. From the position we now occupy, we can only discern the higher links by means of the lower. Let us try to make this fact yet plainer.

It is only by means of our *practical* union with Christ that we have personal evidence of our *saving* union with Him — if I am not in personal subjection to Him, walking with Him in the path of obedience to God's revealed will, then I have no Scriptural warrant for supposing that *my* sins have been pardoned. Again; it is only by means of our saving union with Christ that we obtain evidence of our vital oneness with Him — if I have not forsaken all other claimants to my heart, surrendered to Christ's Lordship, and put my whole trust in His sacrifice for my acceptance with God, then I have no scriptural warrant to conclude that I have ever been born again. Once more; it is only by means of our vital union with Christ that we obtain evidence of our federal and mystical oneness with Him — if I cannot clearly perceive (by means of new sensibilities, new desires, new purposes and efforts) that I have passed from death unto life spiritually, then I have no scriptural warrant to believe that Christ acted as *my Surety.*

From what has just been pointed out it should be quite evident that we are now treating of *the most important aspect* of our many-sided subject — the most important so far as the peace of our souls is concerned, and that we were fully justified in devoting a further chapter to its specific consideration. To be deceived at *this* point is a most serious thing, for it is very liable to have *fatal* consequences. If it is only by means of *practical* union and communion with Christ that I can rightly determine whether or not I have any *saving* union with Him, then how it behoves me to seriously and carefully inquire into my present *practical relations to* the Lord Jesus, and make sure whether I have really taken His yoke upon me, whether I am truly in subjection to His will and am being conformed to His holy image; whether it is my natural inclinations or His exhortations which are really regulating my daily life.

Now taking them in their deepest meaning and fullest scope, all the exhortations of Christ (expressing His claims upon us and His will for us) may be summed up in two words: *"Come* unto me" and *"Abide* in me." The first of these calls is what we have to comply with in order to become *savingly* united to Christ; the second is what we must heed if *practical* union with Him is to be secured and maintained. To "come to" Christ implies the turning of our backs upon all that is opposed to Him, the abandoning of every idol and all other dependencies, the heart going out to Him in full surrender and trustful confidence. To "come to" Christ denotes the turning of the whole soul to a whole Christ, as Prophet, Priest, and King: it is the mind, heart, and will being supernaturally drawn to Him so as to love, trust and serve Him.

"Coming to" Christ is a far, far different thing from raising your hand to be prayed for, or coming forward and taking the evangelist's hand, or signing some "decision" card, or uniting with some "church," or any other of the "many inventions" (Eccles. 7:29) of men. Before any one will or can truly come to Christ, the understanding must be supernaturally enlightened, the heart must be supernaturally changed, the stubborn will must be supernaturally broken. The things of this world have the first place in the affections of the natural man: the pleasing of self is his paramount concern. Christ is too holy to suit the natural man's love of sin; His claims are too exacting to please his selfish heart; His terms of discipleship (Luke 14:26, 27) too severe to suit his fleshly ways. The unregenerate *will* not submit to His Lordship.

Christ must be crowned Lord of all, or He will not be Lord at all. He will brook no rival. There must be the complete heart-renunciation of all that stands in competition with Him: whatever pertains to the flesh must be renounced. The "cross" is the badge of Christian discipleship: not a golden one worn on the body, but the principle of self-denial and self-sacrifice controlling the heart. We must come to Christ as Prophet, to be instructed by Him; as Priest, whose atonement and intercession are to be relied upon; as King, to be ruled by Him. Coming to Christ is a going out of self, so as no longer to rest on anything in self. It is the will bowing to His Lordship, accepting His yoke, taking up the cross, and following Him without reserve. O how very few really do this! To the great majority Christ has to say "Ye *will not come to me* that ye might have life" (John 5:40).

Now as a Scriptural "coming to Christ" is a vastly different thing from how it is represented from the majority of church-pulpits and mission-platforms to-day, so "Serving Christ" is something entirely different from the popular idea which now prevails. That we are saved to serve is a truth written large in the Word: "Ye turned to God from idols, to *serve* the living and true God" (I Thess. 1:9). But serving God *does not mean* that, primarily and mainly, we are called upon to be *"personal* workers" and "soul winners": we are to serve *Christ,* not our fellows. What is a *servant?* He is one that is in subjection to a master: he is one who sinks his own desires and ideas, and carries out the orders of the one who employs him. A "servant" is one who is in the place of subjection, of obedience, regulating his conduct according to the will of another. And *that* is what Christian service consists of: submitting to the authority of Christ, doing His bidding, walking according to His commandments, seeking to please Him in all things — whether He appoints us to plow the ground, mine coal, scrub floors, or preach the Word.

Now *that* is exactly what *practical union* with Christ consists of: it is being taken into His blessed *service:* walking together with Him in the path of obedience to God, with our hearts, minds and wills one with His. Practical union with Christ is but the *wearing of* the yoke which we *took upon us* when we came to Him for salvation. As the married life is the actual carrying out of the solemn vows by the husband and wife at the time of their wedded union, so the Christian life is the maintenance of that relationship which was entered into by the soul when it surrendered to the claims of Christ. At conversion we passed through the "strait gate" of full surrender to Christ, henceforth to tread the "narrow way" that leadeth unto Life for the rest of our earthly pilgrimage. Having come to Christ our duty and our privilege now is to "abide in Him," for only thus will we discharge our responsibilities, promote our well-being, and glorify Him.

The very essence of the Christian life is *to continue as we began:* all spiritual declension, all backsliding, is due to failure at this point. "*As* ye have therefore received Christ Jesus the Lord, *so walk* ye in Him" (Col. 2:6). It is in His essential character as *the Lord* that the world refuses to "receive" Christ Jesus. Like Pharaoh of old, the unregenerate still say "Who is the Lord that I should obey His voice?" (Exod. 5:2). Like the Jews during the days of His flesh, the unconverted declare "*We will not* have this one to *reign over us*" (Luke 19:14). But those who are drawn to Him by the Father (John 6:44) throw down the weapons of their warfare against Him, and give themselves up to be ruled by Him. Christ is "the author of eternal salvation unto all them that *obey* him" (Heb. 5:9). Having surrendered to His claims and received Christ Jesus as "the Lord," the Christian is now to submit to His sceptre: just so far as we do so, is a practical union with Him maintained by us.

"To whom coming, as unto a living Stone" (I Peter 2:4). Let it be duly noted that this is predicated of the Lord's people, and that it is not simply said they "came" to Christ, but "to whom *coming*"! We are to "come to Christ" not once and for all, but frequently, daily; in other words, we are *to continue as we began.* Christ is the only one who can minister to our deepest needs, and to Him we must constantly turn for the supply of them. In our felt emptiness, we must draw from "his fulness" (John 1:16); in our weakness we must turn to Him for strength; in our ignorance, we must apply to Him for wisdom. In our falls into sin, we must seek from Him a fresh cleansing. *All* that we need for time and eternity is stored up for us in Christ. If we have backslidden, let us "repent and do the *first* works" (Rev. 2:4) — cast ourselves upon Christ anew, as self-confessed sinners, seeking His mercy and forgiveness, renewing our covenant to serve and obey.

"Abide in me, and I in you" (John 15:4): we must cultivate fellowship with Christ by subordinating our hearts, minds and wills to Him — if He is to have fellowship with us; for a holy Christ will not commune with any who follow a course of unholiness. The same order is laid down again in the next verse, "I am the Vine, ye are the branches: he that [1] abideth in me and [2] I in him, the same bringeth forth much fruit; for severed from me ye can do nothing." Very searching is this: we need to lay it to heart, and translate into earnest daily prayer. Then the Lord added, "If ye abide in me and *my words abide in you*" (v. 7). Here we are told *how* our practical union with Christ is maintained, namely, by our cherishing His words in our hearts, meditating upon them in our minds, submitting to them with our wills, being regulated by them in our actions. Thus, we "abide" in Christ by being in subjection to Him, by obeying Him.

"If ye keep my commandments, ye shall abide in my love; even as I have kept my Father's commandments, and abide in his love" (John 15: 10). How blessedly this illustrates His declaration "when he putteth forth his own sheep, *he goeth before them*" (John 10:4), and again, "leaving us an example, that we should follow his steps." Christ requires nought from His followers but what He first submitted to Himself. Christ subordinated Himself in all things to God: submitting Himself to God, committing Himself to God. He did not seek His own glory, do His own will, save His own life, plead His own cause, or avenge His own wrong. Self was never a consideration with Him: His only concern was obedience to the Father's commandments, the promotion of the Father's glory, abiding in the Father's love. "I delight *to do thy will*, O my God" (Ps. 40:8) summed up His life.

Christ walked in perfect unison with God. He was of one mind and heart with Him. He had no separate interest from His Father, and no separate joy. His declaration "I and my Father are one" applied as truly to His human walk on earth as it did to the unity of the Divine nature. Whatever touched the Father, equally and in the same way affected Him. "The zeal of *thine* house," He said, "hath eaten *me* up. He pleased not Himself, but as it is written "The reproaches of them that reproached *thee*, fell on *me*." There was perfect harmony of sentiment, unity of desire, oneness in aim between Him and the Father. At the beginning it was "I must be about my Father's business." In Gethsemane it was "Father, thy will be done." At the finish it was "Father, into thy hands I commend my spirit." And to His people He says, "If ye keep my commandments, ye shall abide in *my* love; even as I have kept my Father's commandments, and abide in *his* love."

It was by the keeping of God's commandments that Christ abode in the Father and the Father in Him. Of course, that mutual indwelling never could, through all His perfect lifelong obedience, become more full and complete, in principle and essence, than it was before the incarnation. But to His human consciousness, and in His human experience, the sense of that fellowship must have grown more intense and more precious, as His doing of God's will went on and on to its terrible yet triumphant close. Among the things that the man Christ Jesus learned about obedience through the things which He suffered, must have been the fact that subjection to God carried with it a mighty power to promote and intensify the indwelling of God in man and man in God. And though He learned the griefs and pain which such obedience as He had undertaken to render involved, yet He learned too of its compensating pleasure and joy of abiding in the Father's love.

Let, then, *our* keeping of God's commandments be, in our measure (by the Spirit helping us), like Christ's. In our case, like His, submission to the Divine authority may involve a bitter cup to be drunk and a heavy cross to be borne; for, like Him, we have to learn obedience *by suffering*. But let the obedience we thus learn be of the same sort as His: the giving up of our own wills, always, everywhere. Then, and only then, shall we find how "good and perfect and acceptable" is the will of God (Rom. 12:2). We abide in Christ when our will is merged in His. It is only as we enter in a practical way into His mind and heart, that He enters, experimentally, into ours. This is the secret of rest and repose, of peace and joy, of fruitfulness and usefulness.

That our practical union with Christ, our "abiding" in Him, consists of and is maintained by *obedience,* is also clear from "And he that keepeth his commandments dwelleth in him, and he in him" (I John 3:24). There can be no such mutual indwelling if there is on our part disobedience to the Divine commandments. A course of sinning is altogether incompatible with communion with the Holy One. To abide in Christ is to have our wills merged in His, as His was in the Father's. Thus it is a combination of outward movement and inward repose: the feet acting, the hands busy, yet the heart resting in Him. It is to think, feel, and act as Christ does with regard to God and His law, sin and righteousness, holiness and grace; to entertain the same sentiments with reference to all things.

It only remains for us to glance at another aspect of practical union, and that is, as it concerns *our dealings with the Lord's people.* As the mystical and spiritual union which exists between Christ and His people is evidenced by their practical communion with Him, so the mystical and spiritual union which exists between Christians is to be manifested by a *practical* communion with them. There is a blessed union existing between the saints, as saints, which nothing can sever. They have been made partakers of the same new and spiritual birth; they are partakers of the same heavenly calling (Heb. 3:1); they are partakers of like precious faith (II Peter 1:1). One God is their Father, one Christ is their Lord, one Spirit is their Comforter. They are members of one body, and they have one hope of their calling. Therefore are they exhorted to be "Endeavoring to keep the unity of the Spirit in the bond of peace" (Eph.

4:3). So eminently was that unity evidenced at the beginning we read, "And the multitude of them that believed were of one heart and of one soul" (Acts 4:32). How should it be otherwise, seeing that "They continued steadfastly in the apostles' doctrine and fellowship, and in breaking of bread, and in prayers" (Acts 2:42).

But alas, what an entirely different state of affairs do we now behold in Christendom: we will not say among the Lord's own people, but among those bearing His name. What division, what strife, what jealousy! What sectarian walls and barriers exclude some of Christ's sheep from other members of His flock! "Wherefore receive ye one another, as Christ also received us, to the glory of God" (Rom. 15:7) is the Divine injunction. That does not mean "receive" into church-fellowship (the Roman saints were already in *that* relationship: Rom. 12:4-8), but "receive" each Christian brother and sister *into your hearts,* so that you interest yourself in their welfare, and do all in your power to promote their temporal and eternal interests. But to-day, Baptists, for the most part, will "receive" none but a "Baptist," the Presbyterians none but a "Presbyterian," those known as the "Brethren" none but one who is "identified" with them. That is one reason why — as a protest against sectarianism — the writer remains unattached.

O what a lack of brotherly kindness, tender sympathy, and Christian affection now obtains. Instead of bearing each other's burdens, some seem most pleased when they can add to them. O for grace to sink our petty differences, and seek a practical union and communion with the whole family of God; loving those whom the Lord loves, and walking in affection with those whom He has redeemed with His precious blood. But this too often calls for self-denial and self-sacrifice — *not* sacrificing God's Truth, not sacrificing any Christian principle, but mortifying our carnal pride which loves to have the pre-eminence. O for grace to "know how to speak a word in season to him that is weary" (Isa. 50:4), to "Rejoice with them that do rejoice, and weep with them that weep" (Rom. 12:15), to "lift up the hands which hang down, and the feeble knees" (Heb. 12:12). If we do not, Christ will yet say to us, "Inasmuch as ye did it not to one of the least of these, ye *did it not to me*" (Matt. 25:45).

What a word is this, "Wherefore put away lying, speak every man truth with his neighbor: FOR we are members one of another" (Eph. 4:25). What a *motive* is here presented for Christians being truthful toward their fellow-Christians! By lying to one another they *injure* the union and communion which the members of the mystical Body of Christ have with each other in Him! As another has said "If I lie to my brother, I do the same thing spiritually, as if I used my right hand to stab my left, or as if I used my eye to thrust my leg into a dirty ditch." What high and holy ground is this! O what a spirit of loving communion there should be — *manifested* in a PRACTICAL way — between those who are united to Christ their common Head, and in Him to one another. The Lord be pleased to grant all-needed grace to both writer and reader to act accordingly.

9

Experimental Union

I

WE now will discuss which in some respects, is the most blessed aspect of our theme: for what does our mystical, legal, vital, saving, and practical union with Christ amount to, unless it issues in experimental intimate, precious oneness of heart with Him? This is really the simplest branch of our many-sided subject, yet not a few find it the most difficult: not because of its intellectual intricacy, but because they find it so hard to believe, and harder still to carry out into practice. It seems too good to be true, too blissful for realization in this life, too far above the reach of poor worms of the dust wriggling in the mire. Was it not thus when, as an awakened and convicted sinner, you first heard that Christ was an all-sufficient Saviour? – ah, but *not for* ME. Later, what difficulties presented themselves to your mind: your vileness, your utter unworthiness, your unbelief! What penances, reformations, labors, you supposed were necessary to qualify you for His salvation! But when the Spirit communicated faith, you were amazed at the simplicity of what before had baffled you.

It is much the same in the history of many Christians concerning experimental union and communion with Christ – a conscious, intimate, joyous fellowship with Him who is Altogether Lovely. When they hear or read of this, they conclude that such a blissful experience is not for *them.* Sin is too powerful, too active within, to ever hope for close fellowship with the Holy One in this life. Others may be more favored, *their* corruptions may be more Divinely subdued, but as for *me,* I can only expect to go halting and mourning the rest of my earthly pilgrimage. At best, I can only hope that God will not utterly cast me off, that He will mercifully preserve me from open transgressions which would bring dishonor upon His cause, that He will graciously bear with my innumerable failures, and at last take me to Heaven for *Christ's sake;* but that He should grant me any more than an occasional smile, a sip of His love by the way, is too much for me to expect.

"Ye were called unto *the fellowship of* his Son, Jesus Christ our Lord" (I Cor. 1:9). To whom were those words first addressed? To those who in their unregenerate days had been preserved from flagrant sins? No indeed, some of them had been guilty of the grossest crimes (see I Cor. 6:9-11), but they were "washed, sanctified, justified in the name of the Lord Jesus and by the Spirit of our God." Were they, then, now living unblemished lives, walking in flawless obedience to God's commands? No, far from it; read through the epistle, and observe the many offences which the Corinthian saints had committed. Nevertheless, to them the apostle was moved to say "Ye were called unto the fellowship of his Son." And if *they* were, rest assured Christian readers, that *we* are, too. Though so utterly unworthy in ourselves, still having the flesh unchanged within us, sin ever harrassing and tripping us up; yet "called unto the fellowship of his Son!"

Alas that so few understand of what that "fellowship" should consist. Alas that any Christian should conclude that indwelling sin, with its daily activities, outburstings, and defilements, make "fellowship" with Christ an *impossibility*. Alas that so many suppose that this "fellowship" consists only of an ecstatic experience on the mountain-tops, enjoyed solely by those who gain a constant victory over indwelling corruptions and outward temptations. Were *that* the actual case, the writer would not be penning these lines; rather would he completely despair of attaining unto such "fellowship" with Christ in this life. Ah, my reader, it is those who are still vile sinners in themselves, who find *no* good thing dwelling in their flesh, who are called unto fellowship with God's Son! Surely *that* is indeed "good news." Blessed be His name, the Lord is "a very present help *in trouble*:" for those who are troubled by their futile efforts to heal the plague of their own hearts; troubled over unanswered prayers for grace to subdue their iniquities. Yes, Divine love has made full provision for *such* to enjoy experimental fellowship with Christ in this life.

"This is a faithful saying, and worthy of all acceptation, that Christ Jesus came into the world to save *sinners*; of whom I [not "was," but] *am* chief" (I Tim. 1:15), and it is equally true, blessedly true, that He has *fellowship* with SINNERS. If it were not so, there would be none in this world with whom He could have fellowship, for "there is not a just man upon earth, that doeth good, and sinneth not" (Eccles. 7:20). True, the ineffably holy Christ will not have any fellowship with us in our *sins*, and no renewed heart would desire Him to do so. Nevertheless, it is equally true that He *does* have "fellowship" with sinners: saved sinners, yes; but *sinners* all the same. Did He not have the most intimate fellowship with the apostles? and were they not men of like passions with us? — very far from sinless perfection were they.

But let us now attempt to define *the nature* or character of experimental union and communion with Christ. "There is a friend which *sticketh closer* than a brother" (Prov. 18:24) makes known *His* side of this union; "there was *leaning on Jesus' bosom* one of his disciples, whom Jesus loved" (John 13:23) exhibits *our* side of this communion. The first of these remarkable and inexpressibly blessed Scriptures presents to us an aspect of Truth which some find it difficult to lay hold of and enjoy. In certain circles the exalted dignity of Christ's person has received such emphasis, that a proportionate presentation has not been given of the intimate relations which He sustains to His people: a balance has not been preserved between that in Christ which *awes* and that which *melts* the heart. It is possible to become so occupied with the Lordship of Christ, as to almost (if not quite) lose sight of His Friendship: to be so engaged in rendering to Him the honors which are due Him as God, as to overlook the tender sympathy and compassion which He has for His people as Man.

We are not unmindful of the fact that, in other circles, there has been a deplorable lack of the reverence and homage to which Immanuel is entitled, a fearful cheapening of the truth concerning Him, a light and unbecoming alluding to Him as "Jesus," "our Friend," "our elder Brother," which grates upon the ears and grieves the hearts of those who have been better taught. Yet in our revolt from this unholy familiarity with the Lord of *glory* and the almost total absence of giving to Him the worship which is His due, there is no sufficient reason why we should swing to the opposite extreme, and view Christ as so far above us as to preclude free approaches to and intimate fellowship with Him. He *is* our Lord, and as such we must prostrate ourselves before Him in the dust, and address Him with holy awe. He is *also* our Friend, and as such we should open our hearts to Him with the utmost freedom, casting all our care upon Him, knowing that He careth for us (I Peter 5:7).

Experimental union with Christ is made possible by and is to issue from our *practical* union with Him, that is, our "walking together" in agreement with His revealed will. Experimental communion with Christ is exercised in happy subjection to Him as our Lord, and in intimate intercourse with Him as our Friend. Christ Himself is that "friend which sticketh closer than a brother." This term "friend" tells of the *closeness* of that relationship which Divine grace has established between the Redeemer and the redeemed. It reveals the warm throbbings of His heart unto His own. It gives them full warrant for the fullest confidence and the most unreserved dealings with Him; as it assures of His loving sympathy and deep interest in all that concerns them. There is no aloofness on His part, and there should be no reserve on our part. There should be a readier unburdening of ourselves *to Him* than to our dearest earthly friend or nearest relative.

There are three things requisite in order to our having close communion with one of our fellows. First, that person must be real and present to us: fellowship is not possible with one we know not, or who is far removed from us. Second, we must have a free access to that person, with confidence and boldness toward him: fellowship is not possible where formalities bar our approach and where fear or awe dominates the soul. Third, there must be mutual affection and esteem. Fellowship is not possible where loves exists not or where it has cooled off. Now apply all of this to our present subject. If the soul is to enjoy real experimental union and communion with Christ, He must be a living reality to the heart; faith must bring Him near and give freedom of approach to Him: and the affections must be kept warm and active toward Him; otherwise our religion will quickly degenerate into a mechanical routine, devoid of reality and joy.

In the next place, let it be as definitely insisted upon that, our communion with God and His Christ must be *in the light.* "This then is the message which we have heard of Him, and declare unto you, that God is light, and in Him is no darkness at all. If we say that we have fellowship with Him, and walk in darkness, we lie, and do not the truth; But if we walk in the light, as He is in the light, we have fellowship one with another" (I John 1:5-7). We cannot now give an exposition of this important passage, but must confine ourselves to that which bears directly upon what we are now treating of, namely, the character of experimental communion with Christ. What is it "to walk in darkness?" and what is it to "walk in the light"? The question is one: though viewed from both the negative and positive sides.

The first and most obvious answer must be that, to "walk in darkness" is to conduct ourselves unholily, to follow a course of sin: the works of darkness are the works of the flesh. But we must press the matter more closely home to our consciences. In order to do this, let us consider the leading characteristic of light. The most prominent property of light is its transparency and translucency: it is patent, open, always and everywhere so, as far as its free influence extends. The entrance of light spreads reality all around. Clouds and shadows are unreal: they breed and foster unreality. Light, then, is the naked truth: it makes manifest, it exposes things. Thus the chief conception which this metaphor of "light" conveys is, that of _openness_, clearness, transparency, reality. And that is what God is; that is what Christ — "the light of the world" — is; that is what the Word of Truth is — "a light shining in a dark place."

"The Light shineth in darkness" (John 1:5). He who is the light came to seek and to save those who "sat in darkness" (Matt. 4:16). "For ye were sometime darkness" (Eph. 5:8): what a word is that! — not only that in our unregenerate days we dwelt in darkness, but we _were_ in ourselves "darkness." By the fall we lost that element of clearness, brightness, openness, in which we were created at first. Sin entered, and with sin, shame. The clear and open sunshine of the presence and countenance of Him who is light became intolerable; the covering of fig leaves and the hidingplace of the trees of the garden was preferred. Henceforth, to fallen and unregenerate man, light became offensive: darkness is upon the face of the deep of his heart. Henceforth, darkness is his element: he loves darkness rather than light (John 3:19). Therefore, deception, insincerity, hypocrisy, concealment, characterize him in his attitude toward God.

But at regeneration a miracle of grace takes place: Divine light shines in the heart (II Cor. 4:6), and the consequence is "but now are ye light in the Lord" (Eph. 5:8). The result of this is revolutionizing. Not only is the soul now enabled to see things, and to see itself, in God's light, but he renounces the works of darkness, the "hidden things of dishonesty." He throws off his cloak of pretense, he comes out into the open and truthfully confesses to God what he is. He no longer attempts to cover his sins, or pose as a good and righteous person; but honestly owns himself to be a polluted leper, and incorrigible rebel, an inveterate transgressor, a hell-deserving sinner! "An _honest_ and good heart" (Luke 8:

15) is now his: previously he thought highly of himself and wished others to flatter him; now, he loves *the truth,* and abhors deception and hypocrisy. And, as pointed out in the last article, the believer must *continue* as he began.

It is into the fellowship of Him who is "light" the believer has entered, and if real communion is to be preserved there must be openness and genuineness on his part. Christ will not tolerate any deception: any attempt at concealment or disguise is certain to displease Him. It is both our madness and our loss to try and hide anything from Him. But He is no hard taskmaster; instead, He is full of love and tender mercy. It is written "A bruised reed shall he not break, and the smoking flax shall he not quench" (Isa. 42:3). His ears are ever open unto the cries of His erring people, and their tears of repentance are precious in His sight (Ps. 56:8). Perfect openness and transparent honesty in our dealings with Him, is what He requires; deceit and insincerity He will not tolerate. We cannot walk in the darkness of pretense and have fellowship with Him who is the Light!

"But if we walk in the light, as He is in the light, we have fellowship one with another" (I John 1:7). Note it is not now "as he *is* light" (as in v. 5), but "as he is *in* the light." The thought here is that, the same clear and transparent atmosphere surrounds them both: we walk in the light in which God is: it is the light of His own pure truth, His own nature, of absolute reality. The light in which God dwells is His own light: the light which He *is* Himself. In that light He sits enthroned: in that light He sees and knows, surveys and judges all things. And the light in which we are to walk is identically the same light as that in which God is. The same pure medium of vision is given to us: "In *Thy* light shall *we* see light" (Ps. 36:9). In other words, we must measure everything by God's pure truth and judge ourselves in the light of His holiness.

The same clear-shining, transparent atmosphere of holiness, truth, and love is to surround us, penetrating our inner man and purging our mind's eye, our soul's eye, our heart's eye, that it may see sin as *God* sees it — as "this abominable thing that I hate" (Jer. 44:4); that we may see holiness as *God* sees it — as the inestimable thing which He loves; that all things, all events, all men, all our motives, thoughts, words, deeds, may appear exactly to us as what they appear to Him. It is into a fellowship of *light* we are invited to walk. If there is to be a *real* fellowship, it must be a fellowship of *light,* where there is no compromise, no pretense, no insincerity: where the things of darkness and dishonesty are renounced. But can I, who am so full of sin and corruption, go forth into that light, which is so pure and piercing? Not apart from the cleansing blood of Christ! Thank God for the perfect and ever-availing provision of Divine grace, providing for the removal of every obstacle which my depravity might interpose against walking in the light.

Experimental communion with Christ is the blessed goal towards which all the other unions lead: that the Lord's people may have personal, conscious, intimate, joyous union with Him who loved them and gave

Himself for them — an experience beginning in this life, continuing (more perfectly) throughout the endless ages of eternity. The grand end of our vital, saving, and practical union with Christ is to bring us into *experimental oneness* with Him: that we may drink into His spirit, have His mind, share His joy. Of all the experiences of God's saints on earth *this* approximates nearest to the heavenly bliss. Experimental union consists of knowing, loving, enjoying Christ: it is having plain, practical, personal dealings with Him. A deeper and fuller knowledge of Christ will increase our confidence and joy in Him. The more we are enabled to realize Christ's relation to us and His changeless love for us, the easier and freer will be our approaches to Him.

Experimental union is based upon *faith's realization* of Christ's relation to us and of our relation to Him, enabling the soul to say, "my beloved is mine, and I am his" (Song of Sol. 2:16). It is faith, and nothing but faith, which makes God in Christ real, yea, present, to the soul: "*seeing* him who is invisible" (Heb. 11:27). It is faith, and faith alone, which brings Christ down unto us: "that Christ may dwell in your hearts by faith" (Eph. 3:17). It is faith which gives freedom of approach to Him: "we have boldness and access with confidence by the faith of him" (Eph. 3:12) — the faith of which He is both the Author and the Object. It is only by faith we can enjoy the fact that we were loved by Him from all eternity, and that He now bears us on His heart in the immediate presence of God. "*I live by the faith* of the Son of God, who loved me and gave himself for me" (Gal. 2:20) contains the sum total of all spiritual life and spirituality.

Yet the cementing bond of this union is *love*. Faith unites savingly; love, experimentally. Love is as truly a uniting grace as is faith, though it does not unite in the same way. "God is love, and he that dwelleth in love dwelleth in God, and God in him" (I John 4:16). Where two persons really love each other, their mutual affection makes them to be one: they are wrapped up in each other. So there is a mutual, hearty, reciprocal love, between Christ and believers; He loves them, and they Him; and by virtue of that mutual love there is an intimate, experimental union between them. The husband and wife are one not merely by the marriage covenant — the legal tie and external relationship — but also and chiefly because of the love and affection there is between them. So it is betwixt Christ and His saints: *love*, stronger than death, knits them together.

Experimental communion with Christ, then, consists in basking in the sunshine of His conscious presence: sitting at His feet and receiving from Him as Mary did (Luke 10:39), leaning upon His bosom as John did (John 13:23). The more we are engaged in contemplating and resting in His wondrous and changeless love for us, the more will our poor hearts be warmed and our affections drawn out unto Him. Our daily aim should be a more full and free acquaintance with the Lover of our souls; and this, not so much in a doctrinal way, as in a personal and experimental way, in actual communion with Him. It is in real intercourse with our friends, and in their converse with us, that we get most and best acquainted with them. It is even so with the Lord Jesus Christ, our best Friend. Open your heart freely to Him, and beg Him to graciously open His heart freely to you. Humbly remind Him of His words, "Henceforth I call you not servants; for the servant knoweth not what his lord doeth: but I have called you *friends*; for all things that I have heard of my Father I have made known unto you" (John 15:15).

II

In seeking to define and describe the nature and character of our *experimental* union and communion with Christ it has been pointed out, first, that it consists in a ready submission to Him as our Lord and an intimate intercourse with Him as our Friend: there is no aloofness on His part, and there should be no reserve on ours. Second, it is a walking with Him in the light: where all is open, real, honest, with no concealment or pretense. Third, it is a knowing, loving, enjoying Christ, having plain, practical, personal dealings with Him. Fourth, it is based on *faith's* realization of Christ's relation to us and of our relation to Him: only the exercise of faith will make Him real and consciously near us. Fifth, *love* is the cementing bond of this union: there is a reciprocal affection between the Redeemer and the redeemed. Sixth, it consists of a sitting at the feet of our Lord and receiving from Him, a leaning upon the bosom of our Friend and enjoying His love. Seventh, it is exercised in a real personal intercourse with Him, opening our hearts freely to Him, and receiving free communications from Him.

The great thing for the Christian is to realize that Christ not only gave Himself *for* him, but that He has given Himself *to* him: Christ Himself is mine, my very own! Wondrous, blessed, glorious fact. Oh, for faith to realize it more fully. Oh for grace to act more consistently with it. Yes, Christ Himself is mine: to live upon, to lean upon, to consult, to confide in, to *make use of* in every way I need Him, to have the freest possible dealings with Him. Christ is *mine*: to enjoy to the utmost extent of my heart, to commune with, to delight in. He is ever with me, and under no conceivable (or unconceivable) circumstances will He ever leave or forsake me. He is ever the same: His love for me never varies: He has my best interests at heart. He can satisfy every longing of the soul as nothing else and none other can. He is ready to share with me His peace and joy. O what a happy soul I should be!

What a change it would make in the experience of both writer and reader if we could more fully grasp the amazing and precious truth that the Lord Jesus has not only given Himself *for* us, but that He has done much more — He has given Himself *to* us. CHRIST is ours! Most blessedly is that fact brought out in the wonderful type of Exodus 12: the selfsame lamb whose blood sheltered the Israelites from the Avenger, was theirs to feed upon, to draw strength from, to enjoy (vv. 7-11). Alas how feebly do any of us apprehend the Antitype of this — evidenced in the complaints of our feebleness, leanness, fruitlessness. There is an infinite sufficiency in Christ for time and eternity, and that suffi-

ciency or "fulness" is for us *to draw upon;* but alas, how little we do so.
Surely our deepest experimental need is to be taught by the Spirit — for
He alone *can* teach us this blessed secret, as He ever *does* where there
is a heart really longing to know it — of HOW to make a right and full
use of Christ.

It is only as we really live *upon* Christ that we can truly live *for* Him.
Nor is this the vague, intangible, mysterious thing which human "religion" and Protestant priestcraft would make of it. It is to the Spirit-
taught the most simple, natural, and practical thing for us. First, it is
faith's realization that Christ is truly and actually *mine*; my very own;
mine in an infinitely nearer and dearer way than a mother or wife is
mine. Second, it is faith's realization that Christ is *with* me, near me,
right by my side, "a very *present* help in trouble" (Ps. 46:1), the
Friend who "sticketh closer than a brother." Third, it is faith's realization that *all He has is mine* — IS, not shall be! We are even now
"heirs of God and *joint-heirs* with Christ" (Rom. 8:17). His wisdom,
His righteousness, His holiness, His love, His peace, are *ours.* Fourth,
it is faith's *appropriation* of all this — ah, words easily written, easily understood at their letter-meaning — which enables me to draw from Him,
share with Him, and enjoy what is mine in Him. *That* is "fellowship"
with Christ!

Real and personal *fellowship* with Christ should be made the chief
aim of our souls in all our approaches to Him: in ordinances, means,
and privileges. In public worship, in private reading of the Word, in
our meditation, in prayer, in spiritual conversation with our brethren
and sisters in Christ, free and intimate communion with Him should be
our definite quest. "One thing have I desired of the Lord, that will I
seek after; that I may dwell in the house of the Lord all the days of my
life, to behold the beauty of the Lord, and to enquire in his temple"
(Ps. 27:4): that was the Old Testament way of expressing this truth.
To "dwell in the house of the Lord all the days of my life" did not signify
to spend all his time in the literal tabernacle or temple, but to abide in
conscious communion with Him, enjoying His perfections. *This* the
Psalmist "desired" above everything else, and this he "sought after." So
also must we.

Let us now anticipate an objection: What you have described in the
above paragraphs is indeed a beautiful ideal, but alas, it is utterly im-
practicable for one in such circumstances as I am in. It might be realized
by those who are free from the carking cares of this life, who have not
to battle with the world for daily bread for themselves and those dependent upon them, for such who have time and leisure for holy contemplation and spiritual luxuriation. But for a poor soul like me who scarcely
knows where the next meal is coming from, delighting one's self in the
Lord is not to be attained unto in this life. First we would say, Be not
unduly occupied with God's temporal dealings with you, for His way in
providence is often a great deep. Meditate upon the everlasting covenant of His grace and His boundless love to you. All God's dealings,
even in the most dark and trying dispensations, are in mercy and truth.

He has sworn "I will not turn away from them to do them good" (Jer. 32:40).

If you will but attend to that same word of promise, meditate upon it, and pray over it, your faith will be strengthened, and you will triumph in the Lord and rejoice in the God of your salvation. Remember the faith of Habakkuk; he said "*Although* the fig tree shall not blossom, neither shall fruit be in the vines; the labor of the olive shall fail, and the fields shall yield no meat; the flock shall be cut off from the fold, and there shall be no herd in the stalls: *yet* I will rejoice in the Lord, I will joy in the God of my salvation. The Lord God is my strength" (3:17-19). On God's word the prophet relied. Even though all outward things should, *in appearance*, make against God's word, yet we should believe, with joyful hope, in its sure accomplishment. It will be your wisdom and comfort to leave yourself and every concern with the Lord, committing all, by simple faith, into His hands. "Cast thy burden upon the Lord, and he shall sustain thee" (Ps. 55:22).

We can well imagine other readers saying, *That* is not my difficulty: *my* trouble lies deeper than being occupied with and worried over temporal circumstances, sorely trying though they often are. Such blissful communion with Christ as you have depicted above is impossible for me: how can one so depraved, such a mass of rottenness within, such a spiritual leper, such a miserable failure in everything, ever attain unto intimate intercourse with the Lord of Glory? Ah, *that* is the real problem which weighs so heavily on the hearts of the great majority of truly regenerated souls. Nor can the complacent, self-righteous religionists of the day understand such cases, still less can they minister any help and comfort. Being strangers themselves to the plague of their own heart, having such low conceptions of sin, and still lower of the ineffable holiness of God, being blinded by pride and self-deception, it is utterly impossible that *they* should be able to enter into the anguish of those groaning under sin.

Permit a fellow-groaner to try in his feeble way to point you to "the balm of Gilead." It is *with sin-harassed souls* that Christ holds communion! Ah, *that* is what the haughty Pharisees of the days of His flesh could not understand. They murmured at Him, saying "This man receiveth sinners and eateth with them" (Luke 15:2). It shocked their ideas of religious propriety that He should make so free with those whom *they* considered were so far beneath them spiritually. And if this book falls into the hands of their many successors we would be much surprised if they did not throw up hands of horror against the writer, and denounce such teaching as "dangerous," as "antinomian," as "making light of sin." But this would move us not: it would indeed be deplorable did we receive the approval and commendation of such people. But as of old "the *common people*" heard Christ "gladly" (Mark 12:37), so to-day those who are poorest in spirit will most readily receive His glad tidings.

The gospel is, that it is the LAMB which is given us to feed on. *That* precious title speaks of Christ in His *sacrificial* character. It tells of His amazing grace and matchless love to give Himself to die the death of the Cross for hell-deserving sinners. It tells also of His giving Himself *to* His sinful people, for communion, nourishment, strength, and joy. But more particularly it reveals the perfect *suitability* of Christ for *sinners.* The blacker and viler we see ourselves to be, the better fitted are we for Him whose name is called "Wonderful" — wonderful in His compassion, in His condescension, His readiness to bind up the broken-hearted, His power to heal lepers. His unfailing promise is "All that the Father giveth me, shall come to me; and him that cometh to me I will in no wise cast out" (John 6:37). Nothing honors Christ more than to come to Him *in faith* while feeling our wretchedness, filthiness, and utter unworthiness.

The precious blood of Christ is the only sufficient antidote for a wounded conscience. It is by new acts of faith in His blood that we experience afresh its virtue and efficacy. True, the believer feels the plague of his heart and groans under a body of sin and death, but this should not hinder him from believing — rather should it be an argument to encourage him in believing. The more conscious we are of our polluted condition, the more deeply should we realize our need of that open Fountain "for sin and uncleanness" (Zech. 13:1). "The dying thief rejoiced to see that Fountain in his day, and there may I, though vile as he, wash all my sins away." To it we should be constantly resorting. There is no danger whatsoever to be afraid of trusting that blood too much, or of having recourse to its cleansing too often — rather should we be afraid of trusting it too little. The more frequently we plead that blood before God the more Christ is honored.

"For we have not a High Priest which cannot be touched with the feeling of our infirmities; but was in all points tempted like as we are, yet without sin. Let us *therefore* come boldly unto the throne of grace, that we may obtain mercy, and find grace to help in time of need" (Heb. 4:15, 16). What a precious word is this for sin-harassed souls! First, we are reminded that Christ is our "High Priest," the One who maintains our interests before God. Second, we are assured of His unfailing sympathies: He is one who has "compassion on the ignorant and on them that are out of the way" (5:2). Third, in view of Christ's official relation to and personal interest in us, we are invited to "come boldly [unhesitatingly, confidently, freely pouring out our hearts] unto the throne of grace" — the Mediatorial throne, upon which the eternal Lover of our souls is seated. Fourth, we are to come to that Throne, not only as worshippers to present our offerings of praise, but as sinners "that we may obtain *mercy.*" Finally, access there is given that we may "find *grace* to help in time of need."

What other assurance from Him could we ask for? What further revelation of His heart is needed? A sense of our misery and wretchedness, filthiness and unworthiness, so far from acting as a deterrent, should prove a stimulus for us to come unto "the friend of publicans and sinners." Christ is not like a "fair weather" friend, who fails in the hour of direst need, who turns his back on you when His love, counsel, and help are the most needed. No, no! Christ is that Friend who "loveth at *all* times," that Brother who is "born for *adversity*" (Prov. 17:17). Troubled soul, did you but know Him better, you could not doubt, that; would you but put Him to the proof more, you would obtain fuller evidence thereof in your own experience. Instead of reproving you, He will cordially receive you. It is *faith* which He asks for — faith in His love, His grace, His mercy, His readiness to welcome, to hear our complaints, to heal, to cleanse you.

Faith, dear reader, is neither encouraged nor discouraged by any thing we find in ourselves: it is neither encouraged by our graces, nor discouraged by our sinfulness; for faith *looks out of self unto Another*. Nothing will afford such encouragement to believing prayer as a sight of *the Lamb* on His mediatorial throne (Rev. 5:6). No matter how desperate may be our case, how often we have failed and fallen, how low we are sunk, it is *always* the believer's privilege to turn unto his Redeemer and say, "Look thou upon me, and be merciful *unto me*, as thou usest to do unto those that love thy name" (Ps. 119:132). Oh what incentives, what encouragements He has given us in His Word to pray thus: "very great are his mercies" (I Chron. 21:13). Therein we read of "the multitude of thy tender mercies" (Ps. 69:16), of "his abundant mercy" (I Peter 1:3), that He is "plenteous in mercy" (Ps. 86:5), and that "the mercy of the Lord is from everlasting to everlasting upon them that fear him" (Ps. 103:17).

Very similar as the expressions are in sound, yet there is a vast difference between "Christian experience," and the "experience of a Christian." Real and normal "Christian experience" is for the heart to be occupied with Christ, delighting itself in Him. But "the experience of the average Christian" consists largely of an increasing knowledge of sin and self, and *that* fills him with misery and loathing, and with a sense of emptiness and helplessness. Nevertheless, that only *fits* him the more for Christ — all the fitness He requireth is to feel our need of Him. But alas, only too often *Christ* is excluded from our thoughts; and then the state of our poor minds is very variable, dark, and uncomfortable, afflicted with many disquietudes and sorrows. As we feel sin at work within, we cannot but sorrow; and as we feel sorrow, we are often distracted. Yea, this is ever the case where God leaves us to *reason* about ourselves, to exercise our thoughts on what *we* are in ourselves.

It is in seasons of despondency and sorrow that we most need to turn to Christ and say, "Look thou upon me, and be merciful unto me, as thou usest to do unto those that love thy name" (Ps. 119:132). *This* is to "make use" of Him, to honor Him, to own Him as our loving Friend. When everything appears to be hopeless, go to the throne of grace, for Christ is exactly suited to thee and is all-sufficient for thee. Our desperate case will only serve to draw out His heart, to show forth His grace, to display His compassion, to exercise His mercy, to manifest His all-sufficiency, to endear Himself to our hearts. *His* heart is ever toward us: "Can a woman forget her sucking child, that she should not have compassion on the son of her womb? yea, *they* may forget, yet *will I not* forget thee. Behold, I have graven thee upon the palms of my hands; thy walls are *continually* before me" (Isa. 49:15, 16) He declares. Then why should you doubt His love, or question His willingness to receive you graciously, hear you patiently, and cleanse you effectually?

Oh, my sin-stricken brother, my sin-mourning sister, return unto Him who first sought you out when there was none other eye to pity. Say unto Him, "Hast thou not loved me with an everlasting love (Jer. 31:3); wast Thou not wounded for my transgressions, bruised for my iniquities; so that the chastisement of my peace was upon Thee, that by Thy stripes I might be healed (Isa. 53:5)? Hast Thou not said 'Oh, Israel, return unto the Lord thy God, for thou hast fallen by thine iniquity.'" Take with you words, and turn to the Lord; say unto him, "Take away all iniquity, and receive us graciously, and hast thou not promised 'I *will* heal their backsliding, I *will* love them freely' (Hos. 14:1-3)" Ah, my Christian friend, cannot you see that the Lord permits these sad falls, with the sorrow of soul which they occasion us, to make way for the discovery of His gracious heart, that we may *prove for ourselves* that He IS a Friend that "sticketh closer than a brother!" Earthly friends may fail and leave us; one day soothe, the next day grieve us; but there's One who'll ne'er deceive us, *O how HE loves.*

Experimental communion with Christ requires that we be continually *cleansed by Him*: a fuller consideration of this we must leave (D.V.) for the future; in the meanwhile, let it be pointed out that Divine grace has made full provision for this: "If we confess our sins, he is faithful and just to forgive us our sins, and to cleanse us from all unrighteousness" (I John 1:9). Note well that this comes immediately after, "If we say that we *have no sin*, we deceive ourselves, and the truth is not in us" (v. 8). Sometimes the newly converted soul is favored with such grace, with such communion with Christ, that iniquity hides its evil face, and it seems as though sin in us has been slain. But indwelling corruption soon re-asserts itself; yet pride is unwilling to *acknowledge* it, and the temptation is to gloss it over and call it by some pleasanter name than SIN. But *that*, dear friend, is Satan's effort to draw us back again to "walk in *darkness*" — in deception and dishonesty; and it must be steadfastly resisted.

"If we *confess* our sins:" *that* is to "walk in *the light!*" To "confess our sins" to Him, is to open our hearts to Him. It is to spread our case before Him: concealing, palliating nothing. It is to fully tell Him of all that damps our zeal after holiness, that quenches our love, that makes us miserable in ourselves. It is a laying bare of the whole of our inner man to the loving and wise Physician, who alone knows how to deal with us. And *He* is to be trusted with all the secrets of your soul. He is "faithful and just:" He will not heal your wound slightly: He will set your sins before Him in the light of His countenance, and cause you to loathe them. As you *continue* this frank and open dealing with Him, He will not only "*forgive*" but "cleanse you from all *unrighteousness*" — deliver from deceit and guile, purge from reticence and reserve.

The more we walk in God's light, the more clearly will we see what vile creatures we are, and how far, far short we come of God's glory. The more we cultivate intimate communion with Christ, the more will He cause us to see that what we deemed "trifles" are grievous sins. But if we "confess" them, honestly, penitently, daily, He is "faithful and just to forgive us." Ever remember that He requires. truth in the inward parts," and lies and pretense He will not tolerate. Probably you say, I have confessed my sins to Him until now I am thoroughly ashamed to do so any more. That is pride and unbelief. When Peter asked if he was to forgive his erring brother seven times, the Lord answered, "Till seventy times seven:" that is what GRACE does! Oh my Christian reader, come to this Friend of sinners more frequently, rely upon His promise more fully, and He will not repulse you.

III

Having sought to describe at some length the nature or character of the intimate and precious experimental communion which it is the right and privilege of the believer to have with the everlasting Lover of his soul, we will now pass on to consider the *maintenance* of the same. The Lord has graciously provided full and adequate *means* for this, and it is entirely our own fault if we fail to avail ourselves of them. Neglect of those means produces the same effects upon the spiritual life as neglect of natural means does upon the physical and mental. The body cannot thrive if the laws of health be despised; the mind cannot be developed if its education and discipline be ignored; and the soul cannot be preserved in a healthy state if those things which make for our well-being be slighted. God's blessing rests upon *the use of* those means of His appointing, but He places no premium on slothfulness; and if we are indifferent and careless, then we must expect to be lean and sickly, joyless and fruitless.

Each of us needs to honestly face and seriously answer this question. *How highly* do I *really* value communion with Christ? I am deeply concerned about my temporal prospects; I give much thought to my earthly circumstances; I am at great pains to obtain a living in the world, so that I may have a roof over my head and food and raiment. I am anxious to have a few close friends, and do all in my power to maintain good-will with them. I seek to do my duty by my family. Yes, all well and good; all right in their place. But *their* place is a subordinate one: *Christ* has the FIRST claims upon me. Do I *realize* this? Am I acting accordingly? Am I making it my chief concern to cultivate closer communion with Him? Am I — amidst all the problems, frictions, trials of this life — making *Him* my principal Confidant, Counsellor, Helper? Is it *Him* I am most seeking to please, honor and glorify? If not, is it not high time that I did so?

Do I not owe far, far more to the Lord Jesus than to all my earthly associates and friends, yea, than to my nearest and dearest relatives? And is He not desirous of my treating Him *as the* "friend that sticketh closer than a brother?" Has He not invited me to the most intimate dealings with Him? Is it not my privilege, yea, my bounden duty, *to* give Him the *first* place, each day, in my affections, my thoughts, my plans? Has He not supplied the utmost encouragement for me to cast *all* my care upon Him? Has He not given me promises exactly suited to every circumstance, every difficulty, every need, I may get into? Has He not plainly revealed the *means* which will promote my fellowship with Him? Has He not shown me that neither the presence of indwelling sin nor its breakings forth into activity, need make communion with Him a practical impossibility?

But alas, what vile ingrates we are! what incorrigible wretches! How often have we given the Lord cause to say, "My people have committed two evils: they have forsaken me the fountain of living waters, and hewed them out cisterns, broken cisterns, that can hold no water" (Jer. 2:13)? None but Christ can satisfy the heart, yet we are terribly slow in really believing it. We grasp at shadows, pursue phantoms, seek to feed on ashes, and then wonder why we are so miserable. God will not long allow His people to rest in *things,* or find contentment in their circumstances. He it is who both gives and takes away, who gratifies or thwarts our wishes. We brought nothing into the world, and it is certain we shall carry nothing out of it; therefore, there is nothing in the world which deserves a single anxious thought from us, for we shall soon be at the end of our journey through it.

None but Christ will be sufficient for us when we are called upon to pass through the valley of the shadow of death, and none but Christ can do us any real good now: what we need is to really *believe* that truth. And does not God take abundant pains to prove the truth of it to us? He removes this and withholds that, because He sees that our hearts are too much set upon them. We imagine that a certain thing would be very pleasant and profitable, and fancy that we cannot do without it; if we could but obtain it, we promise ourselves much satisfaction from it. If God grants it to us, do we not find that it is *not* what we expected? We dream dreams, build air castles, live in many a fancied paradise, only to be bitterly disappointed. God's purpose in those disappointments is to wean us from the world, to make us sick of it, to teach us that all down here is but "Vanity and vexation of spirit."

O my reader, it would make much for our peace and blessedness if we committed the management of the whole of our affairs into the hands of Christ. We need to continually pray Him to save us from having any will of our own, to work in us complete subjection to and satisfaction with His holy will. By nature we are full of restlessness, covetousness, discontent — never satisfied with what we do have, ever lusting after what we do not have. But by grace we may live more happily than a prince, even though we possess nothing more down here than bare food and raiment: yea, *shall* do so if we seek and find all our satisfaction in Christ alone. Here is the key to the extraordinary history of Paul and Silas, Bunyan and Rutherford, madame Guyon and many others. Why were they so contented and joyful while lying — some of them for many years — in prison? No doubt God favored them with a double portion of His grace and comfort, yet the real explanation is that their hearts were completely absorbed with Christ.

Now the gracious provisions which the Lord has made for the maintaining of personal and experimental communion with Himself are revealed, first, in the Old Testament Scriptures, particularly in what is recorded therein of His dealings with Israel; and we lose much if we fail to give our best attention thereto. There we see the Lord taking unto Himself a peculiar people out of all the nations of the earth; that which moved Him thereto was His own sovereign grace, for there was nothing in them, more than in others, to commend them to His favor. They were a poor and afflicted people, enslaved, in cruel bondage to the Egyptians. They were an unbelieving and stiff-necked people, slow to appreciate the mercy of God toward them, and slower still to walk worthily of His goodness to them. They were a self-willed, and murmuring people, for after the Lord had wrought marvellously for them, each fresh testing they encountered found them full of distrust and grumbling. Nevertheless, the Lord patiently bore with their waywardness and ultimately brought them into the promised inheritance.

First, the Lord manifested His unfathomable *love* for them. He showed that, when there was none other eye to pity them in their low estate, *His* did; and that when there was no other arm to save them, His would. He heard their cries as they groaned under the lash of their cruel taskmasters; was moved with compassion toward them, and sent a deliverer. Second, He manifested His all-mighty *power*, working such wonders on their behalf as were never witnessed on earth before or since. Pharaoh withstood Him, but he and his hosts were swallowed up in the Red Sea as though they had been so many impotent ants. Wondrously did the Lord work, baring His arm, exhibiting His strength, and demonstrating that with Him all things are possible. Such displays of God's love to and of His might on behalf of Israel, was well calculated to draw their hearts to Him, establish their confidence in Him, and lead them to covet the high privilege of communion with Him. Such was the case: nor were they disappointed, as Exodus 15 shows.

Third, the Lord undertook to graciously act as their Guide, Protector, and Provider. On their journey to the promised land, a wilderness had to be crossed: but they were not left to their own poor resources – the Lord Himself cared for them. A pillar of cloud by day and a pillar of fire by night conducted them across the trackless desert. A supply of angel's food was given for the sustenance of their bodies: this fell within their own camp, so that no arduous journey was required to obtain it, and no charge was made for it. An unfailing supply of fresh water was provided for them by the living stream which gushed from the smitten rock. Infallible assurance was given that while they remained in obedience to God no enemy should stand before them, that *He* would fight their battles for them. No sickness came upon them, their feet did not swell, nor did their clothes become old and worn. Full proof did they have that "Blessed is the nation whose God is the Lord" (Ps. 33: 12).

The Lord was pleased to reveal Himself on the most intimate terms. Their leader, Moses, was permitted to speak with Him face to face, as a man speaketh to his friend; yea, it is recorded that "Moses and Aaron, Nadab and Abihu, and seventy of the elders of Israel *saw* the God of Israel. . . . and upon the nobles of the children of Israel he laid not his hand [in judgment]: also they saw God, and *did eat and drink*" (Exod. 24:9-11) at perfect ease in His presence. Furthermore, God graciously acted as the Legislator of the nation, giving them a complete set of laws which covered every aspect of their life, social, political, and religious. No other people were so wondrously provided for: "He showed his word unto Jacob, his statutes and his judgments unto Israel. He hath not dealt so with any nation: and as for his judgments, they have not known them. Praise ye the Lord" (Ps. 147:19, 20). Those commandments were not grievous, but just, merciful and spiritual, and were designed for the good and well-being of His dear people. In keeping of them there is a great reward.

Finally, complete provision was made for Israel's *failures*. Those laws were not given to sinless creatures, and Divine wisdom devised a method whereby an erring people might continue in communion with Himself, and this in such a way that both His justice would be satisfied and His amazing grace evidenced. This method was a series of oblations and ablutions, sacrifices and cleansings. A priesthood was appointed to serve for God on behalf of the people, and an high priest as their special representative before Him. Peace offerings, sin offerings, and trespass offerings (Lev. 3-5) were appointed to cover the varied offenses of individuals, while atonement was made for all the iniquities of the whole nation on one particular day in the year (Lev. 16). Most blessed of all was the provision made for those who had been defiled by contact with death: here the value of sacrificial atonement was *applied to* them. Obviously the blood of a slain animal could not be preserved, so its "ashes" were laid up, placed in a vessel, and running water put therein, and then sprinkled upon the one needing cleansing (Num. 19).

Full provision, then, was made for the removing of everything unsuited to the holy presence of the Lord. The appointed means were at hand for His people to approach Him without tarnishing the purity of His sanctuary. In the above type (Num. 19) "water" was *not* a figure of the Word, rather was it *the means* for applying the death of the atoning sacrifice. As long as a child of God continues in this sin-cursed world, where everything is defiling and under the sentence of death, and as long as the evil nature remains in him, will pollution be contracted and offenses be committed; and therefore will he need a daily pardon. Therefore, in addition to the general remission of sins which he received at his conversion, he requires a constant application to his conscience — by the Spirit — of the atoning sacrifice of Christ. The blood of the lamb was *shed* once for all at the Cross, but it is *sprinkled* on the believer (i.e., the efficacy of it is applied to him) as often as he needs and his faith appropriates it.

The above type is such as beautiful one that we cannot forbear dwelling on it a little longer. The sacrificial animal was to be a *red* heifer (Num. 19:3) — the color of guilt (Isa. 1:18); yet it must be "without spot or blemish." It had to be one on which a yoke had never been bound, for Christ came to be the Sacrifice of His people of His own free will. It had to be led forth "without the camp" (cf. Heb. 13: 11). It was slain before the priest, but not by the priest himself: so our Saviour was slain by others. The heifer was burned and its ashes mixed with pure water. Now when an Israelite became ceremonially defiled, he was excluded both from the tabernacle and the congregation. But here was the gracious provision made to *restore* him and maintain him in communion with God. Those ashes mixed with water were sprinkled upon him: so it is by the Spirit's re-application of the blood of Christ that those out of communion with the Lord are restored.

Now to His Old Testament people God gave a wondrous manifestation of His love, a full exhibition of His all-sufficiency and readiness to meet their every need, a complete revelation of His will for them in all the details of their daily lives, and then made a most gracious provision to meet their failures and maintain them in fellowship with Himself. Thereby God showed that He was infinitely worthy of their love, confidence, and obedience. But it is in the New Testament that we find the *fullest* occasion for the drawing out of our hearts unto Him, the revelation of the means which He has provided for our personal and experimental communion with Himself, and of the provisions He has made for the maintaining of the same. He has done far, far more for us than He ever did for the nation of Israel: they had but the shadows and the types, whereas He has given us the substance and the antitype. Abundant cause, then, is there for the assuring of our hearts and the drawing out of them in adoring gratitude and praise.

We have received a more signal proof of God's love than did the Hebrews: instead of providing an animal to shelter us from the avenging angel, He gave His own precious Son to be the sacrifice for our sins. He has granted us a more remarkable exhibition of His power: instead of swallowing up Pharaoh and his hosts in death, He has triumphantly brought Christ out of death. So, too, the provisions He has made for us while here in this wilderness-world far excels theirs. We have His completed Word for a lamp unto our feet and a light unto our path, and the Spirit Himself indwelling to guide and govern our wills. Far more intimately has God revealed Himself to us than ever He did to Israel: "For God, who commanded the light to shine out of darkness hath shined *in* our hearts, to give the light of the knowledge of the glory of God in the face of Jesus Christ" (II Cor. 4.6). Even more perfect provision has been made for our failures than was for theirs, for Christ Himself has gone, "into Heaven itself, now to appear in the presence of God for us" (Heb. 9:24), and there "He ever liveth to make intercession for us."

"That which was from the beginning, which we have heard, which we have seen with our eyes, which we have looked upon, and our hands have handled, of the Word of life (For the life was manifested, and we have seen it, and bear witness, and show unto you that eternal life, which was with the Father, and was manifested unto us;) That which we have seen and heard declare we unto you, that ye also may have fellowship with us: and truly our fellowship is with the Father, and with his Son Jesus Christ. And these things write we unto you, that your joy may be full" (I John 1:1-4). We will not give an exposition of these verses, but ask the reader to note well *the order* of truth presented in them. Verse 4 speaks of fulness of joy; and of what is that the outcome? Verse 3 tells us: it is based upon "fellowship" with the Father and His Son; and in what does that fellowship consist? Verses 1, 2 tell us: in a personal, intimate, experimental knowledge of Christ Himself — seeing, hearing, *handling* Him — you only "handle" one close by your side, and one who is dear to you.

It is in intimate fellowship with Christ that real communion with Him consists. It is by the mind being daily engaged with the knowledge-passing love of Christ — meditating thereon, believingly — that the heart is drawn out unto Him. The Christian should seek, above all else, to be occupied with Christ's *love* for him, to value that love far above his own enjoyment of it — the one being the cause, the other but the effect of it. We should esteem Christ's love beyond all the benefits and blessings that flow from it. We should labor to apprehend, from the Scriptures, the freeness, the eternity, the immutability of that love. It is our contemplation of His *love* which admits us into the freest and fullest heart-communion with Him. *That* was the source and spring of Christ's own joy and blessedness — His occupation with the Father's love to Him: note how often He dwelt upon it: John 3:35; 5:20; 15:9; 17:26. The Father's love was precious to Christ, and Christ's should be unto us.

Now all our *enjoyment* of Christ's love is the fruit of knowing and resting in the same, just as it is the true spiritual *knowledge* of Christ which makes way for the exercise of faith in Him. Our deepest need is to know Christ as He is exactly *suited to us* — as the tender mother is suited to her wailing child, as the physician is suited to a suffering patient, as a firm anchor is suited to a storm-tossed ship, as a guide is suited to a traveller who knows not the way, as food is suited to a starving man. Christ, dear reader, is exactly suited to the Christian: suited to everything which concerns him, suited to his every need, his every problem and trial, his every state or case. O to *live on* Christ exactly as He is revealed in the Word. O to *bring in* Christ continually: to make Him our closest Confident, our constant Counsellor, our All in all. He is received into our minds by spiritual meditation in our hearts.

As another has said, "I simply address the Lord Jesus, inwardly in my mind, saying Lord Jesus, look upon me, take notice of all within me, exercise Thy compassion upon me, exactly as my necessities require. Keep, O keep me; bless, O bless, me; defend me for Thy mercies' sake, from sin, the world, and Satan; let me be content to be nothing; do Thou be my all. I call this *communion*. If this be so, then I find it to be more or less my constant practice; because as I cannot live but I must feel sin, so I cannot live but I must look to Jesus for salvation from it, and call on Him to exercise His grace and pity towards me, so long as I am the subject of it. Indeed, I think the greatest communion with Christ, and the Father in Him, through the Spirit, in this present state, is, and doth principally consist in a total renunciation of self, and in a real and actual dependence on the Lord; and the more *simple* this dependence, so much the better."

The *helps* to the promotion of an increased knowledge of, communion with, and joy in Christ, are the reading of the Word — regarding the same as a series of love letters from Him to me personally — spiritual meditation upon what I have read, turning the same into simple prayer.

IV

Christ Himself is mine! *Christ Himself* is thine, dear Christian reader. O that our poor finite hearts could apprehend a little of what that means. Think for a moment of *who He is*: the Brightness of God's glory, the express Image of His person; Immanuel, God manifest in flesh. In Him dwelleth all the fulness of the Godhead bodily. What then cannot He do! All power in heaven and earth is His. Think too of *what He has done* for His people: He became poor that we might become rich, He came to earth that we might go to Heaven, He died that we might live. What must be His love for us! Think of His *present relationship* to us: His righteousness is imputed to our own account, His blood is our purity before God, His fulness is ours to draw upon (John 1:16), His Spirit indwells us; He is our great High Priest on high, ever living to make intercession for us.

Christ is the "friend that sticketh closer than a brother" (Prov. 18: 24). He would have us *come to him continually* (I Peter 2:4) with all our wants, cares, sins, and sorrows; He is able to lift our hearts above them all. None outside Christ is worth a serious thought. O to bask in the sunshine of His conscious presence, to rejoice in His love, to dwell upon the perfect righteousness He has wrought out for us, to be daily occupied with the sufficiency of His atoning blood, to find in Him all that we need for time as well as for eternity. O to *live upon* Christ continually, no matter what you feel or experience in yourself. Let nothing hinder you, my brother, my sister, from keeping up an unbroken communion with your precious Lord and Saviour. This is your right, your privilege, your portion.

Nothing should hinder the Christian from experimental communion with Christ. He should turn *everything* he experiences with regard to circumstances, temptations, sins, friends and enemies, into seeking unto Christ, and finding in *Him* the opposite of all that grieves him in *them*. O to live freely, fully, wholly, on Christ. We shall do so in Heaven, why not do so on earth! Only as the heart is fixed steadfastly on Him is peace and joy our conscious portion. It is only by living *out of* our wretched selves that we can enjoy the person, the work, the fulness of the Lord Jesus. This is the secret of true happiness, and only so far as we find our happiness in Him is practical holiness promoted. His eye is ever upon us, why is not ours ever upon Him? He is the Sum of perfection, the

"Altogether Lovely" One. While we view Him in His peerless excellency, our souls cannot but be enamored of Him.

The greatest loss and misery which can befall us this side of eternity is to be looking off from Christ. None other can do us any real good. But the trouble is in our own proud, legal, self-righteous, deceitful hearts. We are not content to be *nothing* in ourselves, and for Christ to be *everything*. WE want to be something, spiritual "Somebodies." We want to experience something within which will feed our pride and give us satisfaction. We want to feel that we are *better* than when we first came to the Saviour as hopelessly lost, utterly undone, woe-begone, despairing sinners. We may not be quite conscious of this subtle working of pride, but that is what it is, nevertheless. All the fitness He requireth is to feel my need of Him, is as true now as when I first fell at His feet owning myself to be a foul leper.

The whole of practical godliness is summed up in the *denial* or repudiation of SELF. We cannot make Christ our all in all till self be loathed and renounced — by which we mean *all* that pertains to self, good, bad, and indifferent. But this is only possible by the exercise of *faith*, for faith consists in going outside of ourselves to Christ for everything — for strength, for wisdom, for holiness, for peace, for joy. The whole of our salvation is in Him. O to be able to truly say, "My soul shall make her boast *in the Lord*" (Ps. 34:2) — not in my "consecration," not in my growth in grace, not in my knowledge of spiritual mysteries, not in my "service," not in my "victory over sin," not in my spiritual attainments, not in the number of souls I have "won"; but IN THE LORD. O to be done with *religious self!*

Having sought, then, to show again wherein experimental communion with Christ consists, and dwelt upon the means and maintenance thereof, we must now turn to the darker side of our subject and consider the interruption and severance of the same. And in this connection we cannot do better than devote the remainder of this chapter to a careful examination of our Lord's words in Revelation 2:4, "I have against thee, because thou hast left thy first love." As an assembly is but the aggregate of its members and officers, the rebuke to the Ephesian church applies directly unto individual Christians who are in the condition here described. It is one in which *the heart* is not so deeply affected as it once was with the love of God in Christ, nor is there now such devotion toward nor delight in Him; and in consequence, there is a feebler resistance to sin and slackening pursuit of holiness.

It is to be carefully noted that the charge which is here preferred by Christ is not "thou hast *lost* thy first love" (as it is frequently misquoted), but "thou hast *left* thy first love," which is a more definite act, and emphasizes the failure of responsibility. The sad state here depicted signifies a decay in grace, a declension in spirituality, a waning of affection, with the resultant loss of relish for Divine things, growing carelessness in the use of means, and formality in the performance of duty. It is a state of heart that is here in view, which may or may not be accompanied by outward backsliding. The fine gold has become dim.

Christ no longer holds the first place in the soul's affections. Some are conscious of this decay in love, while others aware of it draw the erroneous conclusion they have never sincerely loved Christ at all.

Genuine Christians may find their love for Christ languishing. Just as the body will soon be chilled if, on a winter's day, it leaves the fireside, so the soul's ardor and fervor will quickly wane if the things of time and sense are allowed to crowd out close communion with Christ. But though grace may decay, it is never utterly destroyed; hence the error of speaking about "losing" our first love. The "seed" of God (I John 3:9) remains in His people even when they backslide: it did in David, and in Peter. There is a vital principle communicated in regeneration which is indestructible. So, then, though the Christian's love may suffer a sad abatement, it is never totally extinguished: the acts and fruits of it may be few, its measure may greatly diminish, but the root of it is still present.

That we may the better understand this spiritual disease (and thus be fortified against Satan's lies) let us point out *what it is not*. First, not every distemper or ailment which the renewed heart perceives and mourns over, is a leaving of our first love. Every act of known sin is not apostasy, nor even a degree of it; as every rise of bodily temperature after a meal is not a fever. There are infirmities and failures in the most spiritual saints. As said an old writer, "Alas for the generation of the just, if every vain thought, idle word, or distempered passion, were a decay of love." Nothing is so uncertain as to judge ourselves by particular acts, for in every act love does not put forth itself so strongly as at other times. Some obstructions of love there may be for the present, which the soul takes notice of and retracts with sorrow, but still we hold on our course.

Second, every abatement or absence of transports of soul and mountain-top elations, is not a leaving of first love. At conversion there are strong joys and liftings up of soul upon our first acquaintance with God in Christ, but such an experience is not sustained, nor meant to be so. A healthy person will regularly relish his food, yet he must not expect it to produce such sensations of pleasure as does the first meal to a starving man. At conversion our love shows itself in sensitive expressions, for as yet it is not dispersed and diffused in the several channels of obedience; but when the Christian learns how many ways he is to express his love to God, he may have a true zeal and affection for Him, and become "rooted and grounded" in love, without those ravishments of soul which he experienced when first realizing that his sins were all pardoned and that he was accepted in Christ.

Third, nor must the Christian conclude that his love has decayed because he no longer experiences those conscious goings forth of heart to God as he had *in special seasons*, when God granted him a high day in His courts. There are occasions when God feasts the soul so that it is constrained to say, "My soul shall be satisfied as with marrow and with fatness, and my mouth shall praise thee with joyful lips" (Ps. 63:5). There are times when we are favored with rich experiences of God's love, to which all the pleasures of the creature are no ways comparable. Such are very great mercies, but they are never intended for us to try our state by. A settled calm, a quiet peace of soul, is an even greater mercy than occasional transports of joy. If we preserve our relish for spiritual things it is a surer proof of our standing in grace than in any spasmodic or sporadic raptures.

Though Christians ought not to lightly or rashly judge themselves guilty of a decay in their love, yet on the other hand they should not readily acquit themselves of it, for it is a great evil. The highest degree of love does not answer to the infinite worthiness of Christ, nor to what we owe Him for having rescued us from Hell and secured for us an eternity with Himself in Heaven. But when a believer falls from that measure of love whereunto he had already attained, it is the more grievous, because to now seek his happiness in things, to settle down with a measure of contentment in his backslidden state, is tantamount to saying that he had formerly loved Christ too much, and had been more earnest and diligent in seeking to please Him than was necessary. Thereby he condemns his former love and disesteems Christ as not worthy to be loved with *all* heart, mind, and strength. Moreover, as love decays, so do all our other graces, with their fruits and works. Nor will Christ, who is jealous of His peoples' affection, ignore their growing coldness, but will make them smart for their sin and folly.

It is not without reason then that Christians are exhorted to "keep yourselves in the love of God" (Jude 21). The healthy Christian is still apt to remit something of his delighting himself in the Lord, and his constant duty to honor Him in all things; and at no point does he need to be more upon his guard than in *the preserving of his love*. There is much of self-pleasing in us, love of our own ease and carnal gratification, much lusting after the things of this world, and such a continual opposition of the flesh to the Spirit which ever seeks to draw off from God and heavenly things, that we cannot be sufficiently watchful against everything which has a tendency to quench that spiritual fire which should always be burning in our hearts. Unless we daily heed that exhortation, "Keep thy heart with all diligence" (Prov. 4:23) we shall quickly lapse into that careless and cold state which is the case with the great majority of professing Christians. How much we need to pray for one another "the Lord direct your hearts into the love of God" (II Thess. 3:5).

Many who have left their first love *are little sensible of* the sad fact. One reason for this is that spiritual ailments are not laid to heart till they openly appear in their effects and fruits. A believer may be active in external duties while his love has become cold; the life of his duties may be decayed, though the duties themselves be not left off — as the Pharisees were scrupulous in tithing mint and cummim, but omitted "the love of God" (Luke 11:42). A correct outward deportment is no proof that the affections are still warm toward Christ. As the glory of God is seen leaving the temple of Ezekiel by degrees — first from the holy place, then to the outer court, then to the city, then resting on one of its encircling hills; so it is when Christians grow cold to God. The Lord no longer has the throne of the heart, then secret prayer is neglected, then family worship declines, then public duties become irksome, and then sin begins to lead us into practices dishonoring to Christ; and all because we did not observe and judge the *first declinings*.

Now *the decay of love* is seen in two things: first, in the diminishings of its degree. That love which we are required to give to the Lord consists in valuing and esteeming Him above all else; and this is to be manifested by us in a constant care to please Him, a fear to offend Him, a desire to enjoy Him, a steady delighting in Him. When any of these are abated, as to any considerable degree, then our love is chilling or growing cold. Where love is healthy and the favor of God is highly valued, there is a sincere effort made "that we might walk worthy of the Lord unto all pleasing" (Col. 1:10). But when the heart grows more of less indifferent whether our conduct is honouring to God, and we are more set upon gratifying the flesh, then love is decayed. While His fear be truly upon us we will say, "How then can I do this great wickedness, and sin against God?" (Gen. 39:9).

Now there is in the Christian a yearning to enjoy God in Christ, and a strong tendency of heart toward Him argues a healthy love. When we cannot regard ourselves as happy apart from Him and count all else as dung and dross (Phil. 3:7-9), when we desire a sense of His love and are deeply affected by a lack thereof, we cry "my soul followeth hard after thee" (Ps. 63:8). The Christian longs for sanctifying grace, hungers and thirsts after righteousness, and the perpetual vision of Christ hereafter. But as these desires decrease, so there is a diminishing in the degree of our love. The soul esteems communion with God above all else: "Thou hast put gladness in my heart, more than in the time their corn and their wine increased" (Ps. 4:7); "I have rejoiced in the way of thy testimonies as in all riches" (Ps. 119:14). But when we mourn not for the absence of the light of God's countenance shining upon us, when we cease to esteem His Word more than our necessary food, then our love is waning.

Second, the decay of love is evidenced by the intermission of its acts or effects, for when the heart grows cold and listless it becomes unfruitful. Let us consider some of the principal workings of love *Godward*. These are seen in our thinking and speaking of Him: "I remember thee upon my bed, and meditate on thee in the night watches" (Ps. 63:6); "my meditation of him shall be sweet" (Ps. 104:34). As the wicked are described as those who seldom think upon Him (Ps. 10:4), contrariwise, it is the pleasure of a renewed soul to be much occupied with God's perfections. But when our hearts and minds swarm with vain imaginations and idle dreamings, and thoughts about God are repelled as unwelcome guests, love has decayed. The less our love for God, the less we shall think upon and speak of Him. Again; where love is vigorous, communion with God in prayer and holy duties is ardently desired and earnestly sought: "Seven times a day do I praise thee" (Ps. 119:164). But when communion is neglected, and a sense of

God's presence is not our main object in the use of means, He has to say, "My people have forgotten me days without number" (Jer. 2:32).

Consider the effects of love with respect to *sin*. When the sense of our deep obligations to Christ are warm upon the heart, we are constrained to strive against sin, to resist the lustings of the flesh, and turn with loathing from the temptations of Satan. When overtaken by a fault we bewail it, as she who loved much, wept much (Luke 7:47). The more vigorous our love for God, the stronger our hatred of all which is opposed to Him. But when the conscience has lost its tenderness, evil imaginations are tolerated without remorse, the heart is no longer diligently kept, nor the tongue bridled; then spiritual decay has set in. When a believer makes light of the things which once deeply distressed him, when he grows careless and vain, is venturesome upon temptations and snares, and ceases to groan over his corruptions, then he has left his first love.

Consider the effects of love with regard to *the duties of obedience*. Where it retains its strength love works self-denial, so that the impediments of obedience are more easily overcome. Love begrudges not some expense for the one beloved, and will serve God whatever it costs (II Sam. 24:24). But when every trifle is made an excuse, and that which God requires is deemed too much and exacting, love has waned; an unwilling heart is soon turned out of the way. Again; love makes actions easy and pleasant, and says "His commandments are not grievous" (I John 5:3); therefore when obedience has become a burden and the doing of God's will a hard task, the affections must have cooled off. Finally, love puts life into duties: "fervent in spirit serving the Lord" (Rom. 12:11): without this, His worship is performed perfunctorily, sin is confessed without remorse, and praise is offered without any spiritual melody in our hearts.

In conclusion, let us mention some of *the causes* of love's decay. The evil times in which we live, is one: "because iniquity doth abound the love of many waxes cold" (Matt. 24:12). But though it be hard to maintain our spiritual fires when the world is pouring cold water on them, yet the darker the night the more brightly should real Christians shine. Again; multiplied privileges cloy. The Israelites wearied even of Heaven's manna: "a full stomach loatheth a honey comb." When we were first acquainted with the things of Christ and communion with God, we were greatly enamored, but now they no longer charm. But this should not be: while healthy, the babe wearies not of the breast. Again; neglect and carelessness. The Christian life is a race, a wrestling, a warfare; it calls for diligence and pains. If we neglect prayer, meditation, watchfulness against the encroachments of the world, love will quickly wane. Again, allowed sins: neglect is like not blowing the fire hid in the ashes, sinning is like pouring on oil. To dally with the pleasures of sin soon brings a deadness upon the heart.

Note. For much in the latter part of the above, we are indebted to a sermon by the Puritan Manton.

V

"The backslider in heart shall be filled with his own ways" (Prov. 14: 14). What a sad case is that of the Christian who has lost touch with the Lord, whose sins and iniquities have hidden His face from him (Isa. 59:2)! Formerly, he walked in happy fellowship with Christ, but the light of His countenance no longer shines upon him. Once he was in possession of that peace which passeth all understanding, but now the joy of salvation is no more his portion. One who has "left his first love" has, of course, grieved the Holy Spirit, and hence He *withholds* His comforts from his heart, and consequently he is full of darkness, doubts, and fears as to his state, and can find no rest unto his soul. He has given place to the Devil, only to find him as merciless as the Egyptian taskmasters. He has returned for a season to the pleasures of sin, and now he lies by the wayside, robbed, stripped, wounded, half-dead.

There is no sorrier object in this world than a backslidden believer. His communion with Christ is broken, he has lost his relish for the Word, the spirit of prayer in him is quenched. On the other hand, he has been spoiled for the world, and cannot find that measure of satisfaction in carnal things which the ungodly do. Is, then, his case hopeless? Yes, so far as self-recovery is concerned, for a strayed sheep never finds its own way back again to the fold. The work of restoring backsliders from their spiritual decays is an act of sovereign grace, wrought in them by Him who is of infinite patience and abundant in mercy. When God designs to heal the backsliding of His people, He does so by giving them an effectual call to repentance, and by moving them to use and by blessing unto them those means which He has appointed for their recovery.

To the backslider himself his case appears, at first, desperate, for it is (alas) very much easier to depart from the Lord than it is to return to Him. Having turned his back upon God, it is difficult for him to now seek His face. Why so? Because his heart is so heavily oppressed, his conscience under such a load of guilt, his whole soul filled with shame, while a spiritual deadness seems to paralyse all his faculties. Moreover, severed as he is from communion with the Lord, unbelief is dominant within him, so that he is unable to apprehend the plentitude of Divine grace and the sufficiency of Christ's atoning blood. In such a state he is fully prepared to listen to Satan's lies, telling him that his case is hopeless, that it is quite useless to seek God's forgiveness. Memory, too, will remind him that he has so often in the past confessed his miserable failure to God, that to do so now would be worse than a mockery.

But presently, under the renewing operations of the blessed Spirit, a fresh hope is born within him, and he is made to feel that all is not irretrievably lost. Yet at this stage, it is of deep importance that no means of recovery from spiritual decays be sought unto save those which, for the matter and manner of them, are of *Divine* institution. Alas that so many are misled here. As is often the case with newly awakened souls — who betake themselves to physicians of no value and unto cisterns which hold no water — so not a few convicted backsliders enter upon a course which affords no remedy. It is at this point that Romanism so often gains power over souls who are seeking a relief from a conscience which gives them no respite, for unless the transgressor be under the actual guidance of *evangelical* light, he is easily imposed upon: his distress is so great, his burden so intolerable, that he is ready to listen to almost any comforter, be he a true or a false one.

There are numerous priests and preachers at hand who will counsel those whose conscience is causing them sore anguish to enter upon a course of duties which *God* has nowhere commanded — the confessional, bodily lacerations, pilgrimages, parting with large sums of money for charitable or religious enterprises, are advocated as sure sources of relief; while Protestant quacks will tell the suffering soul that he must quit this habit and give up that form of recreation, etc. etc., if he would obtain the ear of God. This same principle is illustrated in "Wherewith shall I come before the Lord, and bow myself before the high God? shall I come before him with burnt offerings, with calves of a year old? Will the Lord be pleased with thousands of rams, or with ten thousands of rivers of oil? Shall I give my firstborn *for my transgression*, the fruit of my body for the sin of my soul?" (Mic. 6:6, 7) — by such means they hoped to make reparation for their sins and be restored to their former condition. Let great care be taken, then, that the means used for recovery from backsliding be those prescribed *in the Scriptures*.

At no point does the amazing grace of our God appear more conspicuous than is His attitude toward His wayward and wandering children. Their base ingratitude against the inestimable favors they have already received, their wicked unfaithfulness in allowing the worthless things of time and sense to draw their hearts away from the Lord, and the grievous dishonor brought upon His name by their excuseless conduct, instead of causing Him to cast them off in utter disgust, only serve to bring out the changelessness, faithfulness, and abundancy of *His* love. O the superabounding mercies and lovingkindnesses of our blessed Lord unto such worthless wretches as we are. Because God knew how prone His people are unto grievous declensions and spiritual decays, He has graciously recorded in His Word "exceeding great and precious promises" (II Peter 1:4) which are exactly suited to their case: "Return, ye backsliding children, and I will heal your backslidings" (Jer. 3:22); "I will heal their backsliding, I will love them freely; for mine anger is turned away from him" (Hos. 14:4).

Such promises are made good to us by faith's appropriation and by our use of the duly appointed means. But right here a further word of counsel and warning is needed if the exercised backslider is not to miss the goal of his desires: beware of attempting to use those means, and discharge those duties which God requires, in *your own strength*. When backsliders perceive clearly that certain duties are appointed them by God, and they are convinced that they must perform them, they are very apt to act as though such duties were to be executed in their own might. Convicted of carelessness, realizing their sinful neglect of prayer, the reading of the Word, the mortfiying of their members, and other spiritual exercises, and knowing it was their failure to use these means of grace which brought them into their present woeful state, they are now inclined to rush ahead and perform with a will those outward works wherein the duties consist.

Alas, what ignorant, erring creatures we are: how intractable and self-sufficient. When we should be using the strength God has given us, we pretend to have "no prompting of the Spirit," and so rest on our oars. When we should be waiting on the Lord for fresh supplies of grace, we feverishly attempt to act in the energy of the flesh. How slow we are to really believe that humbling word of Christ's "without me ye can do nothing" (John 15:5). Ah, that does not accord with the pride of our hearts, does it, and hence God suffers us to experience many painful failures ere we are willing to receive its truth. Let us, then, seek to be much upon our guard against rushing ahead to perform the duties required unto our restoration, and *leaving the Lord out of* the whole of our efforts. Only God can "heal" us (Exod. 15:26), only He can "restore" the soul (Ps. 23:4). Faith, then, must humbly engage the assistance of Christ and His grace both unto and in those duties, otherwise no matter how earnestly we perform them or how zealously they be multiplied, they will not be effectual unto our recovery.

But it is time for us now to consider those duties which our blessed Lord has appointed for the recovery of His people. "I have against thee, because thou hast left thy first love: remember therefore from whence thou art fallen, and repent, and do the first works" (Rev. 2:4, 5). Having in the previous chapter dwelt upon what is signified by "leaving our first love," we will now turn to the remedy here specified. This, it will be seen, is threefold, addressing the principal centers of our inner being: "remember" is a word for the understanding and conscience; "repent" is spoken to the affections; while "do the first works" is a call to the will: the whole man is guilty when we backslide, and the whole man (all the faculties of the soul) must be operative in returning to our Lord and Saviour. The way of recovery is here clearly defined, and though it involves that which is distasteful to the flesh, namely, the humbling of our proud hearts, yet there will be no restoration to real experimental communion with Christ, and no consequent peace, assurance and joy, until he submits thereto.

First, "*Remember from whence thou art fallen*": this is a call to the backslider to seriously consider his condition, particularly to contrast his present sad case with his former happy one. Recollect what a difference there is between thee and thyself: thyself living and acting in the consciousness and power of the love of Christ, and thyself now in bondage to the power of some worldly or fleshly lust. Call to remembrance that while communion with Christ was maintained that "the joy of the Lord" was thy "strength" (Neh. 8:10), but now that communion is broken, you have neither joy nor strength. Consider what an advantage you once had against the temptations of the Devil and the solicitations of the flesh and the world when your love for Christ was fresh and vigorous, and how much the case is altered with you now — how feeble you present resistance of any sin. Surely you have cause to bemoan "Oh, that I were as in months past, as in the days when God preserved me; and when his candle shined upon my head" (Job 29:2, 3).

"Remember from whence thou art fallen." Recall the "mount of myrrh" and the "hill of frankincense" which once were trodden in fellowship with the eternal Lover of your soul. "In our returning we should have such thoughts as these: I was wont to spend some time every day with God; it was a delight to me to think of Him, or speak of Him, or to Him; now I have no heart to pray or meditate. It was the joy of my soul to wait upon His ordinances; the return of the Sabbath was welcome unto me, but now what a weariness is it! Time was when my heart did rise up in arms against sin, when a vain thought was a grief to my soul; why is it so different with me now? Is sin grown less odious, or God less lovely?" (Thos. Manton).

Second, "and repent." What is evangelical repentance? Its leading elements are conviction, contrition, and confession. Where real repentance is present in the heart there is a true sense of sin, a sincere sorrow for sin, a hearty loathing of sin, and a holy shame for sin. It is called by many names in Scripture: such as, the afflicting of our souls (Lev. 16:29), humbling ourselves (II Chron. 7:14), a broken heart (Ps. 51:17), a contrite spirit (Isa. 66:2), a smiting upon the thigh (Jer. 31:19), mourning (Zech. 12:10), weeping bitterly (Matt. 26:75). "The goodness of God leadeth thee to repentance" (Rom. 2:4), which means, first, it is *by* His goodness that repentance is wrought in us by the gracious operations of His Spirit; and second, that it is *a sense of* His goodness which melts and breaks our hard and stubborn hearts.

The convicted conscience is made to feel how vilely I have requited God for His great goodness to me, and thus sin is embittered to my soul. Thereby I am brought to take sides with God against myself and condemn my wicked wanderings from Him: so far from excusing my iniquities, I now accuse them. The heart is deeply affected by the exceeding sinfulness of sin, and grieves for having offended my loving Lord, for disregarding and opposing my blessed Benefactor, for having so evilly repaid Him, for having so little concern for His pleasure and honor. The soul will now sincerely confess its transgressions, not in a cold and formal way, but out of the abundance of the heart the mouth will now speak: "O my God, I am ashamed and blush to lift up my face to thee" (Ezra 9:6) will be my language.

True Christian repentance is the heart turning from sin and returning to God. In the hour of penitence sin is hated and self is loathed. The deeper the repentance, the fuller will be the confession: there will be a detailed acknowledgement of our wicked conduct, an exphasizing of the enormity of the evil course we have followed. As examples of this let the reader turn to Daniel 9:5, 6 and Acts 26:9-11, and observe *how many aggravations* of the sinning is there mentioned! Further, genuine repentance is always attended with sincere desires and earnest endeavors after reformation of life: "He that covereth his sins shall not prosper; but whoso confesseth *and forsaketh them* shall have mercy" (Prov. 28:12) — as sin is a forsaking of God, so repentance is a forsaking of sin. The language of a contrite soul is, "What have I to do any more with idols?" (Hos. 14:8).

Deeply humbling though the work of repentance be unto us, it is *glorifying to God.* "And Joshua said unto Achan, My son, give, I pray thee glory to the God of Israel, and make confession unto him" (Josh. 7:19); "And if ye will not lay it to heart, to give glory unto my name, saith the Lord of hosts, I will even send a curse upon you" (Mal. 2:2); "And they repented not to give him glory" (Rev. 16:9). It must be so, for repentance is taking sides with God against sin. O how each of us needs to pray for a deeper repentance. Painful though the work of repentance be, yet it issues in pleasant fruits. As one of the Puritans said, "Groans unutterable make way for joys unspeakable." If we sorrowed more for sin, we would rejoice more in the Lord. But let us add that, in cases where true penitents are so bound up within that they cannot pour out their souls in heart-melting confessions before the Lord, yet they can mourn over the hardness of their hearts, and grieve because their sorrow is so shallow.

"Where is the blessedness I knew
　When first I saw the Lord?
Where is the soul-refreshing view
　Of Jesus and His Word?

What peaceful hours I then enjoy'd;
　How sweet their memory still;
But now I find an aching void
　The world can never fill.

Return, O holy Dove! return,
　Sweet Messenger of rest!
I hate the sins that made Thee mourn,
　And drove Thee from my breast.

The dearest idol I have known,
　Whate'er that idol be;
Help me to tear it from Thy throne,
　And worship only Thee."

— Cowper

Third, "And do the first works." Negatively this means, turn your back upon the world, re-enter the lists against Satan, resume the task of denying self and mortifying your members which are upon the earth. Positively it means, return unto the One from whom you so grievously departed, surrender yourself afresh to His lordship, render to Him that whole-hearted obedience which He requires. Make the pleasing of Christ your chief concern, walking with Him your daily business, communing with Him your supreme joy. Re-engage in the fight of faith, take unto you the armor which God has appointed, and give no quarter to your foes. Be diligent in using the means of grace: prayer, the reading of the Word, spiritual meditation thereon, and communing with God's people. Express your gratitude for the Lord's pardoning mercy and restoring grace by now being out and out for Him. "He restoreth my soul" is at once followed by "He leadeth me in *the paths of righteousness* for his name's sake" (Ps. 23:3)!

"And do the first works," then, signifies return to God in Christ. As our departure from the Lord was the cause of all our woes, so our case admits of no remedy till we repent and turn again unto Him. It is blessedly true that Christ purchased grace and pardon for His people, yet these are communicated to them in a way which is becoming to His holiness and wisdom. It would not be for His honor that we should be pardoned and restored without a penitent confession of past sins and an honest resolution of future obedience. Our case is not compassionable without it: who will pity those in misery that are unwilling to come out of it! The sincerity of our repentance is to be evidenced by a hearty determination for the future to live in obedience. In other words, it is not enough that we "cease to do evil," we are also required to "learn to do well" (Isa. 1:16, 17).

"And do the first works." It is not sufficient to bemoan the follies of the past: time present must be redeemed. As there are some sensible of their backslidings who do not actually repent thereof, so there are others who bemoan their sad case yet languish in idle complaints for their lack of love, and make no efforts to recover the same by serious endeavors. Those who are guilty of spiritual decays must not rest until they regain their former mindfulness of God and devotedness to Christ. Spare no efforts in so yielding up thyself to the Lord that *His* interests may again prevail in your heart above all sinful solicitations and vile inclinations. Engage your heart afresh to Christ, make no reservation; let your work be sin-abhorring and sin-resisting each day.

"And do the first works." When a Nazarite had broken his vow, he had to start all over again (Num. 6:12). When we have forsaken the narrow way of obedience to and communion with Christ, God requires us to return to the point from which we wandered. Thus it was with the father of all who believe. Abraham's descent into Egypt was a divergence from the path of faith and duty. And what was the consequence? This, the time he spent there was lost, and he had to return to the point from whence he swerved and begin over again: "And he went on his journeys from the south even to Bethel, unto the place where his tent had been *at the beginning*, between Bethel and Hai; unto the place of the altar which he had made there *at the first*" (Gen. 13:3, 4).

Observe well *the order* which God has specified for the recovery of those who had left their first love. Perhaps we may grasp the force of it better if we transpose it. "Do the first works": "As ye have therefore received Christ Jesus the Lord, so walk ye in him" (Col. 2:6). Ah, but do not overlook the fact that "repent" must precede this renewed activity in the Lord's service: *the past must be put right* before we can again enjoy real communion with Him! God will not gloss over our sins, nor will He suffer *us* to do so: they are to be judged, confessed, forsaken, before new obedience is acceptable to Him. And "repent" is, in turn, preceded by "remember therefore from whence thou art fallen": the more we heed *this* injunction the quicker will our conscience be convicted and the deeper will be our contritions. O that it may please the Lord to bless this chapter to the recovery of some backsliders.

VI

We would ask our readers to please bear with us for writing further on the present aspect of our many-sided subject, namely, the restoration to fellowship with Christ of a backslidden believer. The need for it appears to us so pressing that we feel constrained to make another effort toward helping some of our brethren and sisters who have fallen by the wayside. How many there are who for a year or two seem very earnest and zealous in the Christian life, and then become cold and careless, semi-worldly or weighted down with the cares of this life. Frequently such cases settle down in a state of partial despair: they feel that they are "utter failures," and conclude that daily communion with Christ is not for such as they. Instead of humbly confessing their failures to the Lord and trustfully seeking pardon and fresh supplies of grace, they go halting and mourning the rest of their days.

We greatly fear that there are not a few of God's dear children who, to a greater or less degree, are held captives by the Devil, and are largely ignorant of the means for recovery. It is the duty of God's servants to seek out such and acquaint them with the provisions of Divine grace: not to make light of sin and excuse backsliding, but to faithfully and tenderly point out how much Christ is being dishonored and what they are losing by their conduct, and then to set forth the means which God has appointed for their restoration, particularly emphasising the fact we have a great High Priest who has compassion on them that are out of the way (Heb. 5:2), and is willing and able to save unto the uttermost them that come to God by Him (Heb. 7:25).

Perhaps one of our readers says, But the Lord has turned away from me the light of His countenance, and therefore I have much reason to fear that I am not in His favor. Such an objection is answered in the Charter of Grace: "I *will not* turn away from doing them good" (Jer. 32:40). The Lord has withheld from thee His smile, His comforts, and thou art troubled about it; but that very trouble is for good — it should put thee upon inquiring into the reason for His strangeness toward thee: it should humble thee: it should bring thee into the dust before Him in sincere and contrite confession. And then, thou shouldest exercise thy faith on such a Scripture as this, "For the iniquity of his covetousness was I wroth, and smote him: I hid me, and was wroth, and he went on frowardly in the way of his heart. I have seen his ways, and will heal him: I will lead him also, and restore comforts unto him" (Isa. 57:

17, 18) — it was Fatherly chastisement which smote thee, but His love is unchanged, and He is ready to heal and comfort.

Perhaps another fears that God has not only hidden His face, but has quite forsaken him. He may have done so to thy sense and feeling, yet not so as to His own gracious purpose, which changeth not. Hear how He speaks to thee, distressed one, "For a small moment have I forsaken thee; but with great mercies, will I gather thee. In a little wrath I hid My face from thee for a moment; but with everlasting kindness will I have mercy on thee, saith the Lord thy Redeemer" (Isa. 54:7, 8) — how that should silence thy doubts. How gracious is thy God! How infinitely merciful was it that He should give thee such promises, so suited to thy needs, thy case. How well-fitted is such a word as this to preserve thee under the trials of faith and to bring thee out of them. Read it over and over until the clouds of unbelief are dispersed, and thou art again assured that God has a loving and royal welcome for every returning prodigal.

But possible there is a reader who says, My case is much more desperate. God is incensed against me, and justly so. He has cast me off, and I can expect no more favor at His hands. Once, indeed, I thought that He loved me, and that I loved Him: but I have fouled my garments, fallen into great sin, disgraced my profession. My conscience accuses me of being a dog which has returned to his vomit. I deliberately flouted my privileges, sinned against light, and conviction, and I am verily guilty of that which is not to be found in the truly regenerate. Ah, dear friend, sad indeed as is such a case, yet your language is not that of a reprobate. Thou art fallen into the mire, but are you determined to remain there? You are under a load of guilt, but wilt thou *nurse it*, and so add sin to sin? No matter how vile thy fall, thou canst not be truly humbled for it until thou turnest to God and trustest the plenteous redemption which is in Christ Jesus.

Let us anticipate a possible objection at this point: Is it altogether *wise* to speak so freely of the relief available for even a desperate case? None but a self-righteous pharisee would ask such a question, therefore it is hardly deserving of any answer at all. But for the sake of any who may be perturbed by such a question, let it be pointed out, that there is no subject revealed in Scripture but that the wicked may pervert it (II Peter 3:16). No matter how carefully the truth be presented, how guarded the language used, how well balanced the presentation, those who are determined to do so will wrest it to their own destruction. It is a great pity that some of God's servants do not recognize this fact more clearly, and act accordingly. They are so afraid that a wrong use may be made of what they say, or that their teaching may be denounced as "dangerous," that they are muzzled, and often hold back a most needful and precious part of "the children's bread."

Let us not attempt to be wiser than the Holy Spirit. He hesitates not to tell forth the riches of Divine grace unto the most notorious sinners and the worst backsliders. "My little children, these write I unto you, that ye sin not. And if any man sin, we have an Advocate with the

Father, Jesus Christ the righteous" (I John 2:1): here is a guide for us. First, there is a presentation of the exalted standard which God sets before His people, a pressing of the requirements of His holiness. Second, there is a plain declaration of God's gracious provision for those who sadly fail to measure up to His standard, announcing the freeness of Divine mercy. This is the order for us to follow, and this is the "balance" which we are to observe. First, a stressing of God's unchanging claims, with His hatred of all sin; and then the recounting of the gracious provision made for His failing people. "If any one [of His children] sin," *not* they are cast off by God and forfeit their salvation, but "they have *an Advocate* with the Father." Naught but the apprehension of this latter fact will melt the backslider's heart.

So it is all through the Scriptures. Take Numbers 6, which treats of Nazarite dedication to God. There we have in type the *highest* form of separation from carnal delights and devotedness to the Lord, yet even here we find God anticipating *failure* and providing for it: "And if any man die very suddenly by him, and he hath *defiled* the head of his consecration, then he shall have his head" etc. (vv. 9-12). God knows what we are even after our regeneration, and that there is never a day passes but what we need His pardoning mercy. He knows that while we are left down here, there will always be sin to be confessed, judged, forgiven and put away. And therefore, while He never lowers the requirements of His holiness, yet His grace is ever found amply sufficient for His failing peoples' need, even though that very need be the result of their sins. The preacher is never to excuse sin or lightly regard the declension of saints; yet he must not fail to make clear and present the rich and full provision which a gracious and compassionate God has made for those that wander from Him.

As a further example of what has just been said, let us for a while consider together the precious contents of Hosea 14:1-6. "O Israel, return unto the Lord thy God; for thou hast fallen by thine iniquity. Take with you words, and turn to the Lord; say unto him, Take away all iniquity, and receive us graciously; so will we render the calves of our lips. Asshur shall not save us, we will not ride upon horses; neither will we say any more to the works of our hands, Ye are our gods; for in thee the fatherless findeth mercy. I will heal their backsliding, I will love them freely; for mine anger is turned away from him. I will be as the dew unto Israel; he shall grow as the lily, and cast forth his roots as Lebanon. His branches shall spread, and his beauty shall be as the olive tree, and his smell as Lebanon." This passage belongs as truly unto spiritual Israel to-day, as it applied to natural Israel in the past (Rom. 15:4; I Cor. 10:11).

The name "Israel" is used in Scripture with varying latitude: it has a wider scope when employed nationally, and a narrower when used spiritually. It belongs to all the fleshly descendants of Jacob, but it had a special force unto the elect remnant among them. Inside the nation as a whole were "Israelites indeed' (John 1:47), concerning whom it was said "Truly God is good to Israel, even to such as are of a clean heart

(Ps. 73:1). This distinction is clearly recognized in the New Testament: 'For he is not a Jew, which is one outwardly . . . but he is a Jew, which is one inwardly" (Rom. 2:28, 29); "Behold Israel *after the flesh*" (I Cor. 10:18), which clearly implies there is another Israel "after the spirit!" It has helped the writer much to perceive that the nation of Israel in Old Testament times was a type of Christendom as a whole, and that the godly remnant in that nation foreshadowed the little flock of the regenerate amid the great mass of professing Christians.

"O Israel, return unto the Lord thy God: for thou hast fallen by thine iniquity" (Hos. 14:1). These words, then, had a wider and a narrower application. They were addressed first to the nation as a whole; they were spoken secondly to saved individuals in the nation. Hosea prophesied in very dark times. He lived during the reign of wicked Jeroboam, of whom it is said so often, he "caused Israel to sin;" and while Uzziah, Jotham, and Ahab were over Judah. Idolatry was rampant, yet seven thousand had been preserved from bowing the knee to Baal. History has repeated itself, for our lot is cast in a day when spiritual idolatry is sadly rife, and when many of God's own people are infected and affected by the evil spirit which is abroad. There is much in Hosea 14 which is truly pertinent and of great practical importance for us now. Once we get beneath the different figures there used, their spiritual significance will be readily seen.

"O Israel, return unto the Lord thy God: for thou hast fallen by thine iniquity." How blessedly has God here revealed His desire for backsliders to return unto Himself! The manner in which this call is given is very impressive and heart-melting. "O" is a note of exclamation. It is like one who has done much to help an indigent friend, now surprised and grieved at his base requital, saying, "O John!"; or a devoted husband saying to his unfaithful spouse "O wife!" So God says to those for whom He had done so much, and whose waywardness He has borne with such patience, "O Israel." It is a note of exclamation addressed to their affections. God does not barely say "Israel, return unto me," still less does He gruffly command them so to do; but He tenderly entreats them "*O* Israel return." What *love* that expresses!

The backslider must seriously examine his condition and solemnly consider his sad plight. He has forsaken the paths of righteousness; unless he retraces his steps what will his end be! Let him heed, then, this Divine injunction. "Return": the Hebrew word is very emphatic, yet difficult to reproduce in English — "return *even* unto" or "*quite up to*" is the thought: no partial return will satisfy *His* heart. "Return unto the Lord *thy* God": unto Him who has taken thee into covenant relationship with Himself, who has shown thee such favors; unto Him who alone can do thee any real good. Return unto the One whom thou hast so grievously wronged, so excuselessly insulted, by allowing forbidden objects to draw away thy heart from Him. "For thou *had fallen* by thine iniquity" — into spiritual sloth, into sickness of soul, into a joyless state, out of which none but God can lift you. Then return to Him, for none but He can pardon, cleanse, heal, deliver you from the toils of Satan.

But what is meant by *"return unto* the Lord thy God?" First of all it denotes that the backslider honestly and solemnly face the fact that he has departed from the Lord, that he has followed the evil devices of his own heart, yielded to the temptations of the Devil, entered forbidden paths. Second, it signifies that he must now consider his ways and "cease to do evil." Third, it implies that he judge himself unsparingly for his folly and wickedness, taking sides with God against himself. Fourth, it means that he must humble himself before God, acknowledging his transgressions, confessing his unworthiness, earnestly seeking the Divine mercy. Finally, it includes the setting of his affections again on things above, diligently seeking grace to live as becometh a child of God.

It is not difficult for us to write down what is intended by a "return to the Lord," but it is far from easy for a backslider to carry it out. Satan will make a strenuous effort to retain his victim: if he can no longer allure him with his baits, he will seek to drive him to despair with his accusations, telling him that he has sinned away the day of grace, that he has committed the great transgression, that his case is quite hopeless. Unto any such who may read these lines let us say, Abraham, the father of the faithful, fell into the same sin again and again; David transgressed very grievously; Peter, though definitely forewarned, denied his Master; yet *they* recovered themselves out of the snare of the Devil. Remember is is written, "The blood of Jesus Christ God's Son cleanseth us from *all* sin."

Read through Hosea 13 and note well the condition of Israel at that time: they were guilty of great wickedness, and under the threatening of Divine wrath, yet to them came this tender appeal, "O Israel, return unto the Lord thy God." How that shows us there are no seasons or circumstances which shall obstruct sovereign grace when God is pleased to exercise it toward His erring people. There is "A fountain opened to the house of David and to the inhabitants of Jerusalem for sin and uncleanness" (Zech. 13:1). That Fountain possesses an infinite virtue to wash away every spot and stain of sin. It is a public Fountain standing available for daily use, that befouled believers may wash therein. Does not God say to His erring people "Their sins and iniquities will I remember no more" (Heb. 10:17): then why reject the comfort of such a promise; it is perfectly suited to thy present distress and is the remedy.

"Take with you words, and turn to the Lord: say unto him, Take away all iniquity, and receive us graciously" (v. 2). So desirous is God that His backslidden people turn to Him, He here dictates a prayer for their use: the injured One instructs them! Here God graciously makes known the means of recovery, for so ignorant are we of the way of return that we have to be *told* what to do — "we know not what we should pray for as we ought" (Rom. 8:26)! Yet simple as the remedy appears, it is far from easy to carry out: as a child is slow to acknowledge its naughtiness, so pride of heart in a backslider makes him reluctant to own his iniquities. Alas, how many postpone their restoration by delaying their confession; yet it is to their own great loss and harm that they refuse to acknowledge their sins.

The worse be our case, the greater is our need of coming to Christ. On a bitterly cold day the genial heart of a fire can only be enjoyed by our *drawing near to it;* we cannot bask in the warmth of Christ's love while we determine to remain away from Him, hence the "O Israel, *return* unto the Lord thy God" of Hosea 14:1 is at once followed by "Take with you words and *turn to* the Lord." No empty "words" will suffice: the whole soul must go out to God, so that out of the abundance of the heart the mouth speaks. The one who is conscious that he has left his first love and has a real purpose to return to the Lord, must definitely look to the Holy Spirit to work in his heart the substance of this prayer, so that it truly voices his deep desires.

But why does God order that we "take with us words"? Is He not fully acquainted with the thoughts and intents of our hearts? Yes, but He requires us to humble ourselves beneath His mighty hand, to take unto ourselves the shame of our fall, to stir us up to *feel* the enormity of our crimes. "Say unto him, Take away all *iniquity*": *this* is what is to deeply exercise the penitent's heart — that which has so grievously dishonored the Lord, befouled his own garments, and occasioned such a stumbling block unto his fellows. Repentance is to act itself in prayer, requesting that God will do for us what we cannot do for ourselves — either remove the guilt and defilement of our sins or subdue their raging within. "Take away" the love of, the bondage of, the pollution of, from heart, conscience and life. "Take away *all* iniquity": there must be no reservation: all sin is equally burdensome and hateful to a penitent soul.

"And receive us graciously": faith must individualize it and say "receive *me* graciously": deal with me not according to my evil deserts but according to Thine infinite mercy; look upon the atoning Blood and pardon me; regard me no longer with displeasure, but grant me fresh tokens of Thy favor and acceptance. "*So* will we render the calves of our lips," that is, offer praise unto thee (Heb. 13:15). The *order* is unchangeable: only as the backslider returns to the Lord, humbles himself before Him, repents of his sins, seeks His forgiveness, is he experimentally fitted to be a *worshipper* once more. God will not accept praise of rebels!

"Asshur shall not save us; we will not ride upon horses: neither will we say any more to the work of our hands, Ye are our gods; for in thee the fatherless findeth mercy" (v. 3). The force of these words can best be understood by reading Hosea 5:13; 7:11; 8:8, 9; 12:1 — "horses" were what the unbelieving Hebrews put their trust in during times of war. Fleshly confidence and idolatry were *their* two worst sins, and here they are confessed and disowned; so we must acknowledge and renounce (in detail) *our* sins. The "fatherless" are those conscious of their deep need, helplessness, dependency. O turn to Him and find the Lord "a very present help in trouble."

"I will heal their backsliding, I will love them freely; for mine anger

is turned away from him" (v. 4). This is ever God's response to a returning backslider who penitently confesses his sins and truly desires to
be delivered from a repetition of them. Sin is a disease which wounds
the soul, and only God can "heal" it. When He loves us "freely" He
"manifests himself to" us (John 14:21). "I will be as the dew unto
Israel: he shall grow as the lily" (v. 5): "dew" comes from above, falls
insensibly, cooling the air, refreshing vegetation, making fruitful: it is
a beautiful figure of the Spirit's *renewing* the restored believer, grant-
ing him fresh supplies of grace. The "lily" speaks of lowliness, purity,
fragrance. "And cast forth his roots as Lebanon" (v. 5), that is, be more
firmly fixed in the love of Christ, and so less easily swayed by the
customs of the world and assaults of Satan. "His beauty shall be as the
olive tree" useful and fruitful; "and his smell [the fragrance he emits]
as Lebanon" (v. 6): a restored Christian is a joy to God's servants and
an encouragement to his brethren (see v. 7), others are encouraged
to "return." O what inducements are here set before the backslider *to*
"turn to the Lord": yet *faith* must be exercised so as to *appropriate* the
precious promises of verses 4-8.

10

Glory Union

I

THIS present life, with is continual mixture of good and evil, joy and sorrow, with its constant fluctuations and disappointments, naturally prompts a reflecting mind to the belief and hope of a future life that will be more perfect and permanent; yet that is as far as the unaided intellect can project us. A Divine revelation is indispensable if we are to learn *how* Heaven is to be reached, and of *what* its blessedness consists. By the fall of the first Adam paradise was lost, and only through the last Adam can sinners be restored unto God, and only by the supernatural operations of the Spirit can the hearts of depraved men be fitted for and their steps be directed along the sole way which conducts to the mansions in the Father's House. Vain is human reasoning, worthless the efforts of imagination, when it comes to obtaining a knowledge of that antitypal Canaan which flows with spiritual milk and honey. How thankful, then, should we be for the Word of Prophecy and the light it supplies while we are in this dark world.

That blessed light has been enjoyed by God's elect from earliest times. "As for me [said the Psalmist], I will behold thy face in righteousness: I shall be satisfied, when I awake, with thy likeness" (Ps. 17:15). Here was the blessed sequel to Jehovah's response to Moses: "show me thy glory" had been his request, "thou canst not see my face [in *this* life], for there shall no man see me, and live" was the Divine response (Exod. 33:18-20). But what is, necessarily, denied the saints now, shall be granted them in the future. While in this world indwelling sin raises an insuperable barrier, incapacitating the soul to discern more than a few broken rays of the Divine splendor. But when we "awake," on the Resurrection morn, and sin and the grave are left behind, then will the soul be fitted for the beatific vision, for "the pure in heart shall see God" (Matt. 5:8), see Him then as they cannot now.

When David said "I will behold thy face" he had reference to an *objective* glory, and that, in its most perfect representation; for the *"face"* is the principal part of our persons wherein physical beauty and moral dignity are displayed. When he added "I shall be satisfied with thy *likeness,"* a different concept is before him, another factor is introduced — one which must necessarily enter into the equation of soul *satisfaction.* The most vivid display of the Divine glory, so far from satisfying, will only terrify those who are not *in inward harmony therewith,* as is evident from Revelation 6:16, etc. No sight of God can satisfy any one unless and until his soul be conformed to the Divine image and attempered thereto. Thus we understand the Psalmist to mean, "Hereafter I shall behold the blessed face of God, and be regaled thereby; not only by the vision itself, but because of its transfusing itself upon me, transforming me." It is a Divine glory both revealed and received.

The same wondrous truth is set forth in the New Testament. "For I reckon that the sufferings of this present time are not worthy to be compared with the glory which shall be revealed *in us*" (Rom. 8:18); "For our light affliction, which is but for a moment, worketh for us a far more exceeding and eternal weight of glory" (II Cor. 4:17). The future glory of the saints, then, is not only a *realm* of light and bliss into which they are yet to be conducted, and an *objective* (outward) splendor which will rejoice their hearts, but it is also a glory to be "revealed *in* them," a "weight of glory" *upon* them. "But we all, with open face, beholding as in a glass the glory of the Lord, are *changed into* the same image, from glory to glory, by the Spirit of the Lord" (II Cor. 3:18); the final and perfect degree of this occurring in their resurrection state, at their glorification. All of this is summed up in "When he shall appear, we shall be like him; for we shall see him as he is" (I John 3:2).

There is a most striking and blessed parallel between the last-quoted verse and our opening scripture. The Psalmist said, When I awake," the apostle declares "when He shall appear" — the *same* time-mark or occasion. "I will behold thy face in righteousness" (i.e., none but a righteous person will enjoy this holy privilege): "*we* shall see Him" — the *same* persons, namely, the "sons of God," of whom it is said in the context "every one that doeth *righteousness* is born of him" (I John 2:29)! "I will behold thy face" says David, "We shall see him as he is" says John — the *same* blessed Object. "I shall be satisfied with thy [transforming] likeness. . . . we shall be like him" — the *same* blessed assimilation. What an example of the perfect *unity* of the Scriptures! What a proof that the Old Testament saints were favored with the same light as we are!

Yet notwithstanding the revelation God has vouchsafed us of the life to come, how feebly do we grasp that revelation, how dimly do we comprehend its details; how infinitely it transcends the highest conceptions we can form of it. What we now know of God and His Christ is as nothing to what we shall yet know of Him, yea, in comparison with *that* it scarcely deserves to be called "knowledge": "For now we see through a glass darkly, but then face to face; now I know in part, but then shall I know even as also I am known" (I Cor. 13:12). The fact is that mere language cannot convey to us in our present state any adequate idea of the glory which God has provided for His people. But though a full discovery thereof is reserved till the time of actual possession, yet enough is hinted at to nourish our hopes and gladden our hearts. To make this the more evident unto the reader, let us endeavor to amplify our statement by a presentation of some considerations. We may now form some conception of the Church's future glory.

From the contrast pointed by our present afflictions. That the future bliss of believers is exceedingly great is clear from "For our *light* affliction which is but for a moment, worketh for us a far more exceeding eternal *weight* of glory" (II Cor. 4:17). Now we know that the sufferings of God's people in this world are, considered in themselves, *heavy* afflictions, yea, to some of them, *grievously* heavy. If, then, the trials and sorrows of the most afflicted among the saints are "light" when contrasted with their future happiness, how great must that happiness be! The paucity of human language to express the ineffable joys and pleasures awaiting us at God's right hand, is seen in the piling up of one term upon another: it is a "weight," it is an "exceeding weight," it is a "far more exceeding weight," it is an "eternal weight of glory."

From the reward promised the saints. This is frequently exhibited under the animating figure of the crowns bestowed upon the victors in the Grecian games and upon the military conquerors when they arrived back home in triumph. In those games the great men of the times entered as competitors for the glory of victory, and even kings thought themselves honored by obtaining the prize. The victor was rewarded with a crown of leaves, and was received with unbounded honor by the vast multitudes assembled. Now, after all the self-denials in their training, the unwearied diligence in preparatory exercises, the toils and dangers endured in the arduous struggle, they deemed *this reward* a rich recompense, for it raised them to a pinnacle of glory to be viewed with admiration by all their fellows. Yet, *they* had in view "a corruptible crown," whereas *we* are striving for an "incorruptible" one (I Cor. 9:24, 25). Their crown was the greatest honor this world could bestow, and soon faded and withered. But the Christian's crown shall be bestowed *by God,* and bloom with unfading freshness throughout eternity; and its glory will be viewed by all the principalities of Heaven.

From the scattered hints of Scripture. These are numerous: from them we select two: "And they that be wise shall shine as the brightness of the firmament; and they that turn many to righteousness, as *the stars* for ever and ever" (Dan. 12:3). O ye despised followers of the Lamb, groaning under the reproach of the Cross, lift up your eyes and view this glorious prospect. Behold the heavens studded with their scintillating gems; see those bright orbs darting forth their light; and that is but a faint image of your future glory! "Then shall the righteous shine forth as *the sun* in the kingdom of their Father" (Matt. 13: 43). What object in nature is so glorious as the sun? Who can look on the brightness of his beams? Who can measure the extent and distance of his shining? Such shall be your glory, ye servants of the Lord, who despise the tinsel glory of this world through faith in the Word.

From our relationship to God. We may surely be assisted in estimating the future glory of Christians by the *titles* bestowed upon them from that connection. They are called the children and heirs of God, and it is not possible for the Almighty to invest created beings with a higher honor than that. There is a sense in which both angels and man are, by creation, the sons of God; but it is in a far more intimate and precious sense that believers are called God's *children.* He hath "begotten us again unto a living hope by the resurrection of Jesus Christ from the dead" (I Peter 1:3); "We are all the children of God by faith in Christ Jesus" (Gal. 3:26). We are the children of God, then, as we are *the brethren* of His only begotten Son, and that places us above the highest of the angels. And because we are children, we are the "heirs of God" (Rom. 8:17). O ye tried and troubled saints, who are having such a sore struggle to make ends meet, it shall not always be thus with you. Estimate the inheritance of saints by the riches of God Himself!

From what is said in Ephesians 2:6, 7. "And hath raised us up together, and made us sit together in the heavenlies in Christ Jesus: that in the ages to come He might show the exceeding riches of His grace, in His kindness toward us, through Christ Jesus" — "show" to the heavenly hierarchies. If, then, God intends to make a lavish display of the wealth of His love toward His people, how surpassingly glorious will be such an exhibition! "When the Monarch of the Universe, the God of power and wisdom, declares His purpose of showing how much He loves His people, the utmost stretch of imagination will in vain struggle to form even a slight conception of their glory. All the thrones of Heaven will be filled with wonder, when they behold in their glory 'the men whom their King delights to honour' " (Alex Carson to whom we are also indebted for part of the above).

From the love of Christ for them. Surely that will enable us to form some estimate of the future condition of the saints in glory. Of His immeasurably great love for His people we have the fullest proof in His humiliation and death. Read the history of it, ponder the depths of degradation and ignominy into which the Lord of glory descended, behold Him despised and rejected of men, an outcast from society, and at last a willing sacrifice for His people's sins, and that, even while they were enemies; and then ask yourself, what is *the extent* of His love? It defies description; it is beyond comprehension. Now if He loved us so while enemies, what will He not confer on us as His friends and brethren! Paul taught us to pray that we "might be able to comprehend with all saints what is the breadth and length, and depth and height, and to know the love of Christ which passeth knowledge." If, then, it is a matter of such importance to *know* His love, and if the extent of it is beyond knowledge, what is likely to be the height of glory to which its objects are elevated!

From the reward bestowed on Christ. In John 17:22 we hear Him speak of "the glory which thou hast given me." What is the "glory" which the Father bestows upon the Mediator? It is *the Divine reward* for His stupendous achievements. It is that whereby His infinite merits shall be suitably recompensed throughout eternity. And what a glory that must be: answerable to the dignity of His person, answerable to the revenue of honor and praise which He has brought unto God, commensurate with the unspeakable sacrifice which He made and with the worth of Him that made it! And when *God* gives, He does so in accordance with who He is. O what a "glory," then, must it be with which the Father has rewarded His beloved Son: a transcendant and supernal

glory. And that "glory" Christ shares with His redeemed: "And the glory
which thou gavest me, I have *given them*" (John 17:22). Thus, there is
a *union in glory* between the Church and its Head.

This it is which is the most wondrous and blessed aspect of our many-
sided subject. This it is which is the grand goal which all the other
unions between the Redeemer and the redeemed had in view, namely,
an everlasting union in glory. And this it is which best enables us to conceive of and estimate the marvel, the grandeur, the uniqueness, of this
glory union, namely, that it is the very glory which the Father had given
to the Darling of His bosom, and which Christ will share with those
whom He loved with a love that was stronger than death. "But we
are bound to give thanks always to God for you, brethren beloved of
the Lord, because God hath from the beginning chosen you to salvation
through sanctification of the Spirit and belief of the truth: whereunto
he called you by our gospel, to the obtaining of [not simply "glory,"
but] *the glory of our Lord Jesus Christ*" (II Thess. 2:13, 14) — *that*
was what God had in mind for His people in eternity past: nothing less
would satisfy His heart.

Of old it was revealed "the Lord will give grace and glory" (Ps.
84:11). Here upon earth the saints enjoy Christ in a way of real fellowship, but in Heaven they shall enjoy Him in another and higher manner.
Here Christ communicates Himself to them in a way of *grace,* so that
their present communion with Him and communications from Him are
suited to them as they are sinners in themselves. As thus considered, the
Redeemer in His infinite goodness holds fellowship with His feeble and
constantly-failing people, and as their *Head of grace* He ministers out of
His fulness (John 1:16) every needed supply. But in Heaven He will be
our *Head of Glory,* communicating to us that which will be suited to
our resurrection and sinless state. We shall be as dependent on Him
then for glory, as we now are for grace: *all* will be received *from Him.*
The elect are *"vessels* of mercy" which God hath "afore prepared unto
glory" (Rom. 9:23), and it is out of Christ's fulness they will be *filled,*
so as to be perfectly blessed.

It is to be noted that in John 17:22 Christ employed the past tense:
"the glory which thou gavest me, I *have given* [not "will give"] them."
This may be understood as follows. First, Christ has given the Church
an unimpeachable *title* to the glory which has been bestowed upon
Him. He has acquired the right of this glory for His people: "whither
the forerunner is *for us* entered, even Jesus" (Heb. 6:20): thus it is as
surely ours now as if we were in actual possession of it. Second, He
has given His people the *knowledge* of it: here in John 17:22, and in
such declarations as Colossians 3:4, etc. — "When Christ, who is our
life, shall appear, then shall ye also appear with him in glory." The
promises Christ has given us in His gospel are the root of our future
blessings, and in those promises we have *a lease* to show for it. Third,
He has given us *an earnest* of the same, for by the indwelling Spirit we
have received the "firstfruits" of our inheritance. This it was which enabled the apostle to say I am "a witness of the sufferings of Christ, and

also *a partaker* of the glory that shall be revealed" (I Peter 5:1). Fourth, He gives an actual enjoyment of it to each of the saints as soon as they are absent from the body and present with Himself.

Finally, Christ in this remarkable verse (John 17:22) gives as the reason why He shares with His people the glory which the Father hath bestowed upon Himself: "that they may be one even as we are." Here our thoughts are directed to such a height that our poor minds turn dizzy. The very reading of those words should fill our hearts with holy amazement, as the actualization of them will fill us with admiration to all eternity. The oneness between the Father and the Son is such that They *partake of the same* ineffable blessedness, Each enjoying it equally with and like the Other. And *that* is the pattern and likeness, by way of similitude, of the glory union between the Redeemer and the redeemed! Ours will be like *Theirs!* As the union between the Father and the Son is a real one, a spiritual one, a holy one, an indestructible one, an inexpressibly glorious one, so will be that between Christ and His Church in Heaven.

As we showed in our discussion on Divine union, there is a real union of Persons in the Godhead and a communion among Them, for the mutual converse between the eternal Three are recorded again and again. Now just as the essential happiness of the Three in Jehovah consists in the holy fellowship which they have with each other, so it will be by the Church's heavenly communion with the Father, the Son and the Spirit, in and by the person of the Mediator, that all true blessedness will be enjoyed by us throughout eternity. Even now the saints are admitted unto access to the Father, by the Spirit, through Christ (Eph. 2:18); yet in our glory union with Christ this will be exalted to a far higher degree and we shall be advanced unto much closer and fuller communion with the triune God. "And the glory which thou gavest me I have given them; that they may be one, even as we are one" (John 17:22).

"I in them, and thou in me, that they may be made perfect in one; and that the world may know that thou hast sent me, and hast loved them, as thou hast loved me" (John 17:23). In these words the nature and blessedness of the glory union between Christ and the Church are further opened to us, its blessedness being indicated by the several effects and fruits which flow from the same. Three of these are here noted. First, as that union will affect believers themselves: they are "made perfect in one" Body. Then will all the redeemed "come in the unity of the faith, and of the knowledge of the Son of God, unto a perfect man, unto the measure of the stature of the fulness of Christ" (Eph. 4:13). All differences of opinion, all animosities, all jealousies, shall have vanished forever, and there shall be perfect oneness between them in knowledge, love, and holiness. Second, as this union affects the Church, in connection with the triune God. Being united to Christ, the elect are necessarily united to and interested in all the Persons in Jehovah and as they now have a *grace union* with Them, they shall yet have a *glory union* with Them, which will issue in a communion that will constitute the fulness of their blessedness for ever and ever.

Third, as it affects "the world of the ungodly." Those who have no part or lot in this glory union shall, nevertheless, be given a glimpse of the same, as Dives (for the augmenting of his torment) was permitted to see "Abraham afar off, and Lazarus in his bosom" (Luke 16:23). The sight of Christ's "Queen," standing at His right hand (Ps. 45:9 and cf. Matt. 25:34) "in gold of Ophir" — figure of his glory — will be self-convicting to the reprobate that Christ is what He declared Himself to be; and as they behold the honor which God has put upon the Church, it will openly appear that He has loved them as He loved their Head. And for having despised and rejected Christ, and reproached and persecuted His people, they will be filled with confusion and everlasting shame (Dan. 12:3). But the Church shall be filled with joy unspeakable and have everlasting proof of the wondrous love of God for them.

II

Nowhere in Scripture do we have such a clear and blessed revelation of the Church's future bliss as the Lord Jesus favored us with in John 17. "Father, I will that they also, whom thou hast given me, be with me where I am: that they may behold my glory, which thou hast given me: for thou lovedst me before the foundation of the world" (v. 24). Every word in this verse calls for separate meditation. Once more the Redeemer says, "Father," for He is suing for a child's portion for each of His people: it is not simply wages, such as a servant receives from his master, but an inheritance, such as children receive from their parents — the inheritance being the Father's house, where the Son now is. He had said "Father" when asking for His own glorification (v. 5), and He does so again in connection with the glorification of His saints: addressing God thus, intimated the loving intensity of the Mediator's intercession.

Christ's "I will" here at once arrests our notice — the only record we have of His ever addressing the Father thus, yet it was in as perfect keeping now as His "not my will" in Gethsemane. First, this "I will" was a note of *authority* which became Him who is God and man in one person, to whom had been committed "power over all flesh" (John 17:2). Moreover, He had a perfect knowledge of the Father's will, and as the Surety of His people, Christ was here suing for the fulfilment of that covenant agreement which had been entered into before He embarked upon His great undertaking. Second, it was *a testamentary disposition*: Christ was about to die and therefore said "I will." "When Christ made His will, Heaven is one of the legacies which He bequeathed to us" (T. Manton). The same thought is found again in "I appoint unto you a kingdom, as my Father hath appointed unto me" (Luke 22:29). Third, it also reveals His deep earnestness and full purpose of heart, as the "Master, we *would* that thou shouldest do for us whatsoever we shall desire" (Mark 10:35).

"That they also, whom thou hast given me, be with me where I am."

Nothing gives a lover such a joy and satisfaction as to be in the immediate presence of his beloved. Heaven will not be Heaven to Christ until His glorified Bride is there by His side: then only will He "see of the travail of his soul and *be satisfied*" (Isa. 53:10). Nothing will content the heart of the Head but that His Church should be brought unto the possession of the utmost blessedness, to be continued unto and enjoyed by them forever and ever. It was so that His people might have a clear and comforting knowledge of this that He gave them that exceeding great and precious promise "I go to prepare a place for you: and if I go and prepare a place for you I, will come again, and receive you unto myself; that where I am, there ye may be also" (John 14:2, 3). How this reveals the heart-attitude of Christ unto us!

✓ "Father, I will that they also, whom thou hast given me, be with me where I am." That is in sharp and solemn contrast from "where I am, thither ye cannot come" (John 7:34), spoken to the unbelieving Jews. The wicked have no title, no fitness, no heart to be where Christ is: Paradise is still closed against them by the flaming sword (Gen. 3:24). But it will be the consummation of the believer's happiness to be where Christ is: as the Psalmist declared, "*In thy presence* is fulness of joy, at thy right hand there are pleasures for evermore" (16:11). How utterly different is the attitude of Christ toward His own from that of many of this world, who, when they enter suddenly into earthly riches and honors, quickly forget the fellows and friends of former days. Not so the Lord Jesus: His heavenly glory does not cause *His* love to decay in the least degree or take His mind off His people. They are inexpressibly precious to Him, and He cannot be content unless they are with Him.

It is as though Christ said to the Father, As given to Me by Thee, the elect are My "portion" (Deut. 32:9), My "special treasure" (Mal. 3:17, margin), My "royal diadem" (Isa. 62:3), My "joy" (Zeph. 3: 17): and as their Head and Mediator I express My will, and it is that they shall be raised to the highest pinnacle that it is possible to elevate creatures, that they may be where I am, and that, not in some distant compartment of Thy house, but in My immediate presence, so that they may behold My glory — feasting their eyes and feeding their hearts upon Myself. Surely nothing can convey to our minds, under the teaching of the Holy Spirit, a clearer view of the heart of Christ toward His beloved. O that the blessed Comforter may so shine upon these words of Christ's, and thereby let in such light into our understandings, as may lift our hearts unto a clearer comprehension and greater admiration of His love than we have ever had before.

✓ "That they may behold my glory." This beholding is, first *ocular*. The bodily senses have their happiness as well as the faculties of our souls, and this will be realized in a far nobler and purer degree hereafter. Job affirmed thus when He said, "Though after my skin worms destroy this body, yet in my flesh shall I see God: whom I shall see for myself, and mine eyes shall behold" (19:26, 27) — "see God" in the person of the God-man Mediator. The saints shall then behold the Person who redeemed them, and that nature in which He suffered so much for them. The outward man will be regaled, as truly as the inner. There is a glory to charm our eyes in Heaven: not only the beautiful mansions and the glorious inhabitants, but above all, *the face of the Lamb.* As it is now said of Christ Himself, so shall it yet be the experience of each of His people: "For thou hast made him most blessed forever: thou hast made him exceeding glad with thy countenance" (Ps. 21:6).

This beholding is, secondly, and supremely, *mental and spiritual.* The mind is the noblest faculty, for man is a rational creature, and there is as great an inclination to knowledge in his soul as there is in beasts to carnal pleasures. The drunkard may talk of his delight and the voluptuary of the gratification of sense, but the true delight of the soul is *knowledge,* and therefore it must be satisfied in Heaven, or else we would not be happy. "The pure in heart shall see God" (Matt. 5:8), yet not with the bodily eye, for He who is "spirit" (John 4:24) cannot be viewed by the bodily senses, and therefore is He called "the invisible God" (Col. 1:15). But God has given man, in preference to the beasts, a mind which is capable of knowing Himself, and in our glorified state our knowledge of Him will be immeasurably increased, so that the soul shall be perfectly satisfied with its mental and spiritual sight of Him.

What an affecting sight it will be to behold the glory of Christ! How it will ravish the heart! Abraham was favored with an anticipatory glimpse of it and "was glad" (John 8:56). If old Simeon was contented with a view of Christ as an infant — "Lord, *now* lettest thou thy servant depart in peace, according to thy word: *for* mine eyes have seen thy salvation" (Luke 2:29, 30) — what will be the effect on us when we stand before His very throne! Even now it fills the soul with joy unspeakable when faith and spiritual illumination beholds Him in the Word and through His ordinances, but words cannot express what it will be to behold the Lord in open vision. To behold the King in His beauty, to see the Lamb "as it had been slain" (Rev. 5:6) — still bearing in His body the marks of the cross — will fill us with thanksgiving and praise.

But this glory which the saints are to behold is also a *Divine* one: it will be the luster of the Divine perfections which will be revealed to us through and by Christ, every attribute of God supplying a part, all combining to make up this supreme spiritual splendor. Then will God's unsearchable *wisdom* be more completely opened to us, for in Christ "are hid all the treasures of wisdom and knowledge" (Col. 2:3). Then will God's illimitable *power* be more fully discovered to us: that power which created a universe out of nothing, that preserved His little flock in the midst of a world of wolves, that will make a footstool of all His enemies. Then will God's *holiness* be known in all its loveliness, and joyfully shall we then unite with the angels in crying "holy, holy, holy, Lord God of hosts." Then will God's *love* be seen without a veil: His smile shall never again be checked with a frown, nor the light of His countenance be obscured by any intervening cloud of sin.

Not till the glorified Church reaches Heaven will its union with God in Christ be complete. Union implies more than *relation*: it imports actual *presence*; not physical or local, but spiritual and cordial, by which the sinless soul, with will and affections guided by restored reason and judgment, close with and embrace Him; and He in fulfilment of the eternal counsels, and with infinite love and delight, embraces her. When the soul is perfectly formed according to God's own heart and fully participates the Divine likeness so as to be perfectly like Him, it is fitted for the most intimate communion which is possible between two such natures — the Divine and human. Nor can pen depict the holy bliss of glorified saints from such a love-union, now perfected between the blessed God and them. The likeness of God upon a creature will cause the eternal One to cleave in love to it, and the beholding of His glory by eyes from which the film of sin has been completely removed will make the soul embrace Him as its ravishing portion.

From that love-union in glory will issue everlasting *communion*. "There is nothing there to hinder God and the holy soul of the most inward fruitions and enjoyments; no animosity, no strangeness, no unsuitableness on either part. Here the glorified spirits of the just have liberty to solace themselves amid the rivers of pleasure at God's own right hand, without check or restraint. *They* are pure, and *these* pure. They touch nothing that can defile, they defile nothing they can touch. They are not now forbidden the nearest approaches to the once inaccessible Majesty; there is no holy of holies into which they may not enter, no door locked against them. They may have free admission into the innermost secret of the Divine presence, and pour forth themselves in the most liberal effusions of love and joy; as they must be the eternal subjects of those infinitely richer communications from God, even of immense and boundless love and goodness" (J. Howe, "The Blessedness of the Righteous," 1668).

"Father, I will that they also, whom thou hast given me, be with me where I am; that they may behold my glory, which thou hast given me: for thou lovedst me before the foundation of the world" (John 17:24). In the last clause Christ tells the Father *why* He wills that His elect should be with Him and behold His glory. As the God-man, the Man taken into personal union by the Son, and as such the "fellow" (Zech. 13:7) of Jehovah, He was, from all eternity, the Object of the Father's ineffable love. He was conceived in the Divine mind before all worlds, being the "Firstborn" of all God's thoughts, counsels, designs toward all beings, visible and invisible. Christ, as God-man, was the Center and Circumference as it respected all God's vast designs in grace, nature and providence. Christ's person is infinitely precious in God's sight, and therefore has He placed the highest honor of all upon Him as being the Medium through which the invisible God shall shine forth for all eternity, for *thereby* the Church will perceive *how much* the Father loves Christ and that it is the overflowings of the same which falls on them.

"I will, therefore, that they may behold My personal glory, which Thou has given Me, that from that sight they may have the most enlarged views their minds are capable of, concerning Thy love to Me, and to them in Me, as this will be a perfecting them in the full enjoyment of Thine everlasting love. Thou hast possessed *My* mind with it from everlasting; Thou hast taken *Me* up into the mount of personal union and communion with Thee. I have shone forth before Thee in all My personal glory. I have been in Thy bosom, and been admitted into a full knowledge and enjoyment of all the love of Thine heart. Thou lovedst Me from everlasting, and My whole person, God-man, is the Object of Thine everlasting love. Thou lovedst Me as the Son of God, and as the Son of Man; Thou lovedst Me before the foundation of the world as the Head of the whole election of grace. Thou lovedst Me as Mediator. I am in every sense the Object of Thy love. I would open Thy whole heart to these, Thine, and My beloved ones. I would express it unto them most freely. I would speak out in their hearing the secrets which have passed from everlasting between Thee and Me, that *they may have* the clearest evidence I can give them of it" (S. E. Pierce).

The Lord Christ will shine forth in His personal glory in the view of His saints, and it will be so beheld by them as to be reflected upon them. Our glory in Heaven will not be independent of Christ, nor will it be inherent in ourselves: our everlasting bliss will be received out of the fulness of the Lord of glory. Just as the glory of the sun is subjective in itself, but objective upon others, so it will be in Heaven: we shall be bathed in the effulgence of Him who is Light. We shall be favored with such views of Christ, as God-man, as will forever preclude any possibility of sinning, for our souls will be satiated with *His* perfections, filled with unutterable admiration and adoration. We shall be so completely swallowed up with Christ that we shall no longer have any thought about *ourselves! This it is* which constitutes the very essence of heavenly blessedness: we shall be so thoroughly absorbed with the loveliness of the Lamb as to forever lose sight of, forget, ourselves! The Church will so center as their Portion and Inheritance that communion with Him, through His Christ, will be the fountain of their life for evermore.

Our thoughts have carried us along so swiftly that we must now go back and consider the several steps in the believer's history which is to terminate in this blessed consummation. The first step or stage occurs at *regeneration,* when he is made meet for the inheritance of the saints in light, for it is then there is wrought in him a principle (or "nature") which capacitates his (hitherto depraved) soul to visualize and relish spiritual things. A beggar might gaze upon the glory of a king, and yet be no gainer; but when a regenerated soul looks in faith unto the crucified and risen Saviour he is "saved" thereby (Isa. 45:22). The second step or stage in the soul's journey unto the beatific vision occurs in its practical *sanctification,* which is a gradual process and progressive experience, under which, beholding in the glass of the Law and the gospel the glory of the Lord, he is changed into "the same image" by the Spirit (II Cor. 3:18).

Third, it is *at death* the believer approaches much nearer the goal so longed for by his soul, for then he not only leaves this world behind, but he is forever done with sin — he leaves *it* behind too. Welcome release! How that should reconcile him to the putting off of the body! Passing strange is it from the *spiritual* side of things — though not so from the natural — that the great majority of Christians are as reluctant to leave this world as are the godless, and view with such trepidation the valley of the shadows. Not only is there nothing whatever to be feared in death to the saints — for Christ has extracted its sting — but there is much in it and its attendants that should make it welcome. Sin — that plague of the renewed heart, that monster which is the cause of all our spiritual grief, that vile thing which is ever marring and interrupting our communion with God — will be done with forever. And being done with sin, there will be *an end* to all physical sufferings and mental sorrows. The entail of the first Adam will be finally severed. But this — grand as it is — is but the negative side; consider the positive.

As soon as the Lord is pleased to dismiss any of His saints from the body by death, they are *immediately admitted into Heaven,* and there they behold His glory. Christ's glory is great in the estimation of His people: they have a spiritual perception of it now, but they will have a much greater and grander view of it when removed from this vale of tears, when they are "absent from the body, present with the Lord" (II Cor. 5:8). Therefore was it that the apostle exclaimed, "Having a desire to depart, and to be with Christ; which is *far better*" (Phil. 1:23). Heaven is the habitation of all saints upon their departure from this world, and then they shall enjoy a fellowship with God through Christ which greatly exceeds any they are capable of now. At best our present communion with Christ is but feeble and fitful; but it will not be so always: in the intermediate state the redeemed are with Christ and receive wondrous revelations" (II Cor. 12:7) from Him.

"Blessed are the dead which die in the Lord from henceforth" (Rev. 14:13): not "shall be," but "blessed *are*" they — a Divine declaration which gives the lie to that Christ-dishonoring idea which supposes that at death the souls of believers, in common with unbelievers, pass into a state of oblivion. Yes, "blessed" beyond words are they who die in the Lord, for not only do they leave all sin behind forever, but they are "with Christ in Paradise" (Luke 23:43). True, that blessedness falls short of the final state, nevertheless, in various respects it approximates thereto. There is much in common for believers between death and resurrection, and after the resurrection, though the latter excells the former. Both are termed a "crown" (Rev. 2:10 — immediately after death; II Tim. 4:8 — at the latter day), both are a being "present with the Lord" (II Cor. 5:8; I Thess. 4:17). Both are termed a "sight of Christ" (II Cor. 5:6, 7) — while in the body we walk by faith, but when absent from the body and present with the Lord, walking by sight is necessarily implied (I John 3:2).

Yet great and grand as is the blessedness of the dead in Christ, that which they will enjoy in the resurrection and eternal state shall far surpass it. To the question "How are the dead raised up? and with what body do they come?" the inspired answer is returned, "Thou fool, that which thou sowest is not quickened, except it die; and that which thou sowest, thou sowest not that body that shall be, but bare grain, it may chance of wheat, or of some other grain. . . . So also is the resurrection of the dead. It is sown in corruption, it is raised in incorruption; it is sown in dishonor, it is raised in glory; it is sown in weakness, it is raised in power; it is sown a natural body, it is raised a spiritual body" (I Cor. 15:34-37, 42-44). What a difference are we here taught to expect between the present and the future state of our bodies. From one view, the body that rises is the same that died — personal identity is preserved; but from another view, it is radically changed.

More than a hint of that marvellous change of the believer's body is found in the record of Christ's transfiguration, when "His face did shine as the sun, and His raiment was white as the light" (Matt. 17:2), and when after His own resurrection He passed through closed doors (John 20:19); for it is written that He "shall change our vile body, that it may be fashioned like unto his glorious body, according to the working whereby he is able even to subdue all things unto himself" (Phil. 3:21). And if such a great and grand change is awaiting the believer's body in the resurrection state, who can conceive the change *of the soul* when it is "glorified?" Who is so bold as to define the limits of the soul's capacities and capabilities when freed from the burden of sin and made like Christ (I John 3:2)? Who can estimate the excellency of a glorified soul's operations in connection with Divine things?

III

We now make some reflections constituting a "practical application" of the subject and add a few remarks about the future bliss of the righteous. Our desire is not only to enlighten the mind, but to affect the heart, so that our lives may be more fruitful to the praise of the glory of Divine grace. God has indeed been good in revealing so much concerning that everlasting bliss which awaits His people on High, yet the practical value of such knowledge to us is to be determined by *the effects* which it produces in our daily walk. Those who are going to behold the King in His beauty will surely strive after a closer conformity to His image in this life, and then, conscious of their deplorable lack of such conformity, will not only be filled with grief, but be kept humble in the dust before Him.

First, *a radical change of heart* is indispensable before any depraved member of Adam's fallen race can participate in the inheritance of the saints in light. Moreover, that change must take place before death, for at death each individual goes to "his *own* place" (Acts 1:25) — Heaven or Hell, for which either holiness or sin fits him. Nor does glorification (unlike regeneration) effect any radical change: instead, it is the *perfecting* of what has previously been wrought in a person, No one enters Heaven unless Heaven has first entered him. No one goes to be with Christ unless Christ has first dwelt in his heart. How could those who never had any spiritual love for Him find joy and satisfaction from spending an eternity in His immediate presence? If we have no relish for spiritual things in this life, if our hearts perceive not the supreme "beauty of holiness," then we would be completely out of our element in the dwellingplace of the Holy One, and where none but holy persons are found. Therefore "without holiness no man shall see the Lord."

The natural man has a settled aversion from God. The unregenerate are "alienated from the life of God through the ignorance that is in them, because of the blindness of their heart" (Eph. 4:18), and therefore do they deliberately choose a life that is "*without God* in the world" (Eph. 2:12). True, many of them (like millions of the heathen) assume a religious garb at certain seasons and engage in a round of religious exercises, yet both in heart and practice they are "lovers of pleasure more than lovers of God" (II Tim. 3:4). Press upon such the claims of Christ, tell them He requires the throne of their hearts, seek to set before them the blessedness of a life of obedience to Him and the sweetness of communion with Him, and they will regard you as a fanatic and killjoy. At how great a moral distance, then, are all such souls from heavenly blessedness: either it must be changed to match their corruptions, or their hearts must be changed to suit its purity.

Reader, has *your* heart been so changed that fellowship with Christ is your chiefest delight? O the deceitfulness of the human heart! O the powerful infatuation of self-love! O the fatal delusions of Satan, that so many yet "in the gall of bitterness and the bond of iniquity" should suppose that God can be imposed upon by lip-service or by the labor of the hands. Alas, what multitudes imagine that a few drops of water sprinkled upon them during infancy secures an entrance into Heaven. What multitudes suppose that "joining a church" and financially supporting the minister is sufficient to ensure everlasting bliss. And what countless other thousands persuade themselves that a head knowledge and mouth profession of the Truth is all that is needed. Ah, my reader, thou canst not impose upon God, and never shall you enter *His* kingdom unless thou be born again. Then let each of us seriously and solemnly examine himself.

Second, the soul in which that great change is wrought *eagerly pursues Heaven's blessedness* until it be attained. Perfect conformity to Christ, unbroken communion with Him, is now its supreme desire and quest: let a soul be regenerated and nothing short of this can satisfy it. The deepest longing of a renewed heart is "Lord, lift thou up the light of *thy* countenance upon me" (Ps. 4:6). The giddy crave worldly pleasures, the miser his gold, the ambitious earthly honors, but Christian experience is summed up in, "One thing have I *desired* of the Lord, that will I *seek after;* that I may dwell in the house of the Lord all the days of my life, to behold the beauty of the Lord, and to enquire in his temple" (Ps. 27:4). That which is to afford him *eternal* joy and satisfaction is the object of the believer's *present* desire and delight: a visit from Christ, a smile from Him, a sip of His love, is what he is constantly asking for.

"As for me, I will behold thy face in righteousness: I shall be satisfied, when I awake, with thy likeness" (Ps. 17:15), which is the same as saying, I cannot be satisfied otherwise. But what does that word "satisfied" imply? Hunger is satisfied with food, thirst with water: that which was previously craved is now obtained, and *contentment* follows. Thus, satisfaction of soul necessarily implies *a previous longing* of soul after that which alone can satisfy, a working of earnest desire, a tireless seeking after that which continues to so largely elude us in this life. "With my soul have I *desired* thee in the night; yea, with my spirit within me will I *seek* thee early" (Isa. 26:9) — yes, "seek" after a conscious access to the Lord and a sight of His face, as earnestly, as diligently, as persistently, as the worldling does after carnal things. "Not as though I had already attained, either were already perfect: but *I follow after*, if that I may apprehend (lay hold of) that for which also I am apprehended of Christ Jesus" (Phil. 3:12). That word "attained" has a very small place in the theology of some who are lop-sided on "grace." Yet the apostle hesitated not to use it, realizing that his spiritual longings called for a "following after" on his part.

Here, then, is another point at which we need to test ourselves. It is a contradiction in terms to speak of a soul being "satisfied" in the future if it had no *previous yearning*. In this life there is a restless longing and working of soul: in the life to come the goal is reached and rest (satisfaction) is attained. Thus, if I be seriously minded, if I am concerned about the hereafter, how it behoves me to ascertain whether there be within me a supreme desire, a spiritual appetite, a soul craving which this poor world cannot satisfy, and which stirs me up to seek after Christ now. Or does the language of the Spouse in the Song of Solomon, wherein she expresses her joy and bliss at the brief visits of her Beloved, and her loss and anguish at His departure, strike you as wild enthusiasm? If so, be sure that your heart has not within it that principle which finds its fruition in Heaven. We may ascertain our state by *the objects of our desires*. Make no mistake: that can never be your eternal blessedness for which now you have no relish. Christ will not receive into His presence those to whom it would be a burden.

Third, the knowledge of God and conformity to His image are in their very nature *satisfying* to a renewed soul, and even now *actually do so* in the measure in which they are attained by us. Mere *things* cannot satisfy, for they perish with the using of them. He who hopes to find satisfaction by multiplying his carnal pleasures, or by heaping together material things, is on as vain a quest as if he sought to make a sum by adding together naught but cyphers. But that which shall one day fully satisfy, has in itself an aptness and power to satisfy even now. Happy the soul which has been let into the secret of *where* real satisfaction is to be found, and knows whither to turn his eyes and direct his efforts in the pursuit thereof. Thrice happy those who can say, Give me an experimental, living, efficacious sight of God, and I have enough: "show us the Father, and it *sufficeth* us" (John 14:8).

Let the weary wandering soul turn unto *God*: He will not mock thee with shadows as the world does. "This is life eternal, that they might know Thee the only true God, and Jesus Christ, whom Thou hast sent" (John 17:3). Apart from Christ we cannot know God nor view Him with comfort; but the gospel gives a lovely prospect of Him: the glory of God shines "in the face of Jesus Christ" (II Cor. 4:6), and the more faith beholds Him there, the more does the soul move toward satisfaction. "Godliness with contentment is great gain" (I Tim. 6:6). A vital knowledge of God tends to holiness, and holiness to contentment. Nothing is more analogous to Heaven than the peace and serenity which issues from the believer's present enjoyment of God. He does not wholly conceal Himself from the saints, but favors them with an occasional glimpse of His smiling face, and the degree in which He vouchsafes this blessing brings Heaven into the soul: "They looked unto him, and were lightened" (Ps. 34:5).

Fourth, but inasmuch as the soul's complete blessedness lies in the future, then his happiness in the meantime must largely consist *in hope*. It is the Divine promise that one day there shall be nothing to mar his fellowship with Christ that now supports the saint. It is the assurance that ere long his hunger and thirst after righteousness shall be filled" (Matt. 5:6), and that "no groans shall mingle with the songs that warble from immortal tongues," which comforts the oft cast-down soul. "If we *hope* for that we see not, then do we with patience wait for it" (Rom. 8:25). Yes, it is the exercise of hope which encourages the weary pilgrim to continue plodding on, which nerves the Christian soldier *not* to give up the good fight of faith. It was hope which moved the soul to first seek unto God for mercy, and hope will make its possessor *continue seeking* unto Him till every longing receives its fruition.

Here is yet another point by which to test ourselves. Are our expectations of satisfaction centered in present or future things? They who have received the "firstfruits of the Spirit" cannot but earnestly groan after the harvest itself: "waiting for the adoption, the redemption of our body" (Rom. 8:23). Have you, my reader, been the happy recipient of a bunch of "the grapes of Eschol?" If so, nothing that grows in this wilderness satisfies your palate, and your face will be eagerly turned to that fair Land of Promise of which that "bunch" was but the earnest. If you really have a "good hope through grace" (II Thess. 2:16) then you will, in some measure at least, live upon things future and unseen. "They that are after the flesh do mind the things of the flesh; but they that are after the Spirit, the things of the Spirit" (Rom. 8:5).

Fifth, if we honestly perceive any disposition of soul toward the holy glory of Heaven, any principle within which causes us to pant after God as the hunted hart does after the waterbrooks, then how diligently and zealously should we *seek after the strengthening* and developing of the same, and endeavor to bring our hearts into that temper suited thereto. If we are painfully conscious of how far short we fall of being conformed to the image of Christ, then we should stir up our souls to make more serious efforts after the same. If we are to spend an eternity in His presence, how we should strive after a growing knowledge of God, how we should seek to please and honor Him in all things. Then let us "follow on to know the Lord" (Hos. 6:3), let us spend more time in the "secret place of the Most High," let us make future things the subject of our meditation. (For much in the above paragraphs we are indebted to J. Howe.)

Is it not worth some pains to attain unto the blessedness of Heaven? If athletes undergo such discipline and self-denial in order to obtain a corruptible crown, shall *we* murmur because the turning of our backs upon the world and the mortifying of the flesh are required of us if we are to attain unto an incorruptible crown? Christians are not called to lie upon flowery beds of ease, but to strive against sin, to pluck out right eyes and cut off right hands, to make the cultivation of personal holiness the great business of their present lives. Christ has left his people an example, that they should follow His steps, and His path is not a smooth one, nor did He please Himself. Christ had to "endure the cross" before He was rewarded by the heavenly bliss into which He has entered (Phil 2:8, 9), and unless we take up our cross (that is, live a life of self-sacrifice) Heaven will not be our portion and reward. "To him *that overcometh* will I grant to sit with me in my throne, even as I also overcame, and am set down with my Father in his throne" (Rev. 3:21): *that* is the plainly revealed condition of celestial blessedness.

Once more we say, Can any present sacrifice be too great in view of the future joy? Consider again what the blessedness of the righteous shall consist of: it will be a complete freedom from all that is evil, and the eternal enjoyment of all that is good. When the full number of God's elect have been openly called by the Spirit and vitally united to Shiloh, their living Head, then will take place the solemnization of the nuptials between the heavenly Bridegroom and His Bride. "The king's daughter is all glorious within: her clothing is of wrought gold. She shall be brought unto the king in raiment of needlework" (Ps. 45:13, 14), which was a prophetic statement that receives its fulfillment of the resurrection morning. At that time all her spots and blemishes will be eternally obliterated, and she will shine forth immutably holy, consummately righteous, inestimably pure; thus will she be a suitable Consort for her glorious Husband, being fully conformed to His image.

Then it is that Christ shall "present it to himself a glorious church, not having spot, or wrinkle, or any such thing; but that it should be holy and without blemish" (Eph. 5:27). This is the ultimate end of our redemption by Christ, the perfecting of our sanctification in the life to come. As Mary was espoused to Joseph, before they came together (Matt. 1:18), so the Church is contracted to Christ now, but the marriage is hereafter (Rev. 19:7). He will then take us Home to live with Himself and abide always in His immediate presence. "Thou art all fair, my love; there is no spot in thee" (Song of Sol. 4:7) will be His greeting; "My beloved is white and ruddy, the chiefest among ten thousand" (5:10) will be her response. This presentation of the Church to Himself is Christ's recompense for His sufferings: it is then that "He shall see of the travail of his soul and be satisfied."

It is to be duly noted that the Church's glory in Heaven is the fruit of Christ's death. It is not merited by us but was purchased by Him. "Christ also loved the church and gave himself for it [i.e., in a sacrificial death] that he might sanctify it . . . that he might present it to himself a glorious church" (Eph. 5:25-27). So again, "That by means of death, for the redemption of the transgressions that were under the first testament, they which are called might receive the promise of eternal inheritance" (Heb. 9:15). The following distinctions may help. The electing grace of the Father is the original cause of our glorification. The atonement of Christ is the meritorious cause. Quickening by the Spirit is the efficacious cause. Personal holiness is what *fits* us, for it is the condition without which we cannot obtain eternal bliss (Heb. 12: 14).

In Heaven our communion with Christ will reach its highest perfection, without any possibility of cessation or interruption. Heavenly communion will be our participation with Christ in all the benefits which flow from our union with Him. The glorified Head of the Church will share with His members the high honors which God has conferred upon Him. "The God of peace shall bruise Satan under your feet shortly" (Rom. 16:20): yes, the saints will yet be brought to participate with Christ in His complete triumph over Satan. "Know ye not that we shall judge angels?" (I Cor. 6:3). Communion is *mutual enjoyment,* and Christ will not be satisfied till His blood-bought people be in the same condition as Himself: "That ye may eat and drink *at my table* in my kingdom" (Luke 22:30); yea, "To him that overcometh will I grant to *sit with me* in my throne" (Rev. 3:21). Then it is that He shall say, "Enter thou into the joy of thy Lord" (Matt. 25:21) — an unalloyed and holy joy, a perfect and satisfying one.

The God-man is Lord of angels (Col. 1:16; Heb. 1:4), and since His saints are joint-heirs with Christ, they must *share with Him* in His dominion over the celestial hosts. This is a bold statement, yet it is fully warranted by the teaching of Holy Writ; nor let it appear absurd, though it be so wonderful: if the Son of God condescended to take human nature upon Him, is it incredible that He should raise it to the highest creature dignity? Mark carefully the discrimination of language in the following passage, "And I beheld, and, lo, in the midst of the throne and of the four living creatures, and *in the midst of* the elders, stood a Lamb as it had been slain . . . And I beheld, and I heard the voice of many angels *round about* the throne and the living creatures, and the elders" (Rev. 5:6, 11). The redeemed are *nearer* the Lamb and more intimately connected with Him than the others, for the angels are only in the outer circle.

Above all, we shall be eye-witnesses of the glory which belongs to Christ personally. "And they shall see his face; and his name shall be in their foreheads" (Rev. 22:4). Christ's glory will be beheld by us then to an extent we cannot now conceive: every faculty of soul and body will be refined to the highest degree, suited to the heavenly state, which will immeasurably increase our enjoyment of the beatific vision. The better the sight, the lovelier the object appears; the healthier the appetite, the more delicious the food tastes; the more musical the ear, the pleasanter the melody. So, the holier the soul, the more joyous Heaven's joys and the more glorious its glories. If the queen of Sheba had cause to say of Solomon's glory, "Happy are thy men, happy are these thy servants, which stand continually before thee, and that hear thy wisdom" (I Kings 10:8), then those who shall sit in the immediate presence of the infinitely greater than Solomon will be *superlatively happy*.

In Heaven the Christian will have a constant and satisfying sight of the God-Man, who, as such is "the Lord of glory." In Him the Incomprehensible Three will shine forth in the uttermost display of Their manifestative glory before all the angels and saints. It is *that* which is the blessedness of Heaven, and which each saint shall forever behold, filling them with conceptions of glory as they can never express. The wicked will see Christ in the Day of Judgment, but they will not have an intuitive and supernatural sight of Him. In blessed contrast, it is by a *spiritual* faculty and light that the saints will see Him: it is so now, as He is revealed in the glass of the Word. That spiritual faculty, elevated by the Holy Spirit, will so raise up the mind as to take in larger and larger views of Christ, swallowing up every thought in the contemplation and adoration of the same.

Our life in Heaven will consist in an ever-expanding vision of Christ's manifold glory, so that we shall be eternally admiring, rejoicing in it, having communion with Him over it, giving Him praise for it. The heart will be wholly absorbed in its apprehensions of all "the treasures of wisdom and knowledge" which are now "hid" in Christ (Col. 2:3). We shall be completely lost to everything *but Him!* There will be such an "exceeding and eternal weight of glory" (II Cor. 4:17) on our minds, poising them, as to preclude every wandering thought from Him. The heart will be eternally fixed on Christ as its center. Thus there can be no possibility of sin ever again gaining entrance to our souls. Then will be completely realized that Divine promise, "They shall be *abundantly satisfied* with the fatness of thy house; and thou shalt make them drink of the river of thy pleasures. For with thee is the fountain of life: in thy light shall we see light" (Ps. 36:8, 9).

11

Conclusion

WE have now completed the gamut of our subject. Starting with the *Divine* union that exists between the three Persons in the Godhead, which issues in a perfect communion between Them, we endeavored to show how that made possible the *Mediatorial* union, namely, by the second Person taking into conjunction with Himself the Man Christ Jesus. That is a profound mystery, yet it is food for faith so far as it is revealed in Holy Writ. Then we saw how that the Divine counsels respecting the Mediatorial union laid a foundation for the Church's oneness with Christ. Tracing out the connection between the Church and its Head we have seen that it originated in a *mystical* union before the foundation of the world, when the eternal love of the Triune God chose its members in Christ, and gave it a covenant standing and super-creation subsistence, so that we read of the "grace which *was given us* in Christ Jesus before the world began" (II Tim. 1:9). Thus from all eternity the Church stood in Christ as His mystical Body and Bride.

Now what has just been said above has reference to God's eternal *decree* concerning the same. Descending, then, to the actual *outworking* of that decree, we have seen that the Divine purpose was realized by two things: the Son uniting Himself to us, we being joined to Him by the Spirit. First; in order for the Son to enter this world as the Representative and Surety of His people, it was necessary for Him to become flesh, and by so doing a *federal* union was established, Christ thereby assuming and discharging all the legal obligations of His people: "both He that sanctifieth and they which are sanctified are *all of one*" (Heb. 2:11). This federal union laid the foundation for the sins of His people to be imputed to Christ, and His righteousness to them. Second, the Holy Spirit effects the *vital* union, each of God's elect being livingly "joined to the Lord" so that they become "one spirit," this being essential if they are to partake of the benefits which Christ purchased for them. The same Spirit which indwells Christ in His fulness, now takes up His abode within them.

It is at regeneration the Spirit accomplishes our vital union with Christ, making us living branches of the true Vine; and it is this which makes possible a *saving union* with Him. We are not "saved" until we personally "*believe on* the Lord Jesus Christ; but as saving faith is a spiritual act, one who is spiritually dead cannot perform it. The Spirit supernaturally quickens the soul in order to capacitate it unto a saving faith in Christ. It is the Spirit's quickening of us into newness of life which lays the foundation for feeling our deep need of Christ and casting ourselves upon Him. Until a man be born again he cannot see either his desperate condition or where the remedy is to be found. God must begin "a good work in" the soul (Phil. 1:6) before he will have any heart for Christ. Until we are brought from death unto life the gospel falls upon deaf ears. When the Saviour is embraced by faith all our sins are blotted out, and Christ is "made unto us wisdom, and righteousness, and sanctification, and redemption" (I Cor. 1:30).

At this stage a difficulty presents itself. A vital union with Christ has been effected by the Spirit's quickening operation and a saving union with Christ by our exercise of faith. But the favored one is left in this world, and a sinful nature indwells him: how, then, is *communion* to be maintained between him and a holy Christ? For that, there must be a *practical* union, for "Can two walk together, except they be agreed?" (Amos 3:3). That "agreement" is accomplished just so far as our wills are brought into subjection to Christ's, just so far as we yield to His Lordship or authority over us. "Take my yoke upon you" (Matt. 11:29) is His call to us, and a "yoke" is what *unites together* in a practical way. There can be no communion with Christ outside the path of obedience, and the obedience He requires is that which flows from love and gratitude.

Now there are two chief means Divinely appointed for the *maintenance* of our practical union with Christ, namely, His precepts and His promises. In the one we learn His will, in the other we see His heart: in the one are directions concerning our duty, in the other is comfort and cheer. Whatever be our circumstances, there are precepts to counsel us, and promises to sustain. Yet let it be pointed out that no matter how plainly our duties are set forth in the Scriptures, nor how well-suited the promises be to our varied cases in this world, and no matter how diligently we apply ourselves to the one or the other, they will yield us no relief from the incubus of the flesh until by faith we draw enabling grace from the "fulness" which is in Christ for us (John 1:16). "The life which I now live in the flesh I live by the *faith* of the Son of God, who loved me, and gave himself for me" (Gal. 2:20): faith in His person, in His mediatoral office, in His compassion, in His power.

Having been brought into vital union with Christ our privilege is to continue in communion with Him; having "come unto" Him, our duty is now to "abide in" Him. Yes, says the reader, that would be very simple if I no longer had any indwelling corruptions to plague me; but alas, it is but hypocrisy for *me* to talk about enjoying present communion with a holy Christ. Be careful, dear friend, lest you be found arraigning the wisdom and goodness of God. Has not *He* left the "flesh" within you? — had He deemed it most for His glory and your good, He would certainly have eradicated it. Has He made no provision for His failing people to have fellowship with His blessed Son while they groan because of their sinful nature and its ceaseless activities? Weigh well that question, and go slow in saying that present communion with the eternal Lover of your soul is not for you.

The above difficulty finds its solution in *experimental* union with

Christ. This we entered into at considerable length, because it is at this point that Christians experience so much difficulty. It is hard for them to realize that "there is a Friend which sticketh closer than a brother," whose love for us never wavers, and whose ear is ever open to our most distressful cry. But experimental communion with Christ must be "in the light" (I John 1:5-7): there must be perfect openness and reality in all our approaches to and dealings with Christ. If we come to Him as improverished beggars, He will not turn us away; if we come as conscious and confessed lepers, He will not scorn us; but if we give way to a Laodicean spirit and pretend to be what we are not, He will ignore us.

Experimental communion with Christ consists in basking in the sunshine of His conscious presence: sitting at His feet and receiving from Him as Mary did (Luke 10:39), leaning upon His bosom as John did (John 13:23) — and *they* were of "like passions" as us! The more we are engaged in contemplating and resting in Christ's wondrous and unchanging love, the more will our poor hearts be warmed and our affections drawn out unto Him. Yes, but when I have neglected this privilege, and my heart has grown cold, and I have wandered far from Him, then what am I to do? Do exactly as you did at first: come to Him as the "Friend of publicans and sinners" (Matt. 11:19), cast yourself anew upon His mercy, acknowledge to Him your vileness, ask Him to wash away the filth of your iniquities, plead before Him the promises found in Jeremiah 3:12 and Hosea 14:4, and count upon His faithfulness to do as He has said. Remember that the precious blood of the Lamb is the only sufficient antidote for a wounded conscience: it is by new acts of faith in that blood we experience afresh its virtue.

The cessation of our strivings against sin, the toleration of temptations to sin, allowed indulgence in any sin, snaps this sensitive experimental communion. The loss of our fellowship with Christ is to the believer's soul what the extinction of sight or the absence of light would be to the body. The body might in such a case continue to discharge some of its functions, yet nothing could compensate for the loss of vision. So the soul, deprived of conscious communion with Christ, may, in a measure, perform some spiritual functions but it will go mourning after its lost treasure. The joy of the Lord is the believer's strength (Neh. 8:16), and his joy is commensurate with his fellowship with Christ (I John 3:4). If, then, fellowship with Him be broken, the joy of salvation is lost (Ps. 51:12) as poor David discovered; nor can that joy be regained, till things are put right with the Lord, as the Psalmist also proved.

The only thing which closes our way against renewed communion with Christ is unrepented and unconfessed sins: they are to be *renounced* by godly sorrow, by contrite acknowledgment, by a return to the path of obedience. "They looked unto Him, and were lightened" (Ps. 34:5): "looked" in faith, and were "lightened" by the removal of their load of conscious guilt. Yet let it be pointed out that there must be real diligence and earnestness of soul when seeking restoration of experimental fellowship, for no slothful and formal effort will suffice. "By night on my bed I sought him whom my soul loveth: I sought him, but I found him not" (Song of Sol. 3:1): then is the soul to give way to despair? No, "I will rise now, and go about the city in the streets, and in the broad ways I will seek him whom my soul loveth: I sought him, but I found him not" (v. 2): ah, the Lord *tests* us! "The watchmen that go about the city found me: to whom I said, Saw ye him whom my soul loveth? It was but a little while that I passed from them, but I *found him* whom my soul loveth: I beheld him, and would not let him go" (Song of Sol. 3:3, 4) — that was perseverance rewarded. "O Lord God of my salvation, I have cried day and night before thee: let my prayer come before thee, incline thine ear unto my cry" (Ps. 88:1, 2): yes "day and night" *there* was intensity and importunity!

Finally, remember that the Lord Jesus is the great Physician, Divinely qualified for every wound, malady, want, which sin has wrought in us. Who needs Christ more than *yourself*, when you feel such a vile wretch? Who is there that Christ can get more glory from than by bearing with and cleansing such a one as *you*! The Holy Spirit makes the saint feel sin continually, that he may go continually to the Saviour. The wound is opened afresh to your view, that you may remember afresh it is by *His* "stripes" you are healed. It is the special office-work of the Spirit to continually convict us of sin, and make us inwardly acquainted with it, to the intent that we make more and more *use* of Christ, who is the alone remedy for every part of our spiritual disease.

Many suppose they cannot grow in grace and thrive spiritually unless they are full of comfort, peace and joy. But that is a great mistake. Growth in grace is a growing *in humility*, and thriving spiritually is to decrease in self-love and self-complacency. It is the great work of the blessed Spirit to humble our proud hearts, and this He does by showing us more and more of our nothingness, our utter unworthiness, our rottenness, and this in order to pave the way for exalting Christ, by showing how perfectly suited He is for our every case — for He has mercy on the *leper* who *comes to Him!* The Spirit makes us acquainted with our unutterable depravity and misery, that He may show us Christ's love and mercy. He brings to light our foulness, that He may proclaim the everlasting virtue of Christ's blood. He shows us our emptiness, to make us long after Christ's fulness.

Let it be duly borne in mind that *now* is the season of the Church's *humiliation*, and that those of its members still upon earth have not yet entered into their glorified state. It is very striking to observe that in this too the Church is conformed to the experience of her Head. "The path of the just is as the shining light, that shineth more and more unto the perfect day" (Prov. 4:18), which is true alike of both the Redeemer and the redeemed. By the sovereign grace of God, His elect have been brought into the place of unchanging blessing, yet the manifestation of this and their actual enjoyment of it, is experienced *gradually*, little by little. Then let not the tried and troubled Christian be unduly discouraged because, at present, his waterpot contains only water, and that oftentimes a filthy scum rises to the surface of it. It shall not ever be thus.

Christ is our *Pattern* in all things, as well as the Forerunner. The servant is not above his Master, but must follow His steps. Now a careful study of Christ's history reveals four distinct stages concerning His glory. First, there was *His primo-primitive glory* as the God-man, in the predestinating purpose of God. Not only did God behold in the glass of His decrees the Man taken into union by His Son, so that He could say, "Behold my servant, whom I uphold; mine elect, in whom my soul delighteth: I have put my spirit upon him" (Isa. 42:1) this was in eternity past; "He shall bring forth judgment to the Gentiles" was to occur in the time state; but Christ, as God-man, had a covenant subsistence and was endowed with a glory which far excelled that of the angels. It was to *that* Christ had reference when He prayed, "And now, O Father, glorify thou me with thine own self *with the glory* which I had with thee before the world was" (John 17:5).

That "glory" was His mediatorial glory, for He never relinquished His essential glory as the second Person of the Trinity: He could not do so without ceasing to be God. Thus, the first and original state of Christ was one of celestial glory. So it was with the Church, for the correspondence is perfect at every point, "Blessed be the God and Father of our Lord Jesus Christ, who hath blessed us with all spiritual blessings in the heavenlies in Christ" (Eph. 1:3): that too was "before the world began," for the next verse goes on to state, "according as he hath chosen us in him before the foundation of the world, that we should be holy and without blame before him!" And again we read, "Who hath saved us, and called us with a holy calling, not according to our works, but according to his own purpose and grace, which *was* given us in Christ Jesus *before* the world began" (II Tim. 1:9).

Second, there was *His humiliation state*, when He who was rich for our sakes became poor. The Lord of angels took upon Him the form of a servant. His glory was so veiled, the degradation into which He descended was so deep, that when here He "had not where to lay his head." The state into which He had entered was such that He became "The man of sorrows and acquainted with grief." So it is with His Church collectively, and with its members individually. It is "through much tribulation" that we "enter into the kingdom of God" (Acts 14:22). Sorrow and grief are our present portion: answerable, in our measure, to that through which the Head passed.

Third, there is *His state of exaltation*. This He entered into upon His ascension, when He was "received up into glory" (I Tim. 3:16). He has been crowned "with honor and glory" and set over the creation of God (Heb. 2:7). Yet, as that passage goes on to say, "But now we see not yet all things put under him." No, at present He is "From henceforth expecting *till* his enemies be made his footstool" (Heb. 10:13). Moreover, Christ still lacks the completed and glorified Church, which is His "fulness" (Eph. 1:23). Agreeably to this, when we leave this world, we go to be with Christ which is "far better;" nevertheless, we still lack our glorified bodies — the perfect state is yet future.

Fourth, there is *the ultimate and eternal glory of Christ,* but He will not enter into *that* apart from His Church. The final glorification of both shall occur at the same time. God considers nothing too good or too much for the Bride of His Son, and He will yet endow and enrich her with every spiritual blessing, not only in order to fit her as a suitable Spouse, but elevating her to a state of holiness and happiness, honor and glory, beyond all human and angelic thought, so as to satisfy His own heart as well, and display to all eternity the exceeding riches of His wisdom and grace, and the height and depth, breadth and length of His love toward her. Then shall the glorified Head be glorified in His Body and admired by all them that believe. Then will be fully manifested the original super-creation glory of God's elect.

The future glory of the righteous in Heaven is of such a character that they will be so united unto God Himself, through Christ the God-man as the Medium of it, as for Him to make such a communication of blessedness through our Head, that in the issue of it we shall be "filled with all the fulness of God" (Eph. 3:19). It scarcely needs pointing out that those prayers of the apostle which are recorded in Scripture were indited by the Holy Spirit, and therefore their several petitions are to be regarded by us as so many Divine promises, which, though realized by us in some measure now, will receive their perfect fulfilment in the future. Thus it will be with this most remarkable expression: in the Eternal State the elect shall be granted such communion with the Blessed Three that they will be filled with the life, the light, the love of God.

It is through Christ, yet it is *by the Spirit,* that we have all our knowledge of God. "The Spirit searcheth all things, yea, the deep things of God. For what man knoweth the things of a man, save the spirit of man which is in him? even so the things of God knoweth no man, but the Spirit of God" (I Cor. 2:10, 11). The Spirit dwells in the hearts of believers now on earth, and He will dwell in them in Heaven to all eternity. Therefore is He denominated "The Spirit *of glory*" (I Peter 4:14), for that title *looks forward* to His special relation to us in the unending future. Each Person in the Godhead will therefore have a distinctive part and place in connection with the everlasting bliss of the Church. We shall behold the Father's face (i.e., His revealed perfections), and Christ will be the Medium through which He shines, yet it is by the Spirit we shall be "filled with all the fulness of God." That will be the climax of grace, the consummation of our salvation, and the very zenith of joyous privilege and bliss.

How incapable we are of forming any adequate conception of what it will mean for a soul to be "filled with all the fulness of God!" Not that the finite will ever contain or encompass the Infinite, yet the holy and glorious One shall completely possess and abundantly satisfy our entire beings, spirit and soul and body. The renowned Puritan, Thomas Goodwin illustrated this by the following simile: "So fill you, as the fire of a hot furnace doth a small piece of iron cast into it, when not dissolving it, or converting it into fire itself, yet you see not nor discern the iron, but it appear to be all fire. So the ever-blessed Three will be *all in all* to saints in Heaven, as to fill, penetrate, and so thoroughly possess their understandings, as for them not to mind or think of themselves or of the glory they are possessed of, through their being swallowed up in the thoughts and enjoyment of the glory of the co-equal Three shining on and in and through them."

Christ will everlastingly delight in the Church, and the Church will everlastingly delight in Him. There will be mutual intercourse, an unrestrained opening of heart one to another. In communion *communications* are made by *both* parties. One party bestows favor upon another, and the recipient reciprocates by giving back to the donor, according to the benefit received, grateful acknowledgment: those communications, from both sides, flowing from love and union. Thus we read, "Now ye Philippians know that . . . no church *communicated* with me as concerning giving *and* receiving, but ye only" (4:15). Paul and the Philippian saints were united in heart and had spiritual fellowship together in the gospel (1:5). Out of love to him, they communicated in a temporal way, they being the active givers, he the passive receiver. Then, in return for their kindness, the apostle communicated by acknowledging their beneficence, thanking them for it. This may help us a little to form some idea of what our communion with Christ is Heaven will be like. As the vine conveys sap to the branch, so the branch *responds* by bearing leaves and fruit. Christ will continue to be *the Giver*, and we be the receivers, yet this will issue in the overflowing of our love, and *in return* we shall pour out praise and thanksgiving, adoration and worship.

> "He and I in one bright glory
> Endless bliss shall share:
> Mine, to be forever with Him;
> His, that I am there."